SENDALL IN CYPRUS
1892-1898
A governor in bondage

Diana Markides

Moufflon Publications Ltd., 2014

Cover illustration: J.P. Foscolo photograph, 1894

Published in 2014 by Moufflon Publishing Ltd.
10 Pericleous Street
Lefkosia/Nicosia 1010
Cyprus

distribution@moufflon.com.cy
www.moufflonpublications.com©

© Diana Markides
   The moral rights of the author have been asserted.

No part of this book may be reproduced or transmitted in any form by any means, electronic, mechanical, photocopying, recording or otherwise, without the prior permission of the publisher.

ISBN 9789963642328

Readers: Paul Sharrad, Thelma Blatchford
Editor: Ian Todd
Greek texts: Elena Mina
Watercolours & drawings: Thelma Blatchford
Photoshop work: Andreas Coutas, Sophoclis Karpasites

Graphic designer: Marcia Dallas - imagedesign@cablenet.com.cy

Printer: RPM Lithographica Ltd.

SENDALL IN CYPRUS
1892 – 1898
A governor in bondage

The historian Diana Weston Markides is currently working on a study of the British acquisition and administration of Cyprus in the context of Ottoman bankruptcy 1877-1928. From 1999 until 2004 she was a Senior Research Fellow at the Institute of Commonwealth Studies at the University of London. Her first book, *Cyprus 1957-1963: From Colonial Conflict to Constitutional Crisis, The Key Role of the Municipal Issue* was published in 2001 in the series Minnesota Mediterranean and East European Monographs. The book co-authored with Robert Holland, *The British and the Hellenes: Struggles for Mastery in the Eastern Mediterranean 1850–1960*, (Oxford University Press, 2006) was co-winner of the Runciman Award in 2007. Since then she has published widely on the modern history of Cyprus and the Eastern Mediterranean, taught at the University of Cyprus (ειδικός επιστήμονας) and taken part in many international academic conferences. She lives with her husband, Sophocles, in the village of Fikardou in the Troodos foothills.

For Christina and Ion

National Portrait Gallery bust of Sir Walter Sendall

---

*One step that might be taken
would be, in any case, to have more
of a working governor and less
of a figurehead as
Her Majesty's Representative*

Robert Meade, 2 March 1891

CONTENTS

Preface	*Page 9*
1892	The Peculiar Colonial Context, The Arrival, Taking Stock *Page 13*
1893	Early Tours, Wine Jars and Whirling Dervishes, Nicosia Society, The Law and Order Issue, The Tyranny of The Treasury, The Missing Surplus, The Bridge at Pyroi, The Sultan's Suzerainty, The Significance of Salt *Page 29*
1894	Harriers and Housekeeping, The Elusive Outlaw, The Wine Demonstration in Troodos, Tax Arrears in Paphos, Prisons and Police Again, Rumours of Withdrawal, The Limassol Flood *Page 73*
1895	Troop Withdrawal, Uncertainty about the Future, An Island Abandoned? Political Agitation, Home Leave, Gennadius and Gennadius, A Governor in Bondage *Page 103*
1896	A Warm Welcome Back, Money in Hand, A Start in Tax Reform, 'Natives' in the Executive Council, Fraud in the Public Works Department, Archaeological Activity, *Vakoufs* and *Cadis*, Tennis in Troodos, Rebellion in Crete *Page 133*

1897		An Unfortunate War in Thessaly, Repercussions in Cyprus, Two Key Tax Bills, Queen Victoria's Diamond Jubilee, The Legislative Council Meets at Kykko Monastery, Irrigation Project Set To Go, Enlightening Women, A Moving Farewell *Page 171*

Epilogue *Page 203*

Appendix I *Page 210*

Appendix II *Page 214*

Glossary *Page 215*

Bibliography *Page 217*

Illustrations and Credits *Page 222*

Watercolours and Drawings *Page 225*

Index *Page 226*

PREFACE

A dedication to Sir Walter Sendall, 'a great High Commissioner of Cyprus', can still be found within the neoclassical entrance of Phaneromeni school. I found it a good ten years ago, while researching the history of Nicosia under British rule. His contribution to that distinguished establishment, and to education in Cyprus more generally, has been referred to briefly in one or two local histories, but beyond that little was known about the man who was charged with heading the administration of Cyprus during the last decade of the nineteenth century. Falling between the excitement of the initial British occupation of the island, and the more turbulent early twentieth century, the Sendall years remained shrouded in obscurity.

Who was this Englishman, whose name is still lauded in the heart of old Nicosia? My curiosity was further aroused some years later when, whiling away the time in the National Portrait Gallery in Trafalgar Square, I found myself in room 23 (Expansion and Empire). There, on a pedestal in the centre of the room was an imposing, white marble bust of Sir Walter Sendall, sculpted by Edward Lanteri in 1902.

In recent years my research has gravitated towards the early years of British rule in Cyprus. One area of particular interest has been the extent to which the Cyprus Tribute, the annual sum paid to the Porte out of Cyprus revenues during Ottoman rule, was a consideration in the acquisition of the island, and what effect the diversion of that sum to the Ottoman Debt Charge had on the British administration and its relations with the Cypriots.

Researching into that subject, I found myself becoming absorbed in the atmosphere of the island and the problems of its understaffed administration during the Sendall years. I was impressed by the extent of change and progress brought about in unusually difficult circumstances. In order for the debt charge to be covered, the island was to be run on a shoestring. To make matters worse, its main source of revenue, the tithe on cereals, was afflicted by a global slump in prices, while the island's wine had been locked out of its traditional French market. What part did the Cypriots take in bringing about reform? To what extent did the legislature act as a legislature? What were Sendall's relations with the local politicians? What problems were created by the peculiar status of Cyprus? How did a colonial administration cohabit with a *de jure* Ottoman jurisdiction? What of the Enosis movement? How did the High Commissioner cope, or fail to cope, with the restrictions dictated by the Treasury in London?

The human element is ever present and one is allowed glimpses into the social life of Sir Walter and his wife, Lady Sophia. Snippets from local newspapers offer us lively and humorous images of expatriate concerns. I am grateful to Rita Severis for providing me with a copy of Elizabeth Lewis's rare book, *A Lady's Impression of Cyprus*. This beautifully written record by an astute, observant, and well-connected friend of the Sendalls, has been a constant companion in the course of research. I hope that in drawing together the complex threads of developments during those years, I have also brought them to life.

Many other debts of gratitude have inevitably built up along the way. There is a trail of libraries and archives in England, Athens and Cyprus to whose staff I owe thanks – the National Archive at Kew, the library of the University of Birmingham, the British Library, the London Library, the National Portrait Gallery Archive. I am grateful to Thomas Kiely for introducing me to and guiding me in the British Museum General Archive and for our useful exchange of emails. In Athens, I was thankful to be in the good hands of the staff of the Gennadius library. In Nicosia, the staff of the Laiki Cultural Foundation were always on hand when I needed them. I have made frequent use of the Library of the House of Representatives and, of course, the library of the Cyprus Archaeological Museum. I believe I have become an all too familiar face in the State Archives of the Republic of Cyprus. David Dew kindly offered me access to, and has allowed me to publish extracts from, the unpublished diary of his grandfather, Frederick Alexander Breul.

Eleni Mollinson, as well as Sophocles, have as always, helped me with my Greek translations. Elena Mina has given the Greek texts a final going-over, Marsha has patiently grappled with the graphics and Carol at Mica provided quick and efficient technical services when I needed them. I am grateful for permission to publish contemporary photographs from the collections of Haris Yiakoumis, Kallimages, and Tassos Andreou. Sophoclis Karpasites took over the quality and colour restoration of some of the digital images after the sad death of Andreas Coutas.

Thelma Blatchford's delightful illustrations are an attractive feature of this book. I owe Thelma a special debt of gratitude for her proofreading, editing, encouragement and support over the years.

Robert Holland and Robert Merrillees have read the text at different stages of production and offered helpful comments. Responsibility for its contents remains, of course, entirely mine.

Diana Markides,
Nicosia 2014.

Δουκάνη (threshing board)

1892

The Peculiar Colonial Context,
The Arrival, Taking Stock

In the very early years of British rule, high commissioners freshly appointed to the island of Cyprus tended to arrive in the spring.[1] This was not the consequence of any romantic notion on the part of Her Majesty's Government that the new man should be let down gently. It is true that the dull, drab carriage ride from Larnaca to Nicosia would be brightened by fields of ripening corn and pretty roadside flowers. In those first May days, the sun shone most brightly, the air was soft and gentle and the nights warm. Yet the timing of the transition would be more accurately linked to the stacks of wheat and barley soon to be piled up beside the threshing floors, the most palpable indicator of a new financial year and a new round of tax collecting. The tithe on wheat and barley was the mainstay of the island's revenue and the main task of the new incumbent, as of his predecessors, would be to run the island in such a way that as much as possible of the sum of £92,000, over half the average estimated annual revenue, could be handed over to the Treasury in London for the 'Tribute' payment.

It was during the high commissionership of Sir Walter Sendall that the foundations would be laid for radical changes in the financial management of the island. With the arrival of Joseph Chamberlain as secretary of state for the colonies in Salisbury's coalition government in the summer of 1895, Sendall found a kindred spirit in London. The island would stop being, effectively, a bondholders' milch cow and begin to be perceived as 'an improvable property' in the interest, not only of the Cypriot, but also of the British taxpayer.[2]

We will be looking at the context of these changes and how they came about. What was the relationship of governors to governed? What difference did Sendall, personally, make? In Greek Cypriot historiography, he has been described as the most popular governor, but this popularity has been linked entirely to his attitude to and support for

---

1. Until 1925, when the island was declared a crown colony, the British-appointed governors were entitled high commissioners.
2. Sendall to Ripon, 14 February 1893, CO67/79, National Archives (NA) Kew.

education. The last decade of the nineteenth century generally has received scant attention in academic studies on British rule in Cyprus. The contemporary fanfare of enthusiasm and the plethora of journal articles about the initial British occupation, cultivated deliberately by the Disraeli government, have provided sources for work on the very early years leading up to the establishment of constitutional government in 1882. More recent studies, most notably that of Rolandos Katsiaounis, have probed into the social and economic conditions in the 1880s, but in this and more general works, information on the last decade of the nineteenth century peters out. It has been covered in some depth by Petros Papapolyviou only in connection with the Cretan revolt and the subsequent fleeting Greek-Turkish war in the spring of 1897.

Although the introduction of a constitution in 1882 was a watershed in the way Cyprus was governed, the first partially elected legislature being in place by 1883, it was not until the 1890s that its members actually began to take an active part in the enactment of substantial reforming legislation. This development was itself facilitated by the great steps taken at that time in overhauling fiscal management. A new receiver general and a specially formed committee of the legislative council were key players. The high commissioner made use of Cypriot pressure on the local government, but also Whitehall's restraints on him, to forge compromise bills that would gradually but surely undermine the passive parsimony that underpinned the administrative policy for Cyprus, drawn up in 1883. From that year, the Cyprus government's expenditure was drastically reduced, regardless of revenue collected, reaching an all-time low in the years preceding Sendall's appointment in 1892. By the end of Sir Walter's second year, the 'do nothing policy', as it was termed by *The Times of Cyprus,* had begun to disintegrate, and by the end of his term, had been totally displaced.[3] Towards the end of his high commissionership, in 1897, Cypriots, for the first time, had become entitled to sit on the executive council on a permanent basis. That year, the Public Loan Fund was created, finally securing the retention and more systematic local exploitation of some tax surpluses. It was during 1897 too, that the first loan was taken out by the imperial government for the development of the island. The possibilities of establishing a local bank were being explored in 1896 and the first local bank, the *Tamieftirio Lefkosias,* opened its doors in 1898.

---

3.   *The Times of Cyprus,* 21 March 1890, 'Sir Henry Bulwer inaugurated, or at least put into execution what has been styled as a do nothing policy'.

1. Larnaca, view from the harbour, 1880s

A parallel emphasis was placed during these years on creating an island-wide infrastructure for the movement of goods and people. The building of bridges, until then absent or totally inadequate, was a feature of Sendall's tenure. The much talked of road from Limassol to Paphos was completed and entirely bridged in 1897. External communications were regularized by a weekly steamship service to Alexandria, while the volume of shipping swelled, encouraged by the new regulation regarding shipping dues and a phenomenal growth in trade with Egypt. Primary schools mushroomed all over the island, while secondary education and teacher training were more securely established.

But what was the island like when the Sendalls arrived in Larnaca in the spring of 1892? The ephemeral buzz attending the British occupation in 1878 had long since subsided. After a year or so, the disappointed carpet-bagging merchants that had flocked over, lured by Disraeli's siren song of a great new base, had sold up and abandoned the town to a somnolence only stirred by an occasional vessel anchored off the *scala* or roadstead. The small Ottoman town was still the seat of the European consuls and therefore retained a certain cosmopolitan dignity not to be found in the more bustling commercial centre of Limassol, but 'not a house seemed to have been altered' and the club dances and race meetings of those early years had long since dwindled away.[4] There *was* a new iron jetty at the end of which, on 2 April 1892, a few local officials and notables had gathered to greet the incoming high commissioner and his wife, Lady Elizabeth Sophia, but there was little public interest. The small group on the jetty would have included Claude Delaval Cobham, the distinguished commissioner of Larnaca. It was to his residence, the British Consulate during Ottoman rule, that the little group would have repaired for refreshments. It was perhaps there in the elegant drawing room, with the British coat of arms over the mantelpiece, that the Sendalls began to soak up the nature of their new charge.[5] Cobham, who had been serving in the island since 1879, took a scholarly interest in its history, having a good grasp of Greek, both ancient and modern, as well as Ottoman Turkish. He would be one of the more reliable of the motley band of civil servants with which Sendall was expected to run the administration.[6]

Sir Walter's predecessor, Sir Henry Bulwer, departed quietly the same afternoon for Beirut. After holidaying in Haifa for some months, he would make his way back to England and settle into a long and comfortable retirement in his family home in Norfolk. He was only 56 years of age, eight years younger than Sendall, but he had worn out the Colonial Office's willingness to employ his services further. The way Cyprus was being administered was causing Britain to become 'the laughing stock of the Levant instead of a model of good government'.[7] This was not by any means entirely the fault of the high commissioner, but a growing discontent within the island had signalled the need for a new image.

The paths of these two very different men had crossed on one or two occasions in the course of their careers. An errant offshoot of the

---

4. Alan Harfield ed., *The Life and Times of A Victorian Officer: Journals of Benjamin Donisthorpe Alsop Donne,* (Wincanton 1986), 190. Donne, a lieutenant in the Royal Sussex Regiment, was seconded to the Cyprus Pioneers (subsequently the Cyprus Military Police) from 1880 to 1882. In 1893 he spent a few days in Cyprus on his way home from Egypt.
5. For a description of Cobham's house, which he called *Villa Claudia*, see Alan Harfield ed., *The Life and Times ...* 64-65 and George Jeffery Diary 1 (1898-1921) 1903 section cited in Despina Pilides, *George Jeffery: His Diaries and The Ancient Monuments of Cyprus,* Vol. I, (Nicosia 2009), 85-86.
6. For a description of Cobham by his friend, George Jeffery, see ibid., 85-87.
7. Σάλπιγξ, 14 November 1894.

glamorous Lytton Bulwer clan, Sir Henry had been appointed British Resident on the tiny island of Cythera in 1860 after a gentlemanly education at Charterhouse School and Trinity College, Oxford. The appointment would not have been unconnected with the fact that his uncle, Sir Henry Lytton Earle Bulwer, was the controversial, high-living successor of the great Stratford de Redcliffe as Great Britain's minister to the Porte. A provincial sojourn on Cythera had led in 1865 to the more exotic and exciting post of secretary to his uncle in Constantinople. Tourists visiting Istanbul today are still taken to see 'Bulwer's Pleasure Castle' on the island of Yassiada in the Sea of Marmara. After a year in 'the city of the world's desire' where his duties included entertaining visitors on his uncle's private yacht, the young Henry was eased into a series of colonial postings by his powerful family connections, the apogee of which was governorship of the Natal.[8] It was through this appointment that his career bore on that of Sendall's. But it was the first high commissioner of Cyprus, General Sir Garnet Wolseley, who was initially rushed from the island to Natal where, during Bulwer's first term in office, one bungle after another threatened the British army with defeat at the hand of the Zulus. At the end of Bulwer's term, Sir Walter had been offered the governorship of the Natal for reasons not dissimilar to those for which he would later be offered Cyprus. He had accepted and was about to sail out to Durban, when news arrived of the strong objections of the Pietersburg burgers to this unknown outsider. They announced that they would pay for the return of Sir Henry Bulwer, whom they knew they could manipulate, especially regarding the growing new crisis in neighbouring Zululand. The Colonial Office capitulated and Sendall was pipped at the post. He had to be satisfied with the lesser second-class posting of the Windward Islands in the West Indies. It was this strange blip in colonial appointments that led both men, eventually, to Cyprus. In the view of Sir Robert Meade, by then permanent secretary in the Colonial Office, if the burgers of Pietersburg had not acted 'so unwisely, Sendall would no doubt have moved on from the Natal to a first class career back in 1875'.[9] Instead, Bulwer returned for a second term where, mesmerized by his advisers, he remained paralysed in inactivity as the crisis in Zululand slithered from sporadic hostilities into full-scale civil war. Some insight into the extent

---

8. For the 'frequent' use of patronage for appointments in the Colonial Office in the 1870s and 80s, see Brian L. Blakely, *The Colonial Office 1886-1892*, (Durham N.C., 1972), 116.
9. Minute signed by Robert Meade attached to Sendall to Chamberlain, 18 October 1897, CO67/108, NA.

of this inactivity can be gleaned from the frustrated letter of Rear Admiral Nowell Salmon, who was sent to the Natal in June 1884 to be at Sir Henry's disposal.

> *In quitting the Natal at this juncture, I feel that I am leaving when in my opinion, urgency exists for the employment of every man available in the reserve: but as this does not appear to be the opinion of His Excellency the governor, I have no option but to go on with my ordinary duties.*

The admiral went on to predict that the force at the disposal [of the governor at that time], 'strengthened if need be, by a naval brigade, would be sufficient for the purpose *now*, but that every day lost in indecision will only increase the number of our enemies and decrease the confidence and so lose the support of our friends'.[10] Six months later, Bulwer was recalled to London.

It was in these inauspicious circumstances that Sir Henry found himself governing the island which now paid the interest on the Crimean War loan, negotiated, in no small part, by his uncle in Constantinople. He was offered the high commissionership of Cyprus on his return to London, only on condition he accepted a reduced salary.[11] Bulwer's instructions were simply to collect as much revenue as possible and spend as little as possible. Sir Henry needed little encouragement. Pushing through much needed expenditure in the face of the Treasury's displeasure, required a zeal uncharacteristic of this affable gentleman of leisure. Most of his time seems to have been spent with his entertaining aides-de-camp. And indeed in his aides he found devoted friends, the most famous of whom, Rider Haggard and Tankerville Chamberlayne, followed him from the Natal to Cyprus and would hear not a word against him. They were charming socialites and were prepared to housekeep for him. There was no Lady Bulwer. Haggard remembers his first errand for Bulwer, before travelling out to the Natal as a very young man, was to order an ample stock of good

---

10.   CO179/155, Letter from Nowell Salmon, Rear Admiral and C.-in-C. on The *Boadicia* at Port Natal, to The Secretary to The Admiralty 17 June 1884 (six months before Bulwer's departure). For Bulwer's vacillations, see also Jeff Grey, *The Destruction of the Zulu Kingdom: The Civil War in Zululand, 1879–1884*, (London 1979), 134-138.

11.   See File 27830, 'Salary of High Commissioner' minute signed by Wingfield, attached to correspondence between the Treasury and the Colonial Office considering the possibility of reducing the salary of Sendall's successor, Haynes Smith. 13 January 1898, CO67/109, NA.

2. Bulwer coat of arms – ex-libris in Government House, Cyprus, library book

French wine.¹² Chamberlayne was always reluctant to ride a horse, but had a scholar's interest in the medieval history of the island and loved nothing more than to expound on the subject.¹³ Sir Henry seems to have administered Cyprus as he administered the Natal, by remote control. During his second year, he was already on his way home for a lengthy leave of absence. The minimalist nature of the annual reports and the minor character and small number of bills enacted in the Bulwer years are indicative of the paucity of administrative activity. Although a sound currency and a good administrative framework had been established by Bulwer's predecessor, Sir Robert Biddulph, the Tribute payment was not being sufficiently covered by the annual revenue. In 1883 a senior official of the colonial office, Sir Edward Fairfield, had been sent to Cyprus on a three-month enquiry into the financial management of the island. This had become a matter of some urgency. The government in London was

---

12. See Rider Haggard, *The Days of My Life*, (London 1926), 52-54, especially on housekeeping in the Natal. 'My chief trouble is housekeeping. I have all this house entirely under me and find it difficult work. I have often seen with amusement, the look of anxiety on a hostess's face at a dinner party, but, by Jove, I find it far from amusing now. Dinner days are black Mondays for me.'
13. Elizabeth Lewis, *A Lady's Impression of Cyprus*, (London 1894), 172. For Chamberlayne's reluctance to ride, see Sendall to Ripon, 19 January 1894, CO67/84, NA.

having to pay a substantial annual sum as grant-in-aid to Cyprus to make the Tribute payment possible.

The island had been acquired, in part, to secure the return on the 1855 Crimean War loan. The Porte had defaulted in 1877. The British financial administration of the island after 1878 was intended to relieve the British and French Treasuries who had been obliged, for the previous two years, to pay the influential British and French bondholders the annual interest on this government-guaranteed loan. All the excess revenue of Cyprus had been impounded by the British Government to this end since 1878. This arrangement was formalized in 1881. Five years into the British administration, it had become clear that the island was not footing its share for the servicing of the 1855 loan as planned.[14] Fairfield's mission was to find out why and to propose remedies. His remedy was based entirely on cutting government expenditure. After 1883, on the basis of his suggestions, all idea of investment in the island had been shelved for a regime of extreme parsimony. The expenditure on public works and the civil service, the costliest heads, was targeted for the severest cuts in Fairfield's report.[15]

Fairfield was Bulwer's principal defender in the Colonial Office. He had, after all, been handpicked as a man least likely to baulk at the policy envisaged essentially by him. Moreover, since nothing was to be done, expensive civil servants were dispensable. Bulwer dutifully chipped away at the civil service, even combining the office of chief customs officer with the receiver general so that merchants were obliged to travel to Nicosia to see him.[16] The expatriate inhabitants of the island were shocked. Indignant letters appeared in the press on the iniquities of centralizing government in the hands of the 'departmental clerks at Nicosia, who, together with their heads, are free from even the suspicion of knowledge of the island outside the walls of Nicosia.'[17]

---

14. The arrangement was formalized after three years of negotiation by The Ottoman Debt Administration set up in 1881. See Treasury to Lord Tenterton, 16 February 1881, FO78/3609 and, generally, Turkey: Further Correspondence respecting Ottoman Loans 1876-1878, Part II, Confidential Print No.3849, NA.
15. 'Papers relating to the Administration and Finances of Cyprus', June 1883, C.3661, V11/160, CSA.
16. *The Cyprus Herald*, 11 December 1886. Letter from 'an old resident' to the Homeward Mail, published in *The Times of Cyprus*, 9 May 1887.
17. Letter from 'an old resident' to the Homeward Mail, published in *The Times of Cyprus*, 9 May 1887.

Fairfield noted approvingly that Sir Henry was easing out the chief engineer, Samuel Brown and his assistant, thus getting rid of the spending 'Alexandria ring' responsible for most of the infrastructure constructed in the island since the occupation.[18] He reported with pride that Bulwer had reduced the public works vote from £10,000, the maximum sum allowed by the 1883 directive, to £8,000. Sir Henry also disposed of Falkland Warren, chief secretary to the government since the early days of the occupation. He had become embroiled notoriously in the excavation and sale of antiquities, a not uncommon practice in Cyprus at the closing stages of the nineteenth century.[19] The high commissioner did not intend to replace him. There was no need, he argued, for a chief secretary as well as a chief clerk. These savings were substantially neutralized by the costs arising from the steep increase in the prison population throughout the island. The administration shambled weakly along, but in 1887, the Cypriot population turned dangerously sour.

That year the harvest failed miserably. Since the island lived from hand to mouth, all surplus revenue being hived off to foreign coffers, there was no store of wealth to draw from. The Lords of the Treasury, dissatisfied with the failure of the Cyprus government in collecting taxation arrears and fearing that, following the poor harvest, the arrears would become uncollectible, pressed harder for immediate redemption. Spurred on to greater activity, the receiver general sought to preempt private creditors, pouncing on peasants' property in lieu of tax. Wedding dresses and even underwear, ploughs, oxen, and worse, the land itself, fell beneath the auctioneer's hammer.[20] The regime put in place after the British occupation, whereby the

---

18.   See Bulwer to Knutsford, 24 January 1887, private letter from Bulwer to Fairfield, 26 May 1887 and attached minute written by the latter. 'We are lucky having someone to fight the Alexandria spending ring with which we have been so long burdened in Cyprus [spending on public works]', CO67/46. See also article in defence of Brown, who had been posted to Hong Kong, in *The Times of Cyprus*, 21 March 1890. Two months earlier the paper highlighted the trend with the headline, 'The cry is still they go and yet another good man is lost to the Cyprus colony', *The Times of Cyprus*, 31 January 1890. For Brown's important contribution to Public Works on the island, see Kenneth W. Schaar, Michael Given and George Theocharous, *Under the Clock*, (Nicosia 1995), 11-12, 14-15, 20, 27-28. See also Thomas Kiely and Robert S. Merrillees, 'The Archaeological Interests of Samuel Brown, Government Engineer, and his Circle of Acquaintances in Late 19th Century Cyprus' (forthcoming) for a fuller biographical account of Brown and his association with the island.
19.   See Michael Given, 'The Fight for the Past: Watkins vs. Warren (1885-6) and the control of Excavation', Veronica Tatton-Brown ed. *Cyprus in the 19th Century AD: Fact, Fancy and Fiction*, (Oxford 2001), 255-260.
20.   *The Malta Standard*, 18 April 1887, cited in Rolandos Katsiaounis, *Labour, Society and Politics in Cyprus during the Second Half of the Nineteenth Century*, (Nicosia 1996), p.103.

smallholder had outright ownership of his land, should have been a benefit of British rule, but it meant that the state dealt directly with the individual in terms of tax collection. The collection from each individual of the last penny or the last fig (literally) of the quaint old Ottoman taxes and tithes had the effect of throwing the peasantry into the clutches of the usurious moneylenders.[21] The situation was exacerbated by the fact that the Ottoman tithe on wheat and barley had been substituted in 1882 for taxation to be paid in cash. The strain was felt most of all by the district commissioners on whom the onus of delivering revenue fell. Pressed beyond endurance by the receiver general for greater efficiency in collecting arrears in 1889, Cobham rebelled. He refused to press the Larnaca peasants further, arguing that

> *The difficulties I have met with in collecting arrears of tithes and taxes consist then first, in the poverty of the people. Secondly in the extreme cumbrousness of the machinery enjoined by Ordinance XIV 1882....I could, no doubt [reduce the arrears] at once, but, following the scientific methods of the Receiver General, I could also depress agriculture, diminish the population, decrease cultivation, permanently impair the resources of the government, and discredit the name of England throughout the East.*[22]

The mounting economic crisis took place in an island just waking up to representative organised politics. A constitution had been in the gift of Gladstone's 1882 Liberal government and was willingly offered. It cost nothing and would be some compensation for and, indeed, a diversion from, the stringent taxation regime the local administration was bound to impose. While more representative than most colonial legislatures, the government members depended on the support of the Muslim minority to pass legislation abhorrent to the majority Christians. The support of the Muslim members could not necessarily be guaranteed. The extreme circumstances of 1887 kindled a catholic reaction against a government

---

21. Rolandos Katsiaounis (1996), 98-102.
22. Cobham to Smith, 10 September 1889, CO67/43. NA. This important letter documents the depressed state of Larnaca town and district in 1889 and the impossibility of collecting taxes imposed. Most tellingly, he reports, 'In October 1879, I was directed to issue to the poorer villagers wheat and barley for seed corn. ...the villagers were compelled to repay in money the grain issued in kind at a higher than average price, with interest after one year's delay, of 6%. I need hardly add that this was not exacted without difficulty and murmurings.' Bulwer's only comment was that the quoted paragraph, together with other telling instances of extortion, should be removed if the letter was to be printed.

which was taking much, offering very little and, if an 'old resident' of Larnaca was to be believed, not bothering to heed the warning signs. In an article emphasizing the impossible position in which district commissioners had been placed by the centralising system now enforced by the government, the author, in all probability Delaval Cobham, observed

> To show how grossly ill-informed the government is, it is sufficient to refer to the speech of the High Commissioner delivered on Feb 17 last, in which His Excellency actually congratulates the members on the condition and prospects of the island at a time when famine is staring us in the face.[23]

Legislation by order-in-council, a provision of last resort, was used for the first time during this crisis to ratify the budget rejected unanimously by the elected members of the legislature. Demands and petitions to the government in Cyprus for relief from taxes their crops could not cover, met a wall of silence. Even the most moderate of Cypriot leaders, the Ethnarch, Archbishop Sofronios, reacted in a militant way.

On 8 January 1888, together with a new member of the legislative council (MLC), Achilleas Liassides, Sofronios led a crowd of some thousand Christian and Muslim citizens to Government House to press home their demands.[24] They were met by the acting governor, the commander of the local garrison Colonel Hackett, since Bulwer was enjoying a six-month leave of absence. Similar protests had already taken place in Limassol, Larnaca and Paphos. On 18 January Famagusta followed suit, but there was no official reaction. Egged on by the distressed state of the peasantry, as well as by rising political pressure from the newly educated and more radical members of urban society, the Archbishop agreed to the unprecedented step of bypassing the local government which had failed to respond, and organised a deputation of Cypriot representatives on a mission to London. They were to protest directly to the government at Westminster against the unfair tax burden and to demand, at the same time, a greater share in government. Funding and organising such a journey was no easy task for the Cypriot leaders. There was a long-drawn-out period

---

23. Article signed by 'An old [Larnaca] resident' very probably Cobham, since he refers at length to 'the position of the Commissioners becoming well nigh unbearable', *The Times of Cyprus*, 9 May 1887.
24. George Hill, *A History of Cyprus*, Vol. IV, (Cambridge 1952), 451-452.

during which attempts to persuade the Muslim community to participate failed over the latter's unwillingness to condemn the Tribute.

If there had been any hesitation, it was swept aside by the ruthlessness of the tax collectors. Indicative of their zeal is the fact that there were more forced sales of land in 1888 and 1889 than in 1887, the year the harvest had failed so completely.[25] The persistence of the new secular politicians would, at any rate, allow no backsliding. By the time the deputation actually arrived in London it was June 1889. Headed by the patriarch of the Ancient Church of Cyprus, the delegation found a sympathetic audience from the leaders of the Anglican church. The Archbishop was awarded an honorary doctorate of divinity by the University of Oxford. Although they were eventually received by Lord Knutsford, the secretary of state, the official response to the memorialists took much longer. The secretary of state experienced considerable difficulty in getting Bulwer to complete and send a full report on his version of the situation on the island and the result was not satisfactory.[26] The authorities in Cyprus had attempted to present the memorialists as unrepresentative by instigating petitions against them.[27] In London there was some acknowledgement that the Cypriots' grievances were not without substance. It was in 1887 that the last of the more substantial British-owned companies, formed to attract investment to the island a decade earlier, folded up.[28] But what caused Westminster to sit up and take note was the underlying threat that a refusal to pay taxes, already observed in various parts of the island, might become rampant.[29] In Robert Meade's words, it was time to find 'more

---

25. See House of Commons Parliamentary Papers, c.277 *Cyprus (Enforced Sales): A return showing enforced sales of property in the island of Cyprus for the years 1887, 1888, 1889 (a) at the instance of the island government (b) at the instance of Private Creditors*. This paper was compiled by Robert Wyndham Herbert, the permanent secretary, in response to a question in the House by the member of parliament, Patrick O'Connor. The information took a year and a half to extract from the Cyprus government and was incomplete. The sum of the debt for which the property had been sold, which was specifically sought, was not included. From the statistics it appears that the number of government forced sales increased from 37 in 1887 to 159 in 1889 and the number of private forced sales increased from 309 to 449 over the same period.
26. Herbert found it 'impossible not to sympathise with the Cypriot unofficials (elected members of the legislative council)', and that 'Bulwer's elaborate arguments' for which London had waited for so long, 'only show that we have no decent excuse for the heavy taxation we impose on the island.' Minute (6 June 1891) attached to Bulwer's report on the memorial, CO67/60, NA.
27. Katsiaounis, 188.
28. For an account of companies investing in Cyprus and listed on the London stock exchange, that folded up in 1887, see Gail Ruth Hook, 'Britons in Cyprus 1878–1914', Ph.D. Dissertation, University of Texas at Austin, August 2009, 210.
29. Katsiaounis, 181-185.

3. Portrait of Robert Wyndham Herbert Permanent Under-Secretary of State for the Colonies: 1871–1892 and for the first few months of Chamberlain's government in 1895. He was the brother of Elizabeth Alicia Lewis

of a working governor and less of a figurehead'. The permanent undersecretary, Sir Robert Wyndham Herbert, was becoming increasingly perturbed with the way the island was being administered. It had become clear that not only the high commissioner, but also the receiver general, John Swettenham, would have to go, as questions were raised in the Colonial Office itself as to 'whether the increased revenue his exertions enable us to collect is not too dearly paid for by the discontent now raised in the island.'[30]

Robert Herbert had begun taking a special interest in the island's problems. In the previous year, he had been involved in a failed attempt to persuade the Treasury and the Foreign Office to commute the Crimean War loan. Now the Cypriot leadership had taken the extraordinary step of actually coming to London. This move, on the one hand, indicated the extent of Cypriot dissatisfaction with the local government and, on the other, exposed Whitehall to the inevitable public interest that would

---

30. Minute signed by Robert Meade on 2 March 1891, attached to a memorial sent from Paphos and Larnaca and articles in Cypriot press complaining about oppressive taxation, CO67/51, NA.

attend such an exotic arrival. An increasing number of stories appeared in the British press of the miserable state of the island, while questions were asked in the House about the government's responsibility for the growing number of forced sales of land.[31] Perhaps the last straw for Herbert was the length of time it took for the administration in Cyprus to produce its own information on the crisis, and the inadequacy of this information when it finally arrived. It was clear that some of the Cypriots' not unreasonable grievances would have to be addressed seriously and that Bulwer was not the man to address them. His term was anyway drawing to an end.

So it was that Sir Robert Herbert invited Sir Walter Sendall to cut short his posting in the West Indies and become high commissioner of Cyprus. Son of a Suffolk vicar, his background lacked the glamour and sophistication of Bulwer's. A bright but 'delicate' grammar school boy, he had studied classics at Christ's College, Cambridge. There he gained a first and moved in intellectual circles. He had befriended two somewhat eccentric writers, the novelist Walter Besant and the poet Charles Calverly, whose sister, Elizabeth Sophia, he married in 1870. By this time he was working in the educational branch of the civil service in Ceylon, where he is fondly remembered as the founder of a modern education system.[32] Having been turned down by the burgers in Durban in the circumstances mentioned above, since 1885 he had been governor of the Windward Islands, reorganising the administration from Grenada after their separation from Barbados.[33] It was during a second tour there, that he was summoned

---

31. See Enclosure No.3 in Robert G.W. Herbert, *Cyprus: Enforced Sales....* Bulwer provided a partial response in April 1891 to information sought in July 1890. The figures include only the total annual sum of immovable property whose title was actually transferred, after enforced sales, firstly on behalf of the government and secondly on behalf of private individuals (moneylenders). The report failed to provide further information asked for, viz. the number of donums in each property and the value of the debt for which it was sold. It does show the rapid increase in both government and private forced sales over these years and indicates that the properties sold at auction fetched much less than their registered value.
32. Arnold Wright, *Twentieth Century Impressions of Ceylon: Its History, People and Commerce*, (Sri Lanka, 1999), 221.
33. In Grenada today, one can still walk down Sendall Street and drive through Sendall Tunnel. According to internet guides, the city of St. George's is essentially made up of two parts - the Carenage area and the Esplanade, which are separated by a ridge. Whether you are on foot or in a car, the quickest way to travel from one part to the other is through the 340-foot-long Sendall Tunnel, named after the then governor, Sir Walter Sendall. It is said that he saw the plight of the porters and the horse-drawn carriages that had to ply that route especially during the rainy season, when the unpaved roads were wet and slippery, thus causing great difficulties. As such, the tunnel, started in 1889 and completed in 1894, was to address both the transportation needs and the linking of the town.

home for special duties in Cyprus. At 64, he was ten years older than Bulwer. The salary offered was £4,000, £1,000 more than that of the departing governor. 'It would be impossible', Lord Knutsford observed, 'to get a capable governor for less'. Herbert was known to consider it 'the best and the most important of all economies to secure an efficient Governor'.[34]

It was not only Sendall who was a Suffolk man. East Anglia had acquired a Cyprus connection. The Bulwer family home, as well as that of Rider Haggard, was in Norfolk. The new Cyprus clique hailed from Suffolk. It is quite possible that Sir Robert's briefing of Sendall on Cyprus was not contained within the Colonial Office, but extended to his family home in the village of Ickleton. We know that the Sendalls had associated socially with Herbert's sister Elizabeth Lewis, before they went to the island. She was to refer to them in the introduction to her perceptive book, *A Lady's Impressions of Cyprus,* as old friends. Sir Walter would, in all probability, have met Robert Herbert's close friend, Sir George Bowen, there. He was a retired governor of Queensland, Australia and now lived in Suffolk, on the Herbert family home estate.[35] One can speculate on the possibility of at least one gathering of these like-minded intellectuals before the Sendalls embarked for Cyprus. Bowen's early years had been spent in the Ionian Protectorate where he married the daughter of a Corfiote aristocrat. He was well versed in ancient Greek literature and had written about the Ionians and the Greek mainland. Sendall was also a colonial administrator with a good grounding in classical literature, good enough to edit his brother-in-law, Calverly's, collected poems, many of which were written in Latin or ancient Greek. Sir Walter was a founding member of the Society for Hellenic Studies and would have had much in common with Bowen. At such a Suffolk gathering, there would have been talk of the Eastern Mediterranean, of Egypt, and of British colonial encounters with the Hellenic world…the peculiarity of Cyprus. At any rate a visit to the island was on the agenda. Thence, Elizabeth Lewis and her daughter, together with Sir George Bowen, would travel in 1893 – a journey no doubt designed by the permanent secretary to please his sister and ease the bereavement of his newly widowed friend.

---

34. Minute attached to Ryder, Treasury, to Chamberlain, 28 December 1897, CO67/109. and Blakely, (1972), 116.
35. *The Cladrees,* the home of Sir Robert Wyndham Herbert, is still to be found at Ickleton. It is now the residence of Mr. Beddoes. Ickleton Grange (part of the same property) is the residence of George William H. Bowen Esq. JP.

Δουκάνη, λουρικός και ζυγός (threshing board, harness and yoke)

1893

*Early Tours, Wine Jars and Whirling Dervishes, Nicosia Society,
The Law and Order Issue, The Tyranny of The Treasury, The Missing
Surplus, The Bridge at Pyroi, The Sultan's Suzerainty,
The Significance of Salt*

By the time of the arrival of these visitors to the island early in 1893, Sendall was beginning to pummel and squeeze the administration into shape. He bombarded London with reports on a weekly basis and sought authorization for modest changes. The truth was that he was already more than a little disheartened by his Cyprus experience. The high commissioner was wobbling by the end of 1892, making private enquiries about other postings.[1] The tyrannical regime imposed on the government of Cyprus by the Treasury made life very difficult for a conscientious governor. The onerous Tribute troubled him greatly and the topping-up nature of any grant from Westminster to cover basic expenditure and absolutely no more, meant that it was impossible to budget and plan ahead. Perhaps part of the purpose of the visit arranged by the permanent secretary of such eminent and personable guests, was to sustain Sendall's efforts in the island.

In terms of his immediate environment, the personnel on the island were too few and inadequate to be effective. The administration of Cyprus had been in a sorry state when he arrived in April 1892. A couple of months after his arrival, three of the six district commissioners were on long summer leave, which meant that the already stretched district police commandants (who also directed the prisons in each district) had to do both jobs. Moreover, most of the commandants were 'permanently weak'.[2] One of them, Peter Dudley, had been invalided out of tropical Africa when he landed the Cyprus job in 1890. 'His appointment', reported Sendall, 'has seriously weakened the police administration of the island by putting a confirmed invalid in charge of duties which can only be performed by a man in rigorous enjoyment of all his faculties both of mind and body'.[3] Paphos had been completely abandoned.

---

1.   Sendall to Ripon, 9 May 1893, Add. 3914.f.164, British Library (BL). Sendall angled for the administration of the Straits Settlements, a first-class posting which would secure him a higher pension.
2.   Sendall to Knutsford, 8 July 1892, CO 67/75, NA.
3.   Sendall to Knutsford, 13 June 1892, CO67/80, NA.

> *In Paphos, from where the recently appointed Commandant has just been transferred, after a service there of barely twelve months, to an appointment in another colony, the Commissioner is, at the same time, absent on leave and there is no officer to whom either revenue or police duties can be entrusted. A Commandant cannot be moved from another district because the commissioners are absent.* [4]

On top of that, the secondment of the chief commandant of police, an able man from the Royal Marines, was about to expire. The matron in the hospital had resigned; John Hunter, the director of posts, was an alcoholic depressive.[5] Two new police commandants had been appointed in London but were to prove frustratingly inept postings: the first, Tankerville Chamberlayne, on Bulwer's warm recommendation, and a certain Captain Power.[6] Unwilling to ride a horse, the former was of little use as a police commandant. It quickly became clear that his intention was to take months of leave every summer to be with his Italian wife. Chamberlayne soon found that those halcyon days were over. He never forgave Sendall for not being Bulwer and for not allowing such deviations. Power, a likeable dimwit, tuned out to be a dead weight from the start and the administration spent the following five years trying to ease him out.[7]

Sir Walter was shocked too by the laxity displayed in the learning of local languages. Few civil servants were comfortably conversant with either Greek or Turkish. The money allowance given for those passing language examinations had been abolished in 1888 as an unaffordable and irksome expense. After 1888 the exam was only offered once. With the financial incentive gone, no one turned up and in the past two years no examinations had been held at all. Sendall considered acquaintance with the local languages '*indispensable*' for the district commissioners and the police commandants and desirable in the case of all permanent officials. In this

---

4. Sendall to Knutsford, 8 July 1892, CO 67/75, NA.
5. Sendall to Knutsford, 8 and 25 July 1892, CO67/75, NA.
6. Power and Chamberlayne received their letter of appointment from the Colonial Office on 17 August 1892. See Sendall to Ripon, November 1892, CO67/77, NA.
7. For Power, see Sendall to Knutsford, 3 October 1892. Chamberlayne wrote a whole series of letters to the Colonial Office explaining at length why it was essential for him to take regular leave from the island on at least an annual basis. His slim volume, *Lacrimae Nicossienses: Recueil d'inscriptions funéraires, la plupart françaises, existant encore dans l'île de Chypre, suivi d'un armorial Chypriote et d'une description topographique et archéologique de la ville de Nicosie*, was published in Paris in 1894. Jeffery described it as a book 'of the greatest value, but absurdly affected'. Pilides (2009), 87. Chamberlayne thanks Bulwer effusively in the acknowledgements of *Lacrimae Nicossienses…* but makes no mention at all of Sendall.

he was to find support from the Colonial Office and the examinations were reintroduced. Cobham was made the chief examiner and competence in Greek or Turkish soon became a serious consideration in promotions.[8]

With little money spent on them in the past six years, the few public roads were in a wretched state of repair. The good work done before 1883 was in danger of going to waste. Precious funds from the meagre public works budget had been squandered between 1886 and 1890 in harbour works at Kyrenia, which could be of no consequence to the island's trade. A new protective mole for the tiny port had been designed by Samuel Brown, famous, among other things, for designing the new harbour at Alexandria, but for reasons of economy corners were cut. The length of the breakwater stipulated by him had been reduced after his departure from the island and the mole, damaged twice during construction, was of little use in keeping out the winter storms.[9] Little had been done to extend the road network once the 'spend nothing' policy was strictly enforced, and *The Times of Cyprus* complained in February 1892 that there had been no road maintenance of any significance since Brown's departure for Hong Kong in 1889.[10] The somewhat propagandistic map of Cyprus roads drawn in 1886 exaggerated the government's achievements, including the nature of the road to Paphos. The picture remained exaggerated in the 1891 reprint.[11] Mrs. Lewis, who travelled to Paphos on horseback in February 1893, described the way marked on the map, as a 'partly-made' road, as follows:

> *We then mounted and turning away from the Wine Road, entered upon the field and mountain path dignified by the title, Papho Road....[on leaving Pissouri] we rode over the worst piece of road on our whole expedition..over and over again as we crossed from valley to valley our track was nothing less than an actual staircase, often indeed a staircase composed of rolling stones.*[12]

---

8. Sendall to Ripon, 19 November 1892, CO67/77, NA. See also attached minutes.
9. Andrekos Varnava, *British Imperialism in Cyprus: 1878-1915: The Inconsequential Possession*, (Manchester 2009), 135-139.
10. *The Times of Cyprus*, 28 February 1892.
11. Cunningham to Chief Secretary, 24 September 1886, CO67/42, pointing out the inaccuracies on the index map of the official survey. The map was published without being corrected, on Fairfield's instructions. The same 'imaginary' roads appear in road maps for 1887 and even for 1890. See maps for these years in C.V. Bellamy, *The Main Roads of Cyprus*, (Nicosia 1903) and compare with 1895 map in the same monograph.
12. Lewis, 94-136.

4. Kyrenia Harbour, showing the extended mole

The dire state of road maintenance was not limited to Paphos. In September 1892 *The Times of Cyprus* was grumbling about the 'disgraceful' state of the principal road in Cyprus, the Larnaca-Nicosia road and described the rest of the roads in the island as 'impassable.'[13] An irate letter from Sendall to the Colonial Office demanded an explanation for the shoddy constructions of the public works department, especially as regards the few bridges that had been built. Its director was a lowly unqualified official – a 'practical engineer', Frank Cunningham, promoted in 1888 on a reduced salary to replace the eminent Samuel Brown. He too was absent on leave. Sendall found that those few bridges that had been constructed recently were all of the same design. 'The timbers are covered with earth so that they rot and dangerous holes are covered. Because of the low level of the approach road, flooding torrents can undermine the structure.' Such a bridge had already caused a serious accident.[14]

The problem causing greatest concern to the administration was the phenomenal rise in crime rates in recent years. This was a consequence of the distress caused by the dwindling resources that followed the 1887 drought, but also a symptom of the malfunctioning of the system. There was resentment at the clampdown on the escalating number of taxpayers in arrears. The vulnerability of property, movable and immovable, meant that the peasants, once cheated by corrupt officials, were now fleeced by greedy urban moneylenders in order to pay money taxes.[15] Sendall's government would this year complete the process of returning to collecting tithes on cereals in kind, begun on an experimental basis in 1889, but arrears, and there were many, were paid in cash. Crime for subsistence, but also for revenge, remained a characteristic feature, particularly in the inaccessible Paphos district. Fugitives from the overflowing Ottoman prisons throughout the island found refuge in the craggy rift valleys and became '*klephts*'. They were regarded by the peasants in the area with the terrified awe due to men who stopped at nothing to defy an unpopular system.

---

13. *The Times of Cyprus*, 28 February 1892. For more complaints about this and other roads, see ibid., 3 January 1891, 13 June 1891, 7 February 1892. In April 1892, Bulwer described the road in a somewhat opaque dispatch from Beirut, as having been 'put into a state of thorough repair' but that 'the larger works would be carried on in due course at the proper time'. Bulwer to Knutsford, 6 April 1892, CO67/74, NA.
14. Sendall to Knutsford, 8 July 1892, CO67/75, NA.
15. Katsiaounis, 127.

Government inaction on this matter was now being widely criticized in the local press. It was observed that 'gangs of brigands infest the country, a thing which never occurred during the Turkish administration'. *The Owl* recalled admiringly that Bulwer had regretted that Turkish corporal punishments and summary banishment were no longer available, and agreed with him that they should be reinstituted. 'Cyprus is a hotbed of crime', it opined, 'because of leniency and excellent treatment in prison'. In this context, a new purpose-built prison had been regarded as a first priority since the Bulwer days. Sir Henry had purchased land for the purpose, northwest of Nicosia. The plans for a prison exclusively for long-sentence convicts, complete with treadmill, had already been drawn up and estimates made, but the work had still to be started.[16]

Nevertheless, all was not doom and gloom. The depressed state of the island was not uniform. Bulwer, with the luck that had carried him effortlessly through life, was to preside in his final year, 1891, over a bumper harvest, which alleviated straitened conditions in the Mesaoria plain and secured the largest income from general revenue since the British occupation. An '*annus mirabilis*' for the Treasury in London, not only was the Tribute paid entirely from Cypriot taxes for two years running, but a surplus accrued. In the Mesaoria, the new churches mushrooming in many villages bore witness to the easing of economic circumstances, but also to the end of the subordinate *raya* status accorded to Christians in provinces under direct Ottoman rule.

In the wine-growing districts of Limassol and Paphos the good harvest could not be capitalized on. Sendall was to hear, in the first session of the legislative council after his arrival, of the crisis recently created in the industry. A protective tariff had suddenly been imposed by France, the main destination for the island's wines. To make matters worse, as a result of the new French tariff, the Egyptian market where the Cypriot product hitherto had enjoyed a near monopoly, was flooded with wines from other Mediterranean countries seeking an alternative outlet. The elected members argued for an abolition of the high excise imposed on wine which, in the present circumstances, was likely to bring the industry to its knees. In addition to the *verghi* land tax, the wine-growers were paying 'an *ad valorem* tax of 14 per cent upon their produce. That is to say, 12 per cent

---

16. Sendall to Ripon, 25 November 1892 and attached minutes, CO67/75, NA.

5. The church of Ayios Georgios at Exo Metochi in the Mesaoria plain, ca. 1905

excise duty, 1 per cent under the Field Watchman's Law and, for those in the Limassol district, 1 per cent under the Limassol Roads Law'. A petition from the villagers of Lofou is indicative of the distress in the region. They begged to give the government all the wine the village had produced rather than pay tax on it. There was no market.

> We are ready to deliver the wine on the first demand of the government, or to pour it out in the presence of a government official in order to rid ourselves of the payment of wine duty. We have come to this decision because we are obliged to borrow usuriously to pay this unbearable tax. It is a great misfortune to this year's great vintage.[17]

The high commissioner was able to verify the growing despair and indebtedness of the wine-growers from first-hand experience. It was to the wine districts of Limassol and Paphos that he ventured on what was to be one of many tours of investigation on horseback and under canvas, a move that was as appreciated as it was apparently unusual. His predecessor had

---

17. Enclosure in Sendall to Ripon, 5 September 1892, CO67/77, NA. For interesting details on the problems of the wine-growers, see this lengthy dispatch.

conducted a few royal progresses, not so much to see, as to be seen. Languid and inaccurate images of the country traversed and an abundance of historical and archaeological allusions in *The Times of Cyprus* coverage of these occasions, bear the stamp of Tankerville Chamberlayne. Any specific problems among the inhabitants – in fact the inhabitants themselves – are singularly absent from the reports. When the Cypriots, or 'natives', were referred to they were seen across a void. In a report on the high commissioner's visit to Paphos in November 1886, Chamberlayne referred lyrically to 'men and lads returning at dusk to their homes after a long day's work' and, noting 'the healthy appearance of both men and beasts', concluded that 'their calling is sufficiently remunerative to provide them with all their needs'. In villages, people were 'encouraged to gather around and voice their grievances'. Later in the same text, drawing on his Natal experience, he described such a gathering as an '*indaba*'.[18] But the grievances voiced were rarely recorded or addressed.[19]

---

18. 'Visit of His Excellency the High Commissioner to Paphos', a report in *The Times of Cyprus*, 27 November 1886, almost certainly written by Chamberlayne, I could not find a report of the Karpass visit, but there was a carriage road all the way to Rizokarpasso.
19. I came across only one report of these tours in dispatches – very late in Bulwer's term. It seems there was some prompting from Fairfield. See Bulwer to Knutsford, November 1891, CO67/58, NA. There are brief press references to a visit to the Karpass during the distress there in 1887. This resulted in loans at considerable interest to Karpass villagers and relief work on roads.

6. Gerassimos, Abbot of Kykko
(1845-1911)

The Abbot of Kykko, an elected member of the legislative council, whose monastery Sendall visited on the way from Troodos to Paphos, welcomed the new approach. He spoke with admiration of the high commissioner's rides to various areas 'even in summer......to discover personally the real condition of the island'.[20] Sendall's appearance at the ancient and isolated retreat during his first year, was to be the beginning of a close cooperation with the abbot, which culminated in an extraordinary legislative council meeting held at Kykko Monastery in Sendall's final year.

Riding on down through the mountains to the much neglected town of Paphos, he saw for himself that the road, actually marked on the map published in 1891, simply did not exist. No commissioner's residence being available, Sir Walter set up camp 'in the locality of *Exo Vrissi*, below the windmill'. This report in *The Times of Cyprus* of Sendall's Paphos visit indicates a direct and genuine interaction with the population. Sir Walter 'listened with the greatest attention to matters put to him by local Christian and Muslim leaders and expressed the hope that some of the matters referred to would soon be remedied'. His local visits included a morning

---

20. Address by Abbot of Kykko on the occasion of Sendall's visit to the monastery, received in the Colonial Office on 24 October 1892, CO67/77, NA.

in the boys' school, where he followed a class being taught in the new teaching method now in force in Cyprus. He expressed 'satisfaction' that Mr. Kosmas Lyssiotis, their teacher, displayed 'a great ability to teach the younger boys in an entertaining manner' and 'offered to help the school procure any articles necessary to teach the new method'.[21]

The same paper, observing that such a tour 'requires a deal of energy, especially when it has to be done in the saddle', went on to welcome the new hands-on approach.

> *The Larnaca people did not like the idea, which had become almost universal in the island that complaints were politely acknowledged and pigeonholed. That this system has been resorted to in the past is without doubt and we are glad to see that Sir Walter Sendall likes to see things for himself and if, as we also hear, he has a mind of his own, so much the better.*[22]

Reporting on his tour of the wine district, Sendall concluded that the wine industry was indeed in distress, and suggested a tax cut of 25 per cent to avoid irrevocable decay. His report indicates enormous attention to detail. Grievances arose not only from the amount of tax collected, but the way it was assessed. 'At the moment residue is stirred up and measured with the wine which makes it heavier.' He was sure that the growers would gladly assent to a method of measuring that did not disturb the wine and confessed that he had 'measured a great number of these jars' and, having witnessed the process of making them, had a solution. His dispatch is illustrated with careful diagrams.[23]

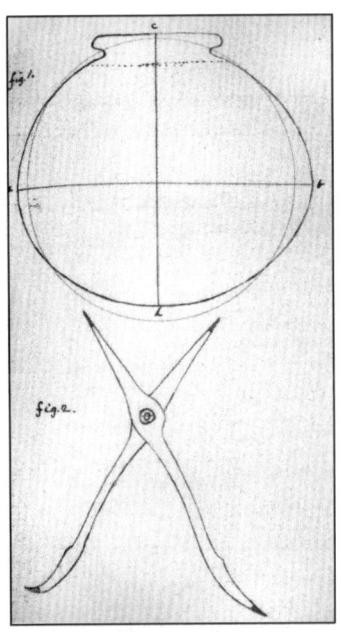

7. Sendall's diagram of a wine jar more suitable for tax assessment

---

21. *The Times of Cyprus*, 8 October 1892.
22. Ibid.
23. It appears in 'Memorandum on the measurement of Wine Jars in Cyprus' written in his own hand and attached to Sendall to Ripon, 5 September 1892, CO67/77, NA.

8. Potters at Phini

He expressed confidence in the future of the wine industry, particularly for the Egyptian market, if it was given a tax break, because of 'the rare capabilities of the soil and the absence of those natural pests that exist in other countries'. The secretary of state for the colonies, Lord Ripon, backed Sendall's plea for a 25 per cent cut in wine tax and for the cost of transport to be deducted from the market price in measuring wine for assessment.[24] Ripon argued that the need to respond generously arose from the fact that the hardship to the wine-growers was likely to be long-term, if not permanent, but tax relief for them was stalled by the Treasury, until such time as the equivalent funds could be found from another 'head'.

The secretary of state also returned to the need for expenditure on penal reform, the Treasury having refused to consider earlier pleas. Bulwer had seriously underestimated the cost of construction of the new central prison – chiefly because his reliance on (unpaid) prison labour had not taken account of the cost of the daily guarding and transporting of the prisoners to and from their current gaol. This was a converted Ottoman caravanserai in the heart of the Old City, the Büyük Khan. The new prison under construction was some way out of town. Sendall argued that convict labour would be extremely slow, while paid free labourers would cost only a little more and the urgently needed modern prison would be available in reasonable time. Either way, the cost would be far greater than Bulwer had estimated. The Colonial Office had suggested that the extra money required be taken from the surplus locust tax fund, but the elected members of the legislative council, Christian and Muslim, had objected. Latterly, the cost of dealing with the annual anti-locust campaign had dropped dramatically, as a result of its success in reducing the pest and because of the new methods used. The surplus, the only substantial sum collected that was not charged to the general revenue, was jealously guarded by the local government as a source of funding small local projects.

Law and Order was a priority and money would have to be spent, even if it meant an increased grant-in-aid. 'The situation cannot be allowed to continue', Ripon wrote to the Treasury. 'It is to a large extent traceable to the weakness and inefficiency of the police, and is susceptible of remedy,

---

24. The tax assessments were made by the district *Medjli Idare*. For a definition of the *Medjli Idare*, see 'Memorandum on the Finances and Administration of Cyprus', Edward Fairfield, June 1882, Enclosure No.1 in Papers relating to the Administration and Finances of Cyprus presented to Parliament June 1883 [c-3661].

Bejuk Khan

9. The Büyük Khan

or, at all events, amelioration. The increase required is £2,907. The scheme for reform submitted by the high commissioner is the result of careful consideration and does not admit of retrenchment.' But the Treasury, not the secretary of state for the colonies, would decide. Cyprus was not a Crown Colony. It was the Treasury that wielded real power over the island. All colonial administrations complained of the tight-fisted nature of the Treasury, but in no other dependent territory did it have such a hold over every penny that was spent. Later in the year, for example, Sendall would be obliged to seek permission to give forage allowance to the chief commandant of police for a much-needed second horse.[25] For the smallest withdrawal, Sendall would have to ask the Colonial Office and the Colonial Office, if it considered the submission justified, would then pass it on to the Treasury. This process was cumbersome for usually the Treasury delayed the process by asking for further explanation. The system was also encumbered by the slowness and irregularity of the mail. A dispatch could take up to four weeks to reach London. It would generally spend at least a month in the Colonial Office, then up to another month in the Treasury.

---

25. Sendall to Ripon, 4 December 1893 CO67/82. For relations between the Colonial Office and the Treasury at this time, see Blakely (1972), 134-141.

Sir Walter might not receive authorization to act, if he received it at all, until three months after the original request had been sent. By the end of his term, he was resorting increasingly to the use of telegrams and from time to time took the initiative without waiting for authorization, in each case being severely reprimanded for doing so.

It was over the law and order issue that Sir Walter first confronted the arrogance with which the Lords of the Treasury dealt with Cyprus, an arrogance which was, in this case, too much even for Lord Ripon. Sensing, perhaps, a way of establishing another 'locust' tax, they suggested there should be 'none of this soft stuff'. Expenditure on education and public works should be suspended throughout the island until law and order had been restored in the area afflicted and this region should be charged a special tax to deal with the problem. Noting that the police and prisons already amounted to a quarter of the whole local expenditure and that an increase of ten per cent was now sought by Sendall 'in order to cope with the state of quasi civil war in the district of Paphos', as they put it, they argued that 'This disgrace to British rule ….. cannot be stopped by teaching the native police reading and writing at the depot, or improving their kits, or by any increase in numbers'. Instead, they proposed:

> *A body of skilled and hardy marksmen …. aided by native guides, should keep up a ceaseless warfare against the brigands, pursuing them into the fastnesses of the hills, until they are extirpated. The energy that defeated the locusts a few years ago would stamp out the brigandage now.*
>
> *It is a mockery to spend more money, as proposed in the present Estimate, in improved land registration, when the tiller of the soil has a cut-throat at his door, or to make school grants for teaching letters to children who are liable to outrage with impunity in their own cottage gardens. Expenditure of these kinds, and that on Public Works, in a measure, might be suspended until the crisis is over.*[26]

The Lords of the Treasury stressed that 'by this or any other means' the secretary of state should keep the estimates of expenditure within a total

---

26. Welby to Ripon, Treasury reaction to the Cyprus estimates for 1893-1894, received in the Colonial Office on 22 February 1893, CO67/83, NA.

of £115,645 for the year 1893-94.[27] This was enough to cause a spark of indignation, even in the dimly lit corridors of the Colonial Office.

'Surely it cannot be supposed', retorted Lord Ripon, 'that it was a feature of the arrangement of 1883, that expenditure was never to grow, *whatever might be the growth of population*'. He pointed out that the annual expenditure of the island had increased by only 5 per cent over the minimum sum required ten years ago, whereas the population had increased by 12 per cent. He stressed that the expenditure sought for police reform was only 11 per cent higher than in 1883 when the vote was established 'and there was little or nothing *then* to indicate the approaching outburst of exceptional crime'.[28] He did not add that this outburst of crime had, in fact, coincided with severe cuts in expenditure that characterised the Bulwer years, combined with very severe tax-collecting methods, enforced at the Treasury's insistence from the late 1880s. Nor did he mention that the police pay was so miserable that the police force, unable to attract recruits, was never less than 180 men short. Ripon insisted that the police must be improved in order to reduce crime, but deemed it unlikely that the increased sums needed for this improvement could be found from economies elsewhere in the budget, 'the expenditure in Cyprus [having been] so carefully supervised, and the policy of effecting reductions so carefully followed'.[29] The Lords of the Treasury remained unmoved.

It was at the beginning of 1893, by which time he had spent nearly a year in the island, that Sendall launched his first assault on this system. 'We shall not be able either to work up an administration in roads, schools, police or reform of education to a satisfactory standard, or to become independent of help from parliament', he informed Ripon, 'unless means can be found *to put the revenue upon a more secure footing* so as to be less liable to violent fluctuations from a more or less favourable season for the crops'.

> *At present, in a bad year, the only expedient resorted to is to reduce expenditure on Public Works with results that are disastrous for the Administration as well as positively wasteful. Roads, on which a lot of money has been spent, deteriorate irreparably.*[30]

---

27. Ibid.
28. Colonial Office to Treasury, 17 March 1893, CO67/83, NA.
29. Ibid.
30. Private handwritten letter: Sendall to Ripon, 14 February 1893, CO67/79.

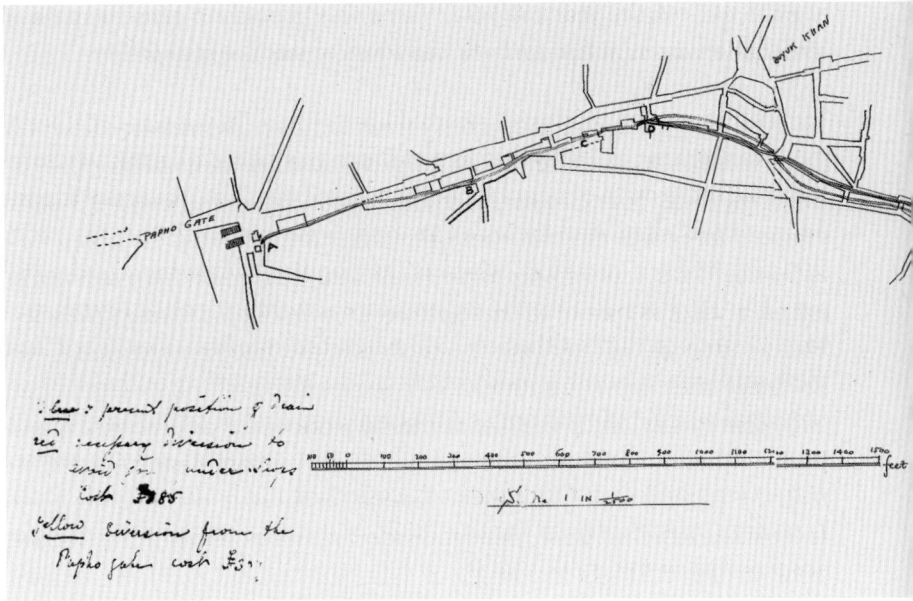

10. Sketch of Nicosia Main Drain, 1896

The key to creating revenue which would negate the need for a grant-in-aid, he believed, was irrigation and more specifically, the building of dams. In his elaborations on how these dams could be built, he alluded to 'an expert from Australia' – none other than Bowen, who was then residing at Government House. It must have been the encouragement of this high official that empowered Sendall to launch such radical proposals - a frontal attack, in fact, on the established principles of Cyprus policy. Sendall had included this proposal in his draft for the annual report to Parliament for 1892. The Colonial Office made sure it was not printed because 'the government would have to respond to questions from the Opposition as to why there was no development on the island when the attitude of the Treasury would make it quite out of the question to entertain your suggestions'.[31]

Sendall wanted to dam the narrow valleys down which the torrents flowed in the rainy season, which he believed could be simply done. He was assured that this was not so and referred to the response to a similar

---

31. Sendall to Ripon, 24 February 1893. This is Sendall's contribution to the annual report for 1892-1893. All the argumentation for investment in irrigation has been struck out, presumably by Fairfield. See also Fairfield minute attached.

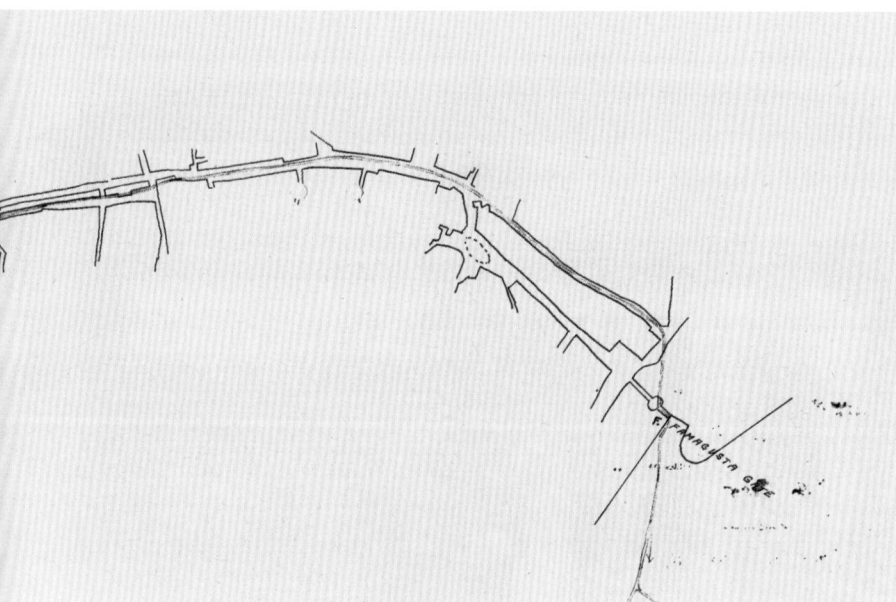

proposal by Kitchener in 1882. The objections lay in the capital required, but also in the difficulties raised by the distances and terrain through which the water would have to be channelled from the western mountain valleys to the thirsty eastern plains.[32] For the moment artificial irrigation, of the kind being successfully implemented on a large scale in Egypt, was considered out of the question for Cyprus. Sir Walter was obliged to focus on less ambitious projects.

One of these had been on his mind since his first arrival in Nicosia. Something had to be done about the stench emanating from the heart of Nicosia. Fears that a cholera epidemic, currently raging in Asia Minor, might permeate the island as well, secured permission from the Treasury for the Cyprus government to guarantee a tiny loan, enabling the capital's municipal council to cover the Pedieos riverbed that traversed the old city.

---

32. Kitchener to Kimberly, 6 September 1882, in Further Correspondence respecting the Affairs of Cyprus, August–December 1882 (Confidential Print). Kitchener is submitting recommendations on a report by Ruddell and Brown for securing a better water supply. Kitchener advocated taking control of the island's water supply and damming the valleys above Limassol. Nothing was decided and nothing was done as a consequence of these reports. It was considered too expensive to bore or dam and too difficult to take over the water supply.

11. Sir Walter and Lady Sendall with Phaneromeni School board, girls and staff, 1894

'It [had] for years stagnated, reeking with every kind of abomination through the most crowded quarter of the town.'[33] Three months later, London having taken that long to nod acquiescence, a contract with the town council was entered into by Hadjizoe of Kaimakli for the execution of the work which would be supervised by an officer of the public works department.

Büyük Kaimakli, a village on the outskirts of Nicosia, was the home of many of the town's master builders. It was flourishing on the growing demand for stonemasons, the prison and the drain being cases in point. The new churches too, complete with bell towers that marked the end of *raya* status, were often the work of Kaimakli masons.[34] The capital with which the Sendalls became familiar had begun spreading beyond the Venetian walls that had contained it since the seventeenth century. In 1893, Emile

---

33. Sendall's annual report for 1892, published in *The Owl*, 19 August 1893.
34. Lewis, 204. Mrs. Lewis also notes the blossoming of 'beautiful woodcarving produced by country carpenters' to meet the growing demand for iconastases and pews.

Deschamps described the tree-lined avenue which led beyond the wooden bridge over the moat at Makridromos (today's Ledra Street) towards the new secretariat as the 'Champs Elysées of Nicosia'. 'Here', he wrote, 'the youth promenade and frequent the many cafes to be found along the way'.[35] The area immediately beyond the walls, south-west of the old city, was becoming a smart modern suburb with a distinctly colonial stamp. Lady Sendall dutifully raised money for the new Anglican church being built there, organising a series of concerts in Phaneromeni girls' school hall at which she played the piano.[36] There was perhaps no other suitable hall, but the venue indicates an early and fairly intimate interaction between the high commissioner and the Archbishop, forged by their mutual interest in promoting education. Moreover, the headmistress of the school, Theano Paroudi, was the betrothed of the high-profile politician, Achilleas Liassides. Both were leading lights in the intellectual life of the capital and, no doubt, saw much of the high commissioner and his 'λαίδη (laidhi)', as she was often referred to in the local press.

Glimpses of the Sendalls' life in Nicosia emerge from the pages of Elizabeth Lewis's book and from titbits in the local papers, particularly the English language rags. That March, there were house guests in residence at Government House. Sir George Bowen, already mentioned, and the Lady Sophia's nephew, John Calverly's son, had been there some days when Elizabeth Lewis and her daughter joined them after their tour of the Limassol and Paphos area. The guests were treated to tours of Nicosia, picnics and expeditions to Kythrea, Buffavento, Bellapais and Kyrenia. Sir Walter was for the most part absent from these pleasant excursions, but he was observed, duty-bound, at a distance. 'It was a daily marvel', noted Mrs. Lewis, 'to see the High Commissioner's large ex-Khedival carriage with a pair of white Russian horses threading their way through the narrow streets and safely turning the sharpest of apparently impossible corners'.[37] Tankerville Chamberlayne, that 'cicerone' who had droned on enlighteningly, as he accompanied the two ladies on the last leg of their ride from Paphos to Limassol, now managed to locate himself

---

35. Emile Deschamps, Στην Κύπρο, τη Χώρα της Αφροδίτης, Greek language edition (Nicosia 2005), 64. The 'Champs Elysées' is now Severis Avenue.
The secretariat further up the same road, was originally intended as a barracks for the Cyprus Military Police. In 1881, it was purloined by the government and adapted to house the central civil service offices of the island and also the new legislative council.
36. *The Owl*, 17 February 1893 and 6 March 1895.
37. Lewis, 198.

12. Road from Kyrenia, ca. 1900

Anglican Church of St.Paul's, Nicosia

in the capital and acted as the visitors' guide around the Frankish monuments. But not in Greek Orthodox Nicosia - it was the Archbishop himself who showed Lady Sendall's party the tiny but 'beautifully painted cathedral church of Ayios Ioannis', received them at his Palace and then guided them around a needlework display put on by the girls of Phaneromeni school.[38]

Both Sendall and his wife, Sophia, were children of Anglican vicars. This churchy background, together with Sendall's classical scholarship and the mutual interest of the two men in education, all provided some sort of common ground for the close relations the high commissioner wanted to cultivate with the Ethnarch of the Cypriot Christians. Sir Walter never missed an opportunity to visit a school. Mrs. Lewis records that he was impressed to find schoolboys at the Hellenic school in Nicosia, 'reading Homer and other classical authors with obvious enjoyment'. But how much more the Archbishop must have enjoyed this unusual interest in and appreciation of Greek education on the part of the new governor.

---

38.   Ibid., 214-215.

The *mufti*, the chief *cadi* and even the sheik of the whirling dervishes were 'at home' in Government House. 'The Cadi, a grand old turbaned Turk … likes to come to receptions', observed Mrs. Lewis, 'and is quite ready for a cup of tea with English ladies'.[39] Both the Christian and Muslim leaders were present for the laying of the foundation stone for the Anglican Church of St. Paul's. The ladies Lewis were there too and the 'jovial and portly Abbot of Kykko'. The church was being built for a second time, to the same design with the same materials, on land donated by Bulwer in what is now Byron Avenue. The land was in all probability acquired from *Evkaf* since it was contiguous with the Muslim cemetery.[40] The stones were retrieved one by one from the abandoned building on the original site on St. George's hill opposite the Secretariat, where subsidence had made the church unsafe. As Lady Sendall laid the first stone, the hymn chosen, appropriately enough, was 'The Church's One Foundation …'.[41]

Agni Michaelides has described the 1890s in Nicosia as a time of 'intellectual renaissance'. The first bookbinder found enough work to establish a business. Cypriot poets began to publish both in the vernacular and in high Greek.[42] Trying to shake off their reputation for dour conservatism, the Nicosia citizens began to organise amateur theatricals in which Achilleas Liassides was a protagonist. Lady Sendall organised musical evenings and no doubt participated in 'book

Phyti embroidery

---
39. Ibid., 200.
40. Bulwer, whose interest in medieval Cyprus was no doubt influenced by his aide-de-camp, Tankerville Chamberlayne, had bought property from *Evkaf* under whose jurisdiction many Lusignan and Venetian monuments lay. He bought, for example, part of the remaining fragment of a Venetian palace in Famagusta, in order to protect it. Jeffery provides us with a photograph of 'Bulwer's Arch' there, before and after repairs. Pilides, Vol.II, 518. For illustrations, see Plate XXXVII.
41. *The Owl*, 8 April 1893.
42. Agni Michaelides, 129-134.

13. Archbishop Sofronios

teas', so abhorrent to Rider Haggard.[43] It was at about this time that building began of a new theatre in the old city near Phaneromeni church. The Papadopoulos Theatre was a replica of a small opera house in Italy and an architectural gem. It reflected the social transformation in urban society under British rule, but its construction was a slow process. Running parallel to the building of the central prison, it would not be completed until 1900.[44] For the moment, school halls, coffee shops and large private houses were the only theatrical venues. During the Christmas season, *The Times of Cyprus* recorded the first expatriate attempt at 'amateur theatricals for a large number of years'. It took place in the home of Dr. Heidenstam, the chief medical officer and his attractive Corfiote wife. The high commissioner and Lady Sendall sat in the front rows in a room which was 'full to overflowing'.[45]

---

43. *A Winter Pilgrimage,* 183. For a typical musical evening organised by Lady Sendall, see *The Times of Cyprus,* 8 February 1894.
44. The theatre, designed by Italian architects, cost about £4,000CY, a large sum in those days. Building began in 1893, but it took seven years to build and was not completed until 1900. It could hold an audience of 600 people. An Italian operetta company was brought over especially for the opening ceremonies. Theatre productions were mainly Greek – ancient and modern – but it was also used by British and Turkish Cypriot enthusiasts: Agni Michaelides, 228-230.
45. *The Times of Cyprus,* 23 December 1893.

There were two key social events annually in Nicosia with a Government House focus. The first centred on the Queen's Birthday celebrations at the end of May and the second was the Nicosia Race Week soon afterwards. The officers and band of the garrison moved up from Polemedia for the duration and Nicosia sparkled. A ball was held at Government House for both occasions. If the Sendalls lacked the *savoir faire* of Bulwer and his 'glamorous' aides-de-camp, whose colourful exertions on these occasions were greatly appreciated by *The Times of Cyprus*, the charm and elegance of the lady hostess clearly compensated, while the iced 'Hock', a refreshing wine/lime/lemon cup drawn from the Sendalls' Carribean years and introduced to Cyprus on this occasion, went down a treat and lingered on in Cypriot colonial circles into the 1950s.[46] 'His Excellency wore small-clothes and white silk stockings', the same paper reported.[47] Sir Elliott Bovill, the attorney general, was in his court dress and many officials in civil service uniform.[48] The more expansive and genuine welcome of Cypriot dignitaries, some of them arriving at the ball in bullock carts, as well as the growing success of native racehorse owners and riders, gave the festive week a less exclusively expatriate character.[49]

At the races the high commissioner and his wife mingled among the crowd and presented the trophies, one of which was for a new race inaugurated by them - the 'Sendall Cup' for the winner of a race exclusively for Cypriot-bred horses.[50] During those last May weeks, 'the regiment' made itself felt in the capital. The band played all over the town and it would be much missed when it returned to Polemedia. It was the absence of social sparkle attending a military or naval presence that provoked the tone of hurt nostalgia in British circles for visits from the fleet, long since departed, 'or even from a lone cruiser'. They needed confirmation that their island mattered, that they were part of a great empire, that their presence in Cyprus had a purpose in the grand scheme of things. *The Owl*'s pining for the excitement of dashing young men in uniform has an almost

---

46. KEO winery produced a fresh white wine named 'Hock' from the fifties.
47. Small-clothes, (according to Grose 1811 Dictionary) were tight-fitting breeches.
48. *The Times of Cyprus*, 31 May 1892.
49. Agni Michaelides, 143. For the success of horses with local owners and riders, not only in Cyprus, but also in Beirut and Egypt, see issues of *The Owl* in 1893 and 1894 where the races are a major feature of the paper. For example, *The Owl*, 18 December 1893 reported that at the Beirut races, eight out of the twelve events were won by the jockey and owner, Agathaclous Michaelides of Limassol. *The Owl* clearly took great pride in this 'well-deserved [Cypriot] success'.
50. *The Times of Cyprus*, 24 May 1892.

14. Government House, Nicosia, in Sendall's time

Jane Austen feel about it.[51] Elizabeth Lewis, perceptive as ever, caught the mood:

> *If the officers' predilections were consulted, they would prefer to be quartered in Nicosia..... Nicosia would be very glad to have them and would, in such a case, form a more brilliant social centre than currently exists on the island.*[52]

If May signalled the peak of the social season in Nicosia, the opening of the legislative council in February surely launched a budding political season. The military band was again summoned from Polemedia, as was a detachment of British troops, to form a guard of honour. The *zaptiehs* wore their turbaned fezzes, the Greek Orthodox dignitaries, *mufti* and *cadi*, turned out in full regalia, the high commissioner and his senior officials were in full dress uniform. In February1893 *The Owl* recorded the largest crowd ever, an indicator of the growing interest in electoral politics. Bulwer had perceived the body as a cosmetic 'advisory council' whose advice he did not seek.[53] It was this failure to consult the Cypriot representatives that, more than anything else, led to the Cypriots taking the extraordinary step in 1887 of bypassing the local government and appealing directly to London, a procedure never considered in Malta, for example, or the Ionian islands during British rule. But Sir Henry had been bypassed before, most famously by Cetshwayo, King of the Zulus, who, in much bloodier circumstances, went to London in spite of Bulwer's repeated efforts to prevent him.[54]

Sendall, in contrast, went out of his way to consult Cypriots at all levels. This, after all, had been Robert Herbert's brief. 'We should run Cyprus more in the manner the Cypriots want', he had observed. Within the parameters of the 1882 constitution, the Cypriot legislators began to take

---

51.   *The Owl,.* 22 September 1894. It advocates that the fleet should visit twice a year at least if the garrison is to be removed.
52.   Lewis, 37.
53.   In Bulwer's opening speech to the legislative council on 17 February 1887, he tells the members he looks forward 'to their advice and assistance in consideration of the several matters which may be brought before you'. See *The Times of Cyprus,* 7 March 1887. It was in the same speech in that same disastrous year that he congratulated the members on 'the general condition and prospects of the country'.
54.   Lord Kimberly considered Bulwer's indecision and procrastination had resulted in the need to concede Cetshwayo a visit to London. Bulwer had been instructed to visit Zululand and discover 'the real feelings of the Zulu' and had failed to do so. See Jeff Grey (1979), 148-150.

The Secretariat and Legislatve Council Hall

a much greater part in the decision-making process. In the spring of 1893, one topic, in particular, was at the heart of political gossip. What had happened to the surplus over the expenditure and the Tribute payment that had been the extraordinary result of the bumper harvest and strict government economies of 1891? The fact that there had been such a surplus, for the first time since 1878, together with the total absence of government spending in the subsequent budget over and above the bare minimum administration costs, led to a series of probing questions into where the money, at least this surplus on the surplus, was.

Achilleas Liassides moved a resolution in the legislative council, based on a proposal made by Sendall himself to Her Majesty's government, that the surplus should be placed on deposit with a view to its application to certain important requirements over and above the usual expenditure, *within the island*. Liassides placed the requirements under three heads: public works, agriculture and education. Spending this money, he said, was basic justice and would benefit the Cyprus government too, by providing more revenue in the long term, and making the population more contented. Sendall warmly supported this resolution.[55] He repeatedly picked up, and even arranged, demands in the local legislature to convince his principals, but also used pressure from Whitehall to modify demands within the council.

---

55. Sendall to Ripon, 22 May 1893 and Enclosure No.7 for text of resolution passed by House of Representatives., CO67/80, NA.

There was enough financial interest in the island for eyebrows to be raised in London at this Cypriot probing. Questions in the House of Commons on 20 May 1893 forced the government to admit to the public (most importantly to the Cypriot public) that any sum remaining from the Cypriot revenue, after the annual interest on the 1855 Ottoman loan had been paid to the Anglo-French bondholders, was placed in a sinking fund for that loan in London. The Treasury was being cornered by Sendall, in cooperation with his legislative council, into spooning out some of the Cypriot money held on account. The secretary of state for the colonies took up the cause. Lord Ripon pointed out that even by their own way of calculating, the Treasury owed the Cypriots £2,000 for each of the years 1889, 1890 and 1891, when, in spite of the growing revenue of those years, the provision for public works had been cut from £10,000 (the sum officially committed in 1883 by the Treasury) to £8,000. 'therefore, in order to place the Home Government beyond criticism, it would only be proper to take advantage of the present prosperity to make up to the island, at least in part, what we withheld in the years above mentioned.' He urged that the money was desperately needed to maintain roads and build bridges. Even the Nicosia-Larnaca road had become well nigh impassable and all the money invested in them in the first - spending - years of British rule, would have been wasted, if repairs were not undertaken in the very near future.[56] The missing surplus had been the main topic for debate in the prolonged session of the legislative council after Easter. The receiver general's fudged response to a direct question on the use to which the surplus was being put 'for the general service of the Government', fuelled a barrage of derisive Cypriot comment. Sendall pressed the point home. 'The more this matter of the disposal of the surplus is not cleared up, the more urgent it will become, both politically and in terms of administering the island half decently.'[57]

After an inevitable delay of six months while the matter was being processed in Whitehall, the Treasury, without admitting any obligation to do so, reluctantly agreed to allow an extra £2,000, the sum deducted from the public works budget during the earlier years, for the 1894 budget for that department. Sendall's government lapped up the extra sum with relish. While most money was spent on accelerating the works on the prison, the autumn being too late for bridge-building before the 'torrent

---

56. Ripon to Treasury, 4 July 1893, CO67/80, NA.
57. Sendall to Ripon, 22 May 1893, CO67/80, NA.

season', one exception was made, that of Pyroi bridge on the main Larnaca-Nicosia road. This became a deliberate showcase project for a government determined to change its image.

The bridge over the broad riverbed at Pyroi, so dilapidated as to have recently caused a fatal accident, was replaced. There was exceptional public interest in this project. The bridge had been described as 'on the point of collapse', in June 1891 but had not been seriously tackled by the government engineer, in spite of the bumper revenue of that year.[58] 'How the Government could have the face to leave such a rotten, patched up structure on the principal highway for so long a time was beyond comprehension', observed *The Owl,* in October 1893, delighted that a new iron structure was in the making. Thenceforth, the Nicosia and Larnaca papers generally maintained a regular bulletin as to the progress on the bridge at Pyroi. The high commissioner was widely congratulated for securing the funds from the home government. The new structure, it was declared, was 'not only serviceable but ornamental'. Sir Walter opened the bridge ceremonially on 25 November 1893.[59] Such ceremony pressed home the good news that some surplus revenue was, at last, being used for the benefit of Cypriot taxpayers. The cavalcade of carriages and carts that trundled across the bridge in Sendall's wake, left the 'do nothing' policy, of which the Treasury and Fairfield remained the chief advocates, stranded on the dusty bank.

The 1893 session of the legislative council did not end until 23 May, the longest session ever, according to *The Owl.* Once the Race Week was over and the heat began to set in, the expatriate families began packing for the hills. The Sendalls' route to Troodos was via Larnaca, where Lady Sendall would go on ahead, by sea to Limassol and thence up the good military road from Polemedia to Troodos. With her she would take the baggage necessary for the long stay and for the entertainments she would prepare and organise for the community encamped there. She and Sir Walter would live at Government Cottage. The other families were all under canvas, but this did not deter them from a full social calendar.

---

58. *The Times of Cyprus,* 18 June 1892.
59. Ένωσις and Φωνή της Κύπρου cited in *The Owl,* 14 October 1892, and *The Times of Cyprus,* 26 November 1892. Progress of bridge reported in every issue of the latter between September and November 1893.

> When all who are usually separated by long and difficult journeys, meet together from the various distant districts for once in the year: the impromptu tea-parties organised under trees; the tennis courts; the presence of the whole military staff and their excellent band playing at the afternoon receptions at Government Cottage; these and many other pleasant things make the annual migration to Troodos a very cheery time to be looked forward to with a good deal of enthusiasm.[60]

En route the Sendalls took the opportunity of staying over for a week in Larnaca with its hospitable district commissioner, Delaval Cobham. When he was on leave they stayed in the ramshackle hostelry. 'The principal inhabitants' thus had an opportunity of meeting Sir Walter and his Λαίδη at levees, afternoon receptions and dinner parties. Niceties would be exchanged and views aired. The gesture was much appreciated, the journey to Nicosia being arduous and there being no hotels.[61] Having waved goodbye to Lady Sophia from the Larnaca pier, the high commissioner would prepare to approach the hill resort from some route he had not yet seen.[62]

It was in the green coolness of the Troodos mountains that Sendall and his team would set to work on the issues raised in Nicosia, both within and without the legislative council, and the matters arising from his tours of investigation. It was a period of analysis of what had passed and preparation for action in the following months. The Queen's Advocate would compile reports explaining the context of the laws enacted, the Treasurer would fine-tune the estimates based, not only on the cash already in hand, but also on the latest assessments of the fetching price for the tithe wheat and barley, still stacked in government stores. Sendall would write despatches to London on these matters, but also on the bills that were not enacted or that there was no time to debate in the busy session of the legislative council.

Of these issues, two stand out: the inclusion of 'natives' within the executive council and proposals for the improvement of education. Encouraging the inclusion of Cypriots in this, the highest decision-making body, was a logical next step for the high commissioner, given his willingness to listen

---

60. Lewis, 335. It was Sir Walter Sendall who modified the name of the Troodos residence from Government House to Government Cottage.
61. *The Times of Cyprus*, 31 May 1892.
62. In 1893 Sendall rode to Limassol with Dr. Heidenstam over the hills through Chirokitia, Lefkara and Ora, which had just applied for a branch road. *The Times of Cyprus*, 1893.

to Cypriot opinion. It was in line too with the permanent secretary's inclination to start governing the island in a way that would begin to accommodate Cypriot aspirations. Cypriot participation in the executive council had been one of the demands of the 1887 memorialists. The issue had been raised again in the last, prolonged session of the legislature and was being aired in the Greek Cypriot press.[63] To continue to deny the Cypriots a voice on the executive council, Sendall argued, would 'be inconsistent with the idea of the constitution as settled by Lord Kimberly in 1882'.

> *The two races conduct themselves with remarkable harmony in the Legislative Council...I believe at the time when the Legislative Council was constituted on its present footing, it was thought probable that the two races would oppose each other and that government, by reason of such opposition, would be able to rule both. Any such conception has proved entirely fallacious. The two races are united in solid opposition to the government.*[64]

The presence of Cypriots on the executive council would, Sendall urged, 'allow the Government to derive the benefit of enlightened natives of the country, not, as at present, in the form of criticism of measures already adopted, but in the form of counsel as to what measures it would be best to adopt.'[65]

There was support in London for this approach. Cypriots were needed on the council, it was argued, 'because the laws prepared there turn so largely on purely local conditions and are so alien to British knowledge and experience that the case for native representation is particularly strong'. The fear raised of subsequent breaches of confidentiality was countered with the following argument. Since the conditions of the administration had been fixed in 1883, nothing had come before the council that would 'cause inconvenience in this respect', while the settled habit of the Cypriots considering themselves in permanent opposition would be broken 'by taking the legislative council, so to speak, into the confidence of the executive'.[66] Sendall had raised the point that it would be difficult to appoint a Turk

---

63. See, for example, *Φωνή της Κύπρου* article, cited in *The Owl*, June 1893.
64. Sendall to Ripon, 18 October 1893, CO67/81, NA.
65. Sendall to Ripon, 18 October 1893, CO67/81, NA.
66. Minute signed by Meade, 30 November 1893, CO67/81, NA.

because none spoke English and the efficient functioning of the executive council demanded the immediacy of a single language.[67] Fairfield displayed an ingrained prejudice as regards 'the natives', characteristic of the Bulwer years. He advised that it would be politic to appoint a Turk as well. No matter if he didn't understand the proceedings since 'he would probably never attend,' and, anyway, in practice, 'the Executive Council would only be the *formal* vehicle. The governor would have his confidential consultations with departmental heads as he does now'.[68] Though by no means ruling out the possibility of natives on the executive council, Ripon ensured a considerable delay by seeking further clarifications three months later from Sendall.[69] Ripon's request did not reach Cyprus until the end of the year, by which time Sendall was becoming impatient. On 19 December, he informed the secretary of state that he would go ahead with the appointment of native members, thereby implementing the Queen's instructions. He observed that he had done this in Barbados with very good results. The Archbishop was the only native that had ever been invited on the executive council. This had taken place only once on an *ad hoc* basis. He agreed with Fairfield on the need for the immediacy of a single language. Since there was no Turk who could speak English, he was going to appoint three Greeks, Paschalis Constantinides, George Shiakallis and Achilleas Liassides. The high commissioner did not advocate the creation of a new body, but proposed including a few members of the legislative council on the existing body on an experimental basis.[70]

The high commissioner was using bulldozing tactics, similar to those he had already used in the financial sphere, to press his principals into action. In doing so, he was slowly but surely beginning to undermine the passivity, inaugurated when the new conditions of the administration were drawn up in 1883. Was this tendency getting dangerous? 'Sendall has shown himself strongly obtuse of late, about the financial restrictions within which we and he have to administer Cyprus', Fairfield had fretted 'He ought to get a wigging.'[71]

---

67. Sendall to Ripon, 18 October 1893. Language difficulties had been Bulwer's pretext for not giving the matter any consideration. See *The Owl*, 10 June 1893.
68. Minute signed by Fairfield, 8 November 1893, CO67/81, NA.
69. Ripon to Sendall, 8 November 1893, CO67/81, NA.
70. Sendall to Ripon, 19 December 1893, CO67/82. He referred specifically to para 3 of the Royal Instructions of 1878, para 39 of Lord Knutsford's despatch dated 6 March 1890.
71. Ibid., Fairfield Minute attached.

The Colonial Office would not be chivvied into hurrying, but Sir Walter's tactics did eventually allow Cypriots to sit, for the first time, in the inner chamber of the decision-making process, a step that would have been unthinkable a few years earlier. It was not until March 1894 that Ripon instructed Sendall formally on the issue. The existing executive council should be empowered, by royal instruction, to name inhabitants of the island to be called 'Additional Members of the Executive Council', to be consulted on specific matters, but not on confidential matters of policy. This would be a three-year experiment.[72] There is no indication here of how many members or which community the members should derive from, but a related minute by Fairfield suggested the places should be offered to one Greek and one Turk with the Turk being replaced by a Greek if the latter declines - 'but the latter should be spoken of as Christians not Greeks', he added out of the blue, 'they might use the latter against us.' Sendall struggled for the following two years to avoid having to receive authorisation from London whenever he wanted to invite the 'native' members onto the council. He insisted that the decision should rest with the high commissioner, intending to ensure their presence most of the time. It was not until 1897 that he gained this concession from the secretary of state.

Sir Walter's affinity for educational matters, displayed prominently in his first posting in Ceylon, came once more to the fore in Cyprus. His classical education facilitated a certain intellectual rapport with the local Greek Christian intelligentsia. He took a special interest in the Hellenic School in Nicosia. In the coming years, he would collaborate with the Archbishop to build a more systematic instruction in the art of teaching within the school. In the meantime, three inspectors from the Greek ministry of education were employed by the government to travel around the village schools teaching the new methods being established in Greece. There surely could not have been a stronger indication than this of the extent to which the Hellenic nature of education within the Christian community was taken for granted in Whitehall, as well as Nicosia, as was the Ottoman nature of the Muslim schools. The island remained Ottoman territory under British administration. When acquiring the island in 1878, Lord Salisbury had not intended to give it the appearance of a British colony, but to demonstrate how an Ottoman province could be efficiently

---

72. Ripon to Sendall, 21 March 1894, CO67/82, NA.

administered by British officials. He hoped thus to persuade the Sultan to extend that beneficence into 'Western Asia'. The policy was to improve the existing systems, not to change them, since retrocession must appear to be the ultimate objective.[73] Although all thought of the British administration of Ottoman Asia had since been abandoned, the Porte would not allow London to forget that the island remained Ottoman. In the context of the Eastern Question it was important for Britain as well that the international status quo remain unruffled. To this end, the Christian community too must remain unruffled. The all-important tranquillity within the island, already tested by financial constraints, depended on British tolerance of cultural diversity.

Within these parameters, in the summer of 1893, Sendall made a start on educational reform. Two government bills were based on drafts that had been submitted to the legislative council in the previous session by Aristotle Paleologos, but had been set aside for the prolonged discussions on financial matters. The Greek Christians had been pressing for educational reform for some years, but had received short shrift when last the matter was raised in 1891.[74] Now the government adopted some of his suggestions and added some of their own. The resulting draft bills being submitted to Whitehall intended to regulate and secure the qualifications and the pay of teachers, until then vague and variable phenomena. Sir Walter secured the inclusion of 'mistresses as well as masters' in this new legislation.[75]

Another matter, this time outside the legislative council, had come to a head in the spring of 1893 and was further considered in Troodos. The tendency of the Porte to cling to any tangible stake in the island led to problems for the local administration when dealing with the plethora of Ottoman institutions they had inherited. Since Cyprus was still under Ottoman suzerainty, there could be no arbitrary British approach. In this context, the incumbent chief *cadi*, Mustafa Ferzi Effendi, had put the cat among the pigeons on more than one occasion. The somewhat ambivalent status of the chief *cadi* in the island and the extent of his powers, as well as that of the Turkish delegate of *Evkaf*, had created ripples between the

---

73. Diana Markides, 'Cyprus 1878–1925: Ambiguities and Uncertainties', Faustmann and Peristianis eds., *Britain in Cyprus: Colonialism and Post-Colonialism 1878-2006*, 19–33.
74. *The Times of Cyprus*, 3 April 1886.
75. Sendall to Ripon, 16 June 1893, CO67/80, NA, and enclosures containing draft bills.

island's Muslim community and the British administration in the past. This year the much-loved Houloussi Effendi, the *mouhassebedji*, who had been the Turkish delegate of *Evkaf* even before the British administration was installed on the island, had died of cholera while on the Hadj.

Sendall was much concerned as to whom Constantinople would now appoint, the 'right' man being essential because of 'the critical state of *vakouf* affairs'. The status of *Evkaf* itself was a matter of debate. Was it or was it not a department of the Cyprus Government? Mrs. Lewis described it as 'The Turkish Public Works Department'.[76] The chief cadi had nominated as Turkish delegate of *Evkaf*, Hadji Hafiz Ziyai Effendi. The high commissioner admitted this man to be a 'most respected' member of the Muslim community, but an ineffectual headmaster of the *Rustye* school, inexperienced in public office and, worse still, in personal financial debt to Ferzi Effendi. Moreover, whereas his predecessors had always acknowledged the authority of the Cypriot *Evkaf* and sought its approval, Ferzi Effendi had ignored it and bypassed the British administration to gain acceptance for his nominee directly from Constantinople.[77] Thus the Turkish ratification appeared to pre-empt the appointment made by Sir Walter and put forward through the British embassy at the Porte.[78]

This was not the only challenge to British control of *Evkaf* generated by the chief *cadi*. Early in 1892, he had awarded the trusteeship of a valuable *vakouf*. He had transferred the *vakouf* to Mehmet Salahi Effendi, without securing the ratification of *Evkaf*. In doing so, he exposed the chaotic state of things in connection with the administration of *vakoufs*, a state, warned Sendall, 'which was likely to cause great embarrassment both to the courts of law and to Her Majesty's Government'. Before the British occupation, the right to award *vakoufs* rested with the sultan, acting through his delegates in Constantinople. This right had never been exercised by the *cadi* alone, in Cyprus, but it had not been officially endowed on the local *Evkaf* either. Nevertheless, many titles *had* been transferred by the local *Evkaf*, on the assumption that enough authority rested within the island.

The British administration had resisted attempts by the Porte to purloin surplus revenues from these *vakoufs*. They acknowledged no more than a

---
76. Lewis, 200.
77. Sendall to Ripon, Troodos, 22 August 1892, CO67/77, NA. See also enclosed minute by Queen's Advocate, dated 28 April 1892.
78. Sendall to Ripon, 20 November 1893, CO67/82, NA.

titular Ottoman role, sending the annual accounts of *Evkaf* to Constantinople simply as 'a matter of courtesy'. Until now, this position had not been challenged, but Ferzi Effendi was much more assertive and aggressive in dealing with *Evkaf* matters than was his predecessor. The question was, 'What validity [was] attached to the *ilam* (edict) of the chief *cadi*? The Queen's Advocate advised that 'if anything was done that could be construed as an admission that the cadi has such power, this would no doubt suit the views of the current Turkish government very well, and they would not be willing to make provision for any other arrangements'.[79] Ferzi Effendi was not popular with the Cyprus government. 'Whatever may be his merits in the eyes of his supporters in Constantinople,' Sendall reported, 'the present Cadi of Cyprus is regarded with grave mistrust by a large section of the community here.'[80] Nevertheless, Ferzi had his supporters. On 2 December the high commissioner sent two memorials from Muslim citizens in Cyprus to Ripon. One urged the desirability of removing Ferzi from office, but the other, with considerably more signatures, pleaded for his retention in the post.[81] The high commissioner stressed the need for the matter to be clarified. 'That the law relating to the appointment of religious offices in Cyprus should be in a state of chaos, so many years after the occupation, cannot but be a matter of concern on account of the large amount of purely secular property, the succession of which is governed by these appointments.'[82]

The British had originally intended to impose a new land tax in Cyprus. Ottoman anomalies were telling factors in the problems of the expensively manned operation to carry out a detailed land survey to this end. In 1893, the land survey was aborted for a more gradual process which put the onus on the landowner, or potential landowner, who could not buy or sell his land without first getting it surveyed and registered. A return to the old Ottoman system of collecting tithes in kind on the key cereal crops had been resorted to once more in parts of the island which were most severely distressed in 1887. This move proved that tithes in kind were infinitely more collectible than cash. In December 1893, the land survey department was streamlined and the government was obliged to become

---

79. Ibid.
80. Ibid.
81. Sendall to Ripon, 2 December 1893, CO67/82, NA. The petition in Ferzi's favour had more signatures than the petition for his removal, but this did not necessarily reflect accurately on the extent of the popularity of the two men.
82. Ibid.

once more a dealer in cereal crops, on the sale of which the administration of the country once more depended. The return to tithes carried the unanimous approval of the legislative council.[83]

The condition of the police and the prisons remained problematical. All the district police commandants were either ailing, absent or inept, and the poor salary of the *zaptiehs* drew few recruits of indifferent quality. The police were 92 men short in the summer of 1893 and by the following year that number was over one hundred. Assistance came from an unexpected quarter, the bishop of Paphos, who suggested a force of 20 special constables to be drawn exclusively from his district. The idea caused much cynicism in the Colonial Office, whose principals envisioned the types who might enlist. Someone annotated in the margin, 'it takes a thief to catch a thief'. But something had to be done about the unruly western district. This is an interesting example of the church and the colonial government collaborating to find a solution to an administrative problem, as they probably would have done in Ottoman times. In the aftermath of the murder of the *mudir* of Paphos, the most notorious crime of the year, security in the Paphos district was at the top of the law and order agenda. The *mudir* had been murdered brutally while touring his district with two salt guards in the process of enforcing the unpopular government salt monopoly.

The arrangements made with the Porte regarding salt generated more problems than revenue for the island's administration. This vital commodity, collected locally from the Larnaca salt lake, had been an important government monopoly in the Ottoman system. On reluctantly handing the island over to British administration, the Porte had insisted on being paid a large annual Tribute in salt. Immediately afterwards, a prohibition was decreed against the sale of Cypriot salt in any part of the Ottoman empire. The expenses of collecting, and most of all guarding, the mountains of salt, which the Porte never bothered to move, far outweighed the sums collected from the sale of salt to Cypriot peasants. In far-flung regions, an arduous and lengthy journey from the salt depots in Larnaca and Limassol, acquiring salt legally was impossibly expensive and time-consuming. Inevitably, this basic ingredient for preserving food

---

83. The elected members reply to the high commissioner's opening speech to the legislative council, 15 March 1893, carried in *The Owl*, 27 March 1893 and Sendall to Ripon, 28 December 1893, CO67/82, NA.

became available under the counter. Offenders against the salt laws, mostly inhabitants of the Paphos and Karpass areas, were flung unceremoniously in gaol. This treatment was much resented. The high commissioner pointed out that the violence provoked by enforcement of this system far outweighed the pettiness of the original offence. In 1893 he alleviated the situation by taking the practical step of opening salt depots in every district – taking the salt to the people.[84] Offenders decreased and revenue from the salt increased.

The overcrowded prisons, then, were not so much a result of a rise in serious crime as a result of the system. A large number of people who were not convicted criminals were being held in prison while awaiting trial. The non-payment of tax, prevalent in the western regions, has been interpreted as popular resistance to colonial rule – and so it was, but not in any organised sense.[85] In countless cases, too, the problem was plain inabililty to pay. Moreover, when a serious crime *was* committed, a large number of people were charged. In 1892, for example, twenty persons were charged with murder, of whom only three were convicted, but all were imprisoned awaiting trial.[86] As a result, in a period which saw the population of the island grow by 13 per cent, the inmates of the central prison had grown by 400 per cent.[87] It was argued locally that the fault lay in the good treatment of the prisoners. Local gaols were not a deterrent. The makeshift prisons, in the Büyük Khan in Nicosia and the old forts in Limassol and Larnaca had no facilities for isolating prisoners and the guaranteed daily meals meant that inmates were often labouring and living under better conditions than they would be at home.

Sendall himself abhorred the perception that had grown up in the previous years of an inherent thuggish lawlessness in the island's population, a perception that would alleviate any pangs of conscience within the British government over the way the Cypriots were being annually fleeced of the product of their labours. 'Cypriots are not hardened criminals', he protested.

---

84. Sendall to Ripon, 16 January 1893, the letter is annotated 'no wonder the law was broken', CO67/77, NA.
85. See, for example, Rebecca Bryant, *Imagining the Modern*, (London 1988), 52-70 and Katsiaounis (1996), 223-226.
86. Cyprus: *Annual Report for the year 1892-1893*, C-7411, 5-6.
87. Sir Reginald Welby, Permanent Secretary to the Treasury, to Under Secretary of State, 25 February 1893, CO67/93.

> *They are essentially a kindly and peaceable people, and unprotected strangers might travel anywhere, under any circumstances and at any time with the most absolute security from molestation. But when he conceives himself to be injured...he sets little value on human life and takes it without remorse in the pursuit of justice in the redress of his private wrongs.*

He advocated 'growth in confidence in the power of the law and respect for its authority as the only sure and certain remedy'.[88] The most important piece of legislation passed in 1893, in respect of judicial procedure, was Law VII (1893). This law made it a crime to change your statement between hearings, thus stifling the not infrequent tendency of criminals and their families to blackmail or bribe witnesses. By the end of 1893 many such small but effective changes in the system were beginning to make a difference. Nevertheless, some improvements, public works, first and foremost, could not be executed without further funding. In the 1894 estimates, the government was pressing again for the extra £2,000 achieved the previous year. The high commissioner also argued for a more generous vote for education. In the annual report for 1892-1893 he highlighted the unsatisfactory nature of the fixed grant for elementary education, unchanged since 1883. It actually penalised the growth of education since the increasing number of schools automatically decreased the grant for each school.

The number of primary schools was growing so fast that the need for an institution equipped to train teachers had become urgent. It was in this connection that the high commissioner took a special interest in the Hellenic School in Nicosia, which was in 1893 reformed and extended to include a lyceum. He saw the school, as indeed did its founders and patrons, as a catalyst for the general improvement of education in the island. The new school, inaugurated ceremonially on 24 December, was to include systematic teacher training in its senior classes. The school was funded by the Cypriot Brotherhood in Alexandria and had achieved recognition by the Greek ministry of education, thus opening the doors to European universities for its graduates.

---

88. Sendall to Ripon, 16 December 1893, CO67/82, NA. Hamilton Lang similarly bears witess to the honesty of Cypriots and how safe travelling in the countryside generally was in the nineteenth century. See R. Hamilton Lang, *Cyprus: Its History, its Present Resources and Future Prospects*, (Macmillan: London 1878), 206-207.

The high commissioner was, of course, present at the opening ceremony. 'It was a pleasing feature', he noted, 'to see the Chief Cadi and the principal Turkish notables associating themselves with their Greek fellow citizens in a work which, should it prove permanently successful, cannot fail to exercise an important influence on the future of the country'. Most of the Nicosia-based English officials were present in the packed assembly room. According to Sendall, 'Scrupulous respect was paid throughout to the person and government of Her Majesty the Queen. Her portrait occupied the chief place in the decorations. The proceedings were opened by Archbishop Sofronios with a prayer, followed by God Save the Queen sung in Greek by the metropolitan choir. The British national anthem was received 'by the assembled audience standing and uncovered'.[89] Mr. Delios, the headmaster, newly arrived from Greece, then rose and delivered a lengthy address, after which the choir and people sang the Greek national anthem. Greek patriotic songs were sung. The high commissioner congratulated the headmaster on the curriculum to be taught. He expressed particular satisfaction that a prominent place was to be given in it to the literature of Ancient Greece. 'The Hellenic Consul then made a few inaudible remarks', *The Owl* noted, 'and the visitors adjourned to the Metropolis [Archbishopric] for refreshments'.[90]

---

89. Sendall to Ripon, 30 December 1893, CO67/92, NA.
90. Ibid and *The Owl*, 3 and 20 January 1894, Michael Volonaki, *Η εκπαίδευσις εν Κύπρω από της Αγγλικής Κατοχής 1878-1912* (Αθήναι 1913), 34-36.

35. Issue of stamps 1894, considered especially beautiful because of the new two-tone colour printing

1894

*Harriers and Housekeeping, The Elusive Outlaw,
The Wine Demonstration in Troodos, Tax Arrears in
Paphos, Prisons and Police Again, Rumours of Withdrawal,
The Limassol Flood*

Nicosia was witnessing the rare phenomenon of a cold winter, cold enough for snow to appear on the Kyrenia hills. This was appropriate weather for the very English Nicosia Harriers. Unlike horse-racing, which was taken up enthusiastically by local owners and riders, hunting hares on horseback remained a pastime for expatriate society, among whom the Boxing Day hunt had become an institution. This year they had met near Margo in the Tymbou area, north-east of Nicosia. Having lost the original hare they,

> *fresh found, and got her away again in full view of the carriages, carts and "bicycles made for two" waiting on the road. "Puss" (the hare) led the field in a large circle and brought them back to the old ground. The field about this time began to trail off in the direction of the Manor House at Margo, where Thompson, who had taken over from Collyer in this respect, laid on a large feast.*[1]

There is no indication that the Sendalls hunted. Sir Walter was still clearly comfortable on horseback, covering the length and breadth of the island in the saddle during his five-year term. As for Lady Sendall, a product of the vicarage, rather than the manor house, her activities were more demure. We know she ran an orderly household. When the couple were reprimanded by the Treasury for ordering some essential equipment for Government House - a chest for plates, on the grounds that there was no evidence that such a purchase was necessary, the high commissioner was careful to point out that there had been no inventory when they arrived. An inventory had now been compiled and deposited with the auditor general.[2]

The first lady took a keen interest in the fine needlework to be found in the island. 'There is a sisterhood', wrote her friend, Elizabeth Lewis,

---

1. See *The Owl*, 3 January 1894, for enthusiasm over Cypriot horses doing well in Beirut, and *The Times of Cyprus*, January, 1891, 92, 93 for more coverage of Boxing Day hunts.
2. Sendall to Ripon, 29 January 1894, CO67/84, NA.

'between the women of Cyprus and those of Ireland, in their natural adaptation of brain and fingers to cunning art embroideries'. The fear had already taken hold among the expatriate ladies that the finer work was dying out. Lady Sendall took it upon herself to create incentives for the skill to be handed down to the next generation. An exhibition of Cypriot needlework and hand-weaving was set up at the Imperial Institute in London, and an outlet for sales created in Chelsea.[3] In January 1894, she persuaded Sir Walter to dig deep in his pocket and fund a stall for Cypriot needlework at the Chicago exhibition of embroidery. By March, the high commissioner had received a cheque for $69.15 cents from Her Majesty's ambassador in Washington, being the proceeds of the sale of Cypriot needlework. This success led Sir Walter to enquire into the possibilities of setting up a permanent outlet in the United States.[4]

One of the oldest *lefkaritika* cutwork *(kopta)* designs representing the river *(potamos)* on the edge of the cloth. The *potamos* was always the main feature of the old lefkaritika. This one is known as *klonotos monos*

---

3.   Lewis, 203-204.
4.   Sendall to Ripon, 29 January 1894. CO67/84 and letter from Julian Pancroft to the Earl of Kimberly enclosed in Ripon to Sendall, 23 March 1894, CO67/85, NA.

An energetic fund-raiser, Lady Sendall worked hard for local charities, particularly the lepers. This was an interest perhaps inspired by the Sendalls' close friendship with Frederik Carl von Heidenstam, who, like George Bowen, had an attractive Corfiote wife.[5] He had been in the island since Ottoman times and was fluent in Turkish and Greek. In 1893 he had been appointed chief medical officer and was one of the (*ex-officio*) members of the legislative council. He accompanied the high commissioner on many of his tours of inspection. Sendall makes special mention in his despatches of how immensely helpful he was.[6] As a doctor, Heidenstam was loved and respected. He took a scientific interest in meningitis and leprosy. Lady Sophia contributed to efforts to make the lepers as comfortable and happy as possible. Before she left the island, she had collected in England and in Cyprus, enough money to build a Greek Orthodox church for the 80 or so lepers in the leper colony outside Nicosia.[7]

As leading lady, she was bound to head fund-raising for the rebuilding of the Anglican church, whose foundation stone she had laid. Sendall had paid out of his own pocket for the removal of building material from the abandoned site on St. George's hill to the new building site, but found no sympathy in London when he asked for money for a wall around the Anglican cemetery. It was some way out of Nicosia, he explained, and needed protection from vandals. Fairfield did not see why the Anglicans needed a cemetery at all. Why should they not be buried in Greek Orthodox cemeteries, the Greek Orthodox church having shown a willingness to include them there? He thought the new church quite unnecessary. Drawing on his own experience on a three-month tour of inspection in the island, he observed that the room in which services had been held was never full. They were very lucky, he thought, not to have to pay their vicar, Josiah Spencer, who was the government's inspector of schools, and had, indeed, 'caused a deal of trouble' in that capacity, although he was now accepted.[8]

In fact, in the 1890s, in a move perhaps accelerated by the visit of Archbishop Sofronios to the Archbishop of Canterbury a year or two earlier,

---

5. See Rita Severis, *The Swedes in Cyprus*, (Nicosia, 2008), 158-177 for information on Heidenstam.
6. Sendall to Knutsford, 4 July 1892, CO67/75, NA.
7. *Cyprus: Annual Report for the Year 1897-1898*, 93.
8. Sendall to Ripon, 8 May 1894 and attached Fairfield minute, CO67/86, NA.

the Anglican church began to see Cyprus as fertile ground for greater interaction with the Greek Orthodox Church. As well as the archbishop, we know that the bishop of Paphos and the abbots of Kykko and Macheras were on cordial terms with British officials as they had been, on the whole, with the Ottomans. Elizabeth Lewis's observations indicate that there was much talk at the time of 'common ground' between the two churches and of building on these excellent relations to set up a higher school which would 'remedy' the 'shortcomings' of the Church of Cyprus and 'redirect its religious spirit'.[9] Two years later, in 1896, the Rev. H. F. Duckworth was sent out as envoy by the Eastern Church Association. He was 'to acquire knowledge and experience of the administration, life and influence of the Orthodox Church of the island; and also to assist the chaplain (Spencer) in ministering to the English residents there.' He was to 'devote himself assiduously' to the study of the modern Greek language and the doctrine of the Eastern Church with a view to paving the way to closer relations. Duckworth certainly studied the church and wrote about it and about his sojourn on the island.[10] He also gave free English lessons at the Pancyprian Gymnasium. The work allowed him more intimate relations with the Greek Orthodox community. The school was located conveniently close to the archbishopric, facilitating contact with the Archbishop and his entourage.

Spencer's own relations with the Greek Orthodox Church had not been so smooth. Sendall was clearly wary of Spencer's connections with the Eastern Church Association, in view of the fact that his role of school inspector classified him as a member of the Cypriot civil service. He particularly resented the publication of the Association's intentions by Spencer in the Nicosia paper, *Phoni tis Kyprou* in September 1894.[11] He could do without Anglo-Cypriot spiritual jealousies and suspicions confounding the anomalies and antagonisms within this dependency. The Porte's resistance to the whittling away of Ottoman jurisdiction on the island was expressed chiefly in the defence of its Muslim institutions and the civic prerogatives they provided for the Muslim population. At the

---

9. Lewis, 212-214.
10. Sendall to Ripon, 7 September 1894 and attached leaflet published by The Eastern Church Association. Duckworth's publications include *Greek Manuals of Church Doctrine*, H.T.F. Duckworth. (London: Rivingtons, published for the Eastern Church Association, 1901). See also H.T.F. Duckworth, *Some Pages of Levantine History,* (Toronto 1906), Chapter I: 'Great Britain and Cyprus – a rider to the Eastern Question'.
11. Ibid.

same time, Greek Orthodox culture and symbols were absorbed into modern nationalist trends that sought to resist any hint of interference with the autonomy of the church. The aims of Sendall's government were much more mundane. In 1894 all mental and physical effort focused on making maximum use of every man and every penny the government could command to provide the basics of a good administration.

The cold weather that winter suppressed the stench that was once again permeating the heart of Nicosia, in spite of the new covered main drain. The trouble, the engineers together with the municipality discovered, was that individuals had drilled into the new covered drain and continued to drop through the holes the putrefying matter they had once thrown into the riverbed. The seasonal sluicing of the drain by the occasionally flooded Pedieos river was totally inadequate. Once the sluices were connected to the Arab Ahmed aquaduct and the holes sealed, the citizens once more enjoyed purer air.[12]

The town within the walls was soon to be rid of another unsightly feature. Every day a motley convoy of bullock carts would trundle out from the Büyük Khan, through the Paphos Gate toward Ayios Andreas, carrying short-term convicts to work on building the new prison. They were guarded by a few mounted *zaptiehs*. As Sendall had predicted, using convicts had proved very slow and not all that economical. They had to be guarded all day until they were returned safely to their cells in the Khan. During the day they provided shoddy and reluctant work. But at last, the first new prison block was almost complete. Once all was ready, the labour force would be housed on the job.

Of more salacious interest to all the inhabitants of the island was the news that Yiallouris, the notorious bandit charged with murdering the *mudir* of Paphos, had been tracked down on the island of Samos. He had been extradited to Cyprus, tried and found guilty of murder on 13 February. To Sendall's dismay, the Queen's Advocate had subsequently advised that the trial was invalid, because Yiallouris had not been extradited to face the murder charge, but other earlier charges. Sendall was confronted with a conundrum. The only reason individuals had dared to come forward and bear witness against him was because he was under arrest. It was very

---

12. 'The Insanitary State of Nicosia Town', Report, 29 April 1894, SA1:2069/94, CSA.

15. Nicosia within the walls (a *khan* behind the St. Sophia/Selemiye Mosque)

important, now that the notorious brigand *had* finally been found guilty, that he hang. If the public sensed that he might be released, the witnesses would be too frightened to come forward in a new trial. The issue had, in fact, become bogged down in the Porte's determination to treat Cyprus as a mere province, an integral part of the Ottoman Empire. Therefore, when Yiallouris was sent to Constantinople for re-extradition to Cyprus, this time on the specific charge of the murder of the *mudir* of Paphos, the Porte refused to cooperate, Cyprus not being under foreign jurisdiction. The solution lay in playing down the word 'extradition', sending him from Constantinople to the Lebanon from which, because of that province's special status, he could be appropriately shipped to Cyprus.[13] It took a whole year to have Yiallouris hanged. This much-travelled villain became the talk of the island. A racehorse was named after him to amuse the gentry, but by the peasants he was held in awe for his defiance and his habit of slipping away. Perhaps not unconnected with the problems of convicting Yiallouris was the second amendment, rushed through the legislative council in March 1894, to the law on judicial proceedings enacted the previous year. Now evidence given at a first hearing would be put into a deposition that could be treated as evidence, even if contradicted in a second hearing.

The complications created by the Turkish government over Yiallouris's extradition were characteristic. It seemed to the British that the Porte never lost an opportunity to stake a claim of some kind or another on the island, in an attempt to inject some substance into the Sultan's shadowy suzerainty. Such interventions complicated efforts to create order out of the anomalous legacy of the Cyprus Convention, which among other things hampered efforts to increase the area of land under cultivation, complicated the collection of revenue and left the broke administration with a mountain of unsellable salt to guard. In this context, Sendall confronted the corrupt exploitation of these anomalies in a landmark case, in which *Evkaf* had sought to sell to a new lucrative buyer a large tract of land which they had already sold years earlier to peasants. The current smallholders were to be evicted. The case was overruled just as *Evkaf* were about to take steps to enforce the eviction order 'which, with the full knowledge and consent of Bulwer's government,' they had obtained in the

---

13. Sendall to Ripon, 14 July 1894, and enclosure No.1, J.P. Taylor, British Consular Court at Constantinople to Sendall, 28 June 1894, CO67/88, NA.

same court, on the eve of Sendall's arrival, two years earlier. This would have implicated the government in a course which might have 'serious and embarrassing results'. The original purchasers were reinstated. The high commissioner's 'judicious and well-timed exertions' were appreciated in London because they ensured that 'a dangerous precedent was not set against the peasant who cultivated the land' and produced the revenue.[14]

Sir Walter continued to probe into the possibilities of disentangling the government from the vague, but persistently demanded, land claims on behalf of the Sultan. The fact that a landowner had just won a case against the government of Cyprus for preventing the cultivation of land over which the Sultan had dubious claims, set a precedent. The high commissioner hoped that this would lead to the cultivation of other land claimed by the Sultan. Much of this land had been delimited as government forest, but there were tracts of arable land that could not fall into the forestry category. Extending cultivation and setting a limit to the Sultan's interventions on the island were together important enough matters to concern the Foreign Office. After the high commissioner had drawn attention to the problem, the Porte's assertions of authority over *vakouf* lands were dealt with summarily by the Foreign Secretary, who insisted that

> *The Sultan has vested in Her Majesty's Government, full powers for making Laws and Conventions for the government of the island in Her Majesty's Name. No reservation as regards the regulation of vakoufs is made. ... No room is left for the legislative intervention of the Sultan in any matter so long as the British administration of Cyprus continues...Her Majesty's Government, while recognising that the Sultan retains sovereignty over Cyprus, must adhere to the contention that His Majesty the Sultan is precluded by [the convention] from intervening in the affairs of the island...If the income from these lands were withdrawn from the island, there would be no means available for maintaining the mosques.*[15]

The 1894 session of the legislative council was opened in mid-February, a month earlier than in previous years, in view of the more substantial role it was now playing in the enactment of legislation intended to reform and

---

14. Sendall to Ripon, 4 May 1894, and attachments, CO67/85. Also Sendall to Ripon, 7 June 1894, and attached minutes, CO67/86, NA.
15. Ibid.

16. *Zaptiehs* in Famagusta, August 1897

improve, rather than simply regulate. *The Owl* observed that the Government Gazette was bursting with bills to be laid before the council, both by the government and private members. Committees of members were created to look into two key matters: education and police reform.

The decision to replace the much hated turban with the fez for *zaptiehs*, *The Owl* believed, signalled the start of a reformed police force and, indeed, a start was being made in 1894 from top down.[16] First, there was a tactical weeding out of weak commandants; Chamberlayne, for example, was transferred from the police force to the customs in Larnaca, a job he could do easily, where he would not be missed when on one of his frequent extended but unpaid leaves, and where he would find a matching intellect in Delaval Cobham. Neither Chamberlayne nor Bulwer ever quite got over the fact that Sendall turned down Chamberlayne's application to be commissioner of Kyrenia, giving the job to a much younger man.[17] As compensation, Chamberlayne was to be acting district commissioner during Cobham's absence from Larnaca.

The police commandant to be appointed there was Theodore Mavrocordato, a very capable policeman who had married the daughter of the Anglican chaplain in Limassol. Sir Walter later tried, but failed, to send him to London for special training. Mavrocordato, as commandant, would normally have acted in the district commissioner's absence.[18] With Chamberlayne standing in as district commissioner, he would now be free for essential police work. One of Sendall's protégés, the excellent Percy Algernon Ongley, already acting commandant, was made permanent and chosen to tackle the most challenging district, Paphos. The new policeman from Ireland, Clarence Wodehouse, was put in Limassol. Such juggling of the staff and their responsibilities was a way of maximising whatever available talent there was. The high commissioner seems to have been equally aware of the importance of image. Undermanned, overworked and thoroughly demoralised, the old and seasoned troopers were being

---

16. *The Owl*, 1 March 1894.
17. Sendall to Ripon, 12 March 1894, CO67/84, NA.
18. Sendall to Ripon, 21 April 1894, CO67/85, NA. Theodore Mavrocordato was a Levantine who married the English daughter of the Anglican chaplain to the garrison at Polemedia. He was very highly thought of by Sendall, who pressed for him to acquire special training with the metropolitan police. The idea was rejected in London, but he did become police commandant of the Limassol District and took a major part in the hunt for the Hasanpouli. He was a friend of Rider Haggard's. See Haggard, (1926), Chapter V, 52-91.

replaced by immature lads 'of a far from desirable stamp'.[19] The shortage of police had led to thoughts of importing men from Egypt, but Sir Walter baulked at a move sure to cause resentment among the Cypriots.[20] Instead, a commodious recruitment and training depot for *zaptiehs* was constructed on the prominent bastion, visible to all those leaving and entering the city through the Paphos Gate. A manual of instruction in English, Greek and Turkish aimed at literate recruits.[21] The system was not foolproof. One literate and willing recruit, Savvas Tserkezis, describes walking all the way from Larnaca with a friend to join the *zaptiehs* in Nicosia, only to be told, after hanging around outside the recruiting office for two days, that the recruiting officer was ill and that they might as well go away.[22]

There remained the creation of the special force for the Paphos district, an issue with which the law and order committee of the legislative council was absorbed. It recommended a special force that would not be restricted to Paphos alone, but funds were limited and recruits unwilling. By the end of the year, the district commandant had found only twenty-four suitable men, but this was a start, and they would be paid for by the money gained by the failure to find recruits in the regular police. The regular police was 80 short, the special police would have 80 men. Was the experiment going to work? The Paphos district was in the greatest need. The list of inhabitants who had failed to pay taxes was greater in Paphos than elsewhere. One reason was that arrears had to be paid in cash, a commodity not easily available in these remote regions where much trading still took the form of barter. The collectors' attempts to recoup arrears by grabbing bullocks, ploughs and bedsteads, made them extremely unpopular and achieved poor results.

In September, the high commissioner toured the Paphos district. 'I can confirm', he reported to London, 'the inability of the villagers to pay their taxes because they have no means of disposing of their produce'. The solution Sendall proposed was that the government should collect arrears in kind instead of in cash. It would be more collectible and therefore

---

19. *Cyprus: Annual Report for the Year* 1893-1894, 31.
20. Sendall to Ripon, 30 January 1894, CO67/84, NA.
21. Sendall to Ripon, 23 April 1894. See also attached Police Instruction Manual, in English, Greek and Ottoman script, printed at the Government Printing Office in Nicosia, CO67/85. See also *Cyprus: Annual Report for 1893-1894*, 23.
22. Savvas Tserkezis, Ημερολόγιον του Βίου μου, (Nicosia 2007), 98-99.

ultimately create more revenue – fewer arrears would have to be written off. The Treasury's response infuriated Sir Walter. If the farmers could not sell the grain, they argued, how could the government? 'How grievous will be the government position if the peasants chose to pay all their taxes in that very unsellable commodity.' His Excellency pointed out that the government was in a much better position to find a market than the Paphos peasants. Only grain that could be 'disposed of at best advantage' would be taken. The villagers could not sell because there was no road to Ktima, their main trading centre or to Paphos, the only port in the district. 'If only this government could be credited with the possession of a little intelligence', he complained privately, and asked his close associate in the Colonial Office, Robert Meade, now the permanent secretary, to make his sentiments known to the Treasury. Their Lordships nitpicked and delayed, and finally condescended to agree to the high commissioner's proposal. By the time notice of their acquiescence reached Nicosia, the tithe collectors, who would have taken in the arrears as well, had finished their rounds and departed. The chance of recouping a large portion of arrears was lost.

This story encapsulates the frustrations created by the Treasury's stranglehold on the local administration. Sir Walter's arrears scheme worked very successfully in the following years, and he linked it to another – the demand for a new government steam-powered patrol boat. The old customs cutter, purchased fourth-hand in 1878, was no longer seaworthy. There was much paranoia in Constantinople at the time, of Armenians smuggling guns into Turkey, and Sendall took advantage of this and the presence of cholera in Asia Minor to argue for a patrol boat to enforce quarantine regulations and to waylay illegal immigrants and smugglers. His own priority was to use the boat to convey the good quality tithe grain grown in the north coast and the Karpass where 'it [was] difficult to get vessels to land', to the government stores on the south coast, where it could be more easily sold and despatched. He predicted correctly that because of low wheat prices, the government would be driven to export more and more grain on its own account. Such a vessel was eventually delivered to Cyprus, but not until after Sendall had moved on. Nevertheless, he exported the very first shipment of good quality Cyprus wheat to Britain. This contract with grain merchants in Hull resulted in a regular and lucrative trade.[23] In the absence of a patrol boat on the east coast, he

---

23. Sendall to Ripon, 4 June 1895. Also table demonstrating savings to be made, CO67/92, NA.

established a troop of quarantine guards who were so successful at catching illegal immigrants that the fines they paid amply covered the cost of their maintenance.

An overly ambitious and hopelessly unsuccessful enterprise had been Sendall's attempt to replace, or at least join, Russia as a major supplier of wheat to British forces in the East. He was inspired by an article in the *The Daily Graphic* which reported that grain was to be stored 'on an immense scale' in granaries at Valetta to be a reserve in case of war. Letters were despatched to the Admiralty, making the case for Cypriot grain, and a sample shipment was ordered. Sadly, the wheat had not been properly cleaned. The Cyprus government's facilities were rough and ready. In his haste to prepare the cargo for Malta, the receiver general had 'planted a winnowing machine in the centre of Pascotini Street, a narrow but much used thoroughfare of Larnaca', observed *The Times of Cyprus*. 'To pass anywhere near is to be smothered, with "official chaff" and "weavils"'(sic).[24]

The lot of the peasants, not only in Paphos, but in the Limassol wine district, continued to be distressed by the French prohibition against imported wine. The expanding and lucrative market of earlier years had resulted in more and more land being turned over to viticulture so the decline was dramatic. The wine district, thanks to the military road to Troodos and the new wine roads, was in relatively close communication with its port, the most modern and politicised town on the island, Limassol. Limassol's wealth turned on the export of wine and the income generated by the presence of the British garrison at Polemedia. The Christian and Muslim elected members of the legislative council had combined to reduce excise further and to have it assessed at the port, instead of the villages, so that the government would bear the cost of transport. This was out of the question as far as London was concerned. Sendall's attempts to reduce excise and improve the methods of assessment had been marginal, while the lot of the wine-growers became daily more critical.

As concern grew through the summer as to how the year's grape harvest was to be disposed of, fearful rumours began to circulate that the British garrison was to be withdrawn, a rumour that was met, initially, with indignant disbelief. The island was soon agog. Why should they go to

---

24. *The Times of Cyprus*, 19 May 1894.

17. View of Limassol from the *SS Jumna*

Malta? Wasn't this a *strategic* colony?[25] The Colonial Office had sounded out the high commissioner on the matter in the spring. By the early summer the papers were beginning to pick up the story, by September the withdrawal of the garrison was transformed in the local press into 'the withdrawal of Britain', giving rise to endless speculation as to the future status of the island. Retrocession to the Porte was most greatly feared by the Greek Christians. Sendall warned that this was a bad time to withdraw the garrison. The general drop in incomes because of the waning wine industry made the income from military spending in Limassol even more important. At the same time, 'mischievous and exaggerated comments' in the press, on the 'increasingly strained' relations between 'the two races' exacerbated a situation which might become difficult to deal with 'if the native police were the only available force'. The local papers, especially the Limassol papers, whipped up the stories of tension to prevent the withdrawal, but actual strife could not be ruled out. By the summer, the high commissioner was enquiring nervously whether he could be informed about any gunboats in the vicinity once the troops were withdrawn. 'The prevailing uncertainty', he warned, 'has now extended to the whole political future of the island.'[26]

The situation was serious enough for the two elected members to whom Sendall was closest, to travel up to visit him at Government Cottage in Troodos. An exceptionally good carriage road to the summit would have allowed Liassides and Constantinides to make the journey from Platres in 25 minutes.[27] Their purpose was to express their concern at the turn of events. The rumoured abandonment of the island by Britain was at the top of the agenda, but with the grapes about to be harvested, the plight of the wine-growers which would depend on the new tax law enacted by the legislature in May and now awaiting ratification from London, was a matter of great urgency.

There had been much discussion in the last session of the legislative council as to alternative sources of revenue in the event of the wine excise being reduced. The draft law submitted to London had relied, among other

---

25. *The Owl*, 15 and 22 September, 20 October 1894.
26. Sendall to Ripon, 10 April 1894, CO67/85, NA.
27. *The Times of Cyprus*, 26 September 1893, describes 'a four-wheeled American carriage belonging to a sporting advocate trotting along [the Platres – Troodos road] at quite a respectable rate'.

things, on increasing the import duty on tobacco. Liassides had a special interest in reintroducing the cultivation of tobacco, a crop whose cultivation on the island had been prohibited since Ottoman times. Much tobacco was imported for cigarette factories, by far the most successful industry on the island, catering for an insatiable local consumption, but also for export to Syria.[28] No doubt his special interest in legalising local cultivation was instrumental in motivating his suggestions for a hiked-up import duty on that commodity. While trying to reassure his Cypriot visitors that troop withdrawal did not mean abandonment, Sendall could not confirm that the new tax legislation had been given the go-ahead, as they had hoped. The two councillors left Government Cottage, as concerned as they had been before their visit. On their departure, Sir Walter telegraphed London for a statement by the secretary of state confirming that Britain was not withdrawing from Cyprus.

It was in this strained atmosphere of uncertainty about the future that the wine-growers of the Limassol district were organised by the two members of the legislative council who represented them, Socrates Francoudes and Ioannis Kyriakides, into participating in 'the most dramatic and numerous demonstration for a common purpose' undertaken since the British occupation. Kyriakides was the son of a wine-grower from Zoopygi. Francoudes was a prominent Limassolian.[29] Their action belies the self-seeking, usurious characters since attributed to the Cypriot legislators. They were taking energetic and serious action on behalf of their constituents. This most eloquent act of protest took place not in Limassol, but in the mountains. The wine-growers gathered in Perapedi, in the heart of the wine district, from virtually every wine village in the Limassol and Paphos districts. They then walked a good ten miles up the steep mountainside to Troodos to see the high commissioner personally and hand him their resolution. Let us turn to Sendall's own description of this extraordinary event.

> *In the course of the morning I received an intimation that a deputation was about to proceed to Troodos for the purpose of presenting the memorial. The whole body of villagers accompanied the deputation and since the precincts of the cottage were too small, I*

---

28. Diamond Jenness, *The Economics of Cyprus: A survey to 1914*, (Montreal 1962), 82, 178.
29. For biographical notes, see Coudounaris, 2010, 275 and 626.

walked a short distance along the road and met them at a convenient spot. There were at least 3,000 of them collected from all parts of the wine district and massed together on the hillside which rises steeply up from the road, they presented a striking and interesting spectacle. With the exception of a few schoolmasters and village priests, there was no one in the whole assembly above the condition of a peasant, and a more orderly crowd it would be impossible to see anywhere.

During the reading of the memorial, about which I shall speak presently, your lordship's telegram, informing me that England had no intention of abandoning Cyprus was put into my hands, and at the conclusion of the proceedings, I read it out to the people. It was received with the utmost enthusiasm and with hearty cheers for HM the Queen, the crowd dispersed as peaceably as they had come.[30]

Sir Walter was clearly moved by this large group of desperately earnest men who had walked so far up the mountain, not in anger, but in the belief that if they approached him personally, he would help them. He did his best. Arguing that the wine excise grew year by year increasingly unproductive, he suggested to the secretary of state that 'its temporary suspension would affect the revenue only to a moderate degree, while it would put heart into the cultivators and enable them to wait with some hopefulness for better times'. He urged the Treasury to 'free the wine industry altogether from every fiscal burden and leave it to itself for a time'. If the experiment failed then the industry should be allowed to die, 'but looking at the superlative natural excellence of the Cyprus product' this [was] a result which was scarcely to be apprehended. What was certain was that it would be killed off if the government continued to force the cultivators to pay money tax on wine they could not sell. During the period of suspended taxation, the wine-growers would be educated to make wine after the example of the Cyprus Wine Company [31] - particularly to demonstrate how unnecessary it was to use gypsum and pitch, which spoiled the naturally well-flavoured wines. The revenue lost could be made up by raising the duty on petroleum and tobacco and increasing the price of salt. With his usual tone of assumption that London would go along with him,

---

30. Sendall to Ripon, Troodos, 10 September 1894, CO67/89, NA. See Zanettos, 1911, 819.
31. Jenness, (1962), 201. The Cyprus Company's wine won a French award in 1896, having already built up to a considerable standard by 1892. See article headed 'Growing Popularity of Cyprus Wines: A Dividend of six per cent' in *The Times of Cyprus,* 27 October 1892.

Sendall told the secretary of state that he would hold a special meeting of the legislative council in early November to enact the changes.[32]

Sir Walter would not receive a reply from London for months. He set off from Troodos on a second tour of the problematical Paphos district, sending his newly appointed chief secretary, Arthur Young, through the Tylliria region. Young was the first competent and conscientious chief secretary appointed to that position. Colonel Falkland Warren had arrived on the island in 1878 as part of the occupation force under Sir Garnet Wolseley. He had, during his long term as chief secretary, become notoriously involved in the export of antiquities, had quarrelled with Bulwer and had been sent to Ceylon. In the meantime the work of the chief secretary had been, in theory, undertaken by the chief clerk, William Bennett, but in effect, the government remained without a responsible officer at its head. In a private letter to Ripon, Sendall made it clear he did not think Bennett up to the job of chief secretary.

A Sandhurst man who had been appointed commandant of the Cyprus Pioneer Force in 1878, Young had gained some notoriety as candidate for Famagusta, where he was district commissioner, in the elections for the legislative council in 1886. The local politicians had combined to prevent the intrusion of officialdom into the only political platform to which they had resource.[33] Sir Walter was quick to spot Young's ability, moving him from Famagusta to head the land registry office in Nicosia and, when the opportunity arose, making him his right-hand man.[34] His wife, Lady Evelyne Anne, worked closely with Lady Sophia on welfare and fund-raising committees.

In the Paphos area, Sendall was accompanied on his tour of inspection by the energetic George Smith. The district commissioner appointed at the end of 1892 was beginning to make a difference. A small hospital, a new salt depot, and petitions from the villagers for grain to be exported from the even more remote village of Polis, rather than carried laboriously by pack animals to Paphos, reflected new dynamics. This time there was no

---

32. Sendall to Ripon, Troodos, 10 September 1894, CO67/89, NA.
33. George Hill, *History of Cyprus*, Vol. IV, (Cambridge 1972), 441-442.
34. Sir Arthur Henderson Young, CMG, KBE, GCMG became high commissioner of Malaya in 1906 and subsequently governor of the Straits Settlements. He had married Lady Evelyne Anne Kennedy, daughter of the second Marquis of Ailsa, in 1885. See Wikipedia.

need to set up camp. George Smith and his wife had made themselves a comfortable home. Elizabeth Lewis had stayed there a year earlier.

> *One step more, and we found ourselves lapped in luxury. Tea, comfortable rooms in a new wing all to ourselves, warm baths…and in the drawing-room later, a magnificent and courteous tabby cat couched before a brilliant coal fire, and any amount of books and newspapers made us exalt in the sensation that we were civilized beings after all.…The drawing room opens into a fine arcaded balcony-terrace, which leading by a flight of stone steps into the well-watered garden, vivid with the green and gold of orange trees and bathed in a sea of almond-blossom, overlooks, from the high limestone cliff, the azure Paphian sea.*[35]

Sendall and his aide-de-camp, Captain Fielden, returned to Troodos from their tour of Paphos suffering from a bad bout of malarial fever. Sir Walter blamed the fever on 'an unhealthy campsite' during the tour. He was aware of the island-wide nature of the malarial scourge, particularly prevalent in the western valleys of the Troodos range. He had earlier launched a pilot scheme by which quinine was available for sale in the village stores of the most badly affected areas, a scheme which met with considerable success.[36] The high commissioner and Lady Sophia remained in Troodos until the end of October, thereby gaining some space for Sir Walter to convalesce, but not to stop working. The mailbags from Troodos were heavy with dispatches for London.

A few days after the Sendalls' return to Nicosia, three urgent telegrams arrived from Limassol: from the mayor, from the acting district commissioner, and from the colonel of the Connaught Rangers, bearing news of disaster. 'Town utterly wrecked by flood', wrote Colonel Brooks. 'Every available man helping. Twenty bodies already found. State of inhabitants wretched. Have provided shelter and food for as many as require it. Will wire again tomorrow'. The high commissioner responded immediately to all three, 'I shall be with you tomorrow'.[37] Indeed, he did arrive the next day to behold a scene of utter devastation.

---

35. Lewis, p.137.
36. Sendall to Ripon, Troodos, 20 October 1894, CO67/89 and Sendall to Ripon, 12 January 1894, CO67/84, NA.
37. Telegram from Clarence Wodehouse to Sendall, 12 November, Colonel Brooks and Mayor

> The town was inundated from end to end, the water in the streets at the western end reaching a depth from three to eight feet. It flooded through the doors and windows of houses and brought down walls, most of which were of mud brick. A mosque on the left bank was totally destroyed. A Greek church on the opposite bank of the river was cut in two and an entire row of houses disappeared without trace.[38]

The morning after his arrival, Sendall gathered together district officials, the mayor and principal townsmen and the military officers from Polemedia to work out a plan of action. The town was divided into districts, each one in charge of a responsible person who undertook to find labourers and to personally superintend the work of cleaning the streets. The military depot provided picks and shovels. Dead animals lay all over the place in the hot sun. Every available soldier in the half battalion stationed at Polemedia had been marched down to the town as soon as the flood was reported They worked non-stop, carrying every animal corpse they could find to the end of the jetty and throwing it into the sea. One hundred and thirty one corpses of horses, mules and donkeys were disposed of in this way.[39]

According to the Captain of *HMS Arethusa*, dispatched post-haste to Limassol, 'it was the high commissioner's prompt arrival from Nicosia that galvanized the panic-stricken inhabitants into helping to clear the debris'. Sendall found them sorrowful, but friendly wherever he went. The fact that 'half of Limassol had accommodated the other half' eased the housing problem. Those who could not be accommodated by friends or relatives were given shelter by the garrison at Polemedia. A party of bluejackets from the *Arethusa* was placed at the disposal of the town and undertook the demolition of the condemned buildings, 'amongst which the most difficult to deal with was the minaret of the mosque, a stone tower of a considerable height and dimensions whose foundations had been completely undermined. It was most skillfully demolished with cotton

---

of Limassol to Sendall, 13 November, Sendall reply, 13 November 1894. A report by the Limassol police commandant and acting commissioner, Wodehouse, recorded 22 deaths – '15 Turks and 7 Christians'. See Report attached to Sendall to Ripon, 2 December 1894, CO67/88, NA.
38. Sendall to Ripon, 20 November 1894, CO67/88. See also *The Owl*, 24 November 1894, for coverage of flood and Sendall's movements.
39. Ibid., and the Wodehouse Report on the flood.

18. A view of Limassol after the flood, 1895

charges'.[40] With the price of food already rising fast, Sir Walter decided to prevent racketeering by having bread baked by the public authorities.

On returning to Nicosia, the high commissioner focused on fund-raising both for the immediate emergency and for essential flood protection works.[41] These had not been carried out after the 1881 flood, and the town was paying for that omission. But neither grants nor loans, nor contributions from fund-raisers were forthcoming from Britain, either for relief or for flood works. This, in spite of the fact that Sendall had appealed to the Lord Mayor of London and sent photographs, wondering 'if any movement [had] been set on foot in England' to raise contributions.[42] The Greek government sent money for rebuilding schools. The Sultan sent money to relieve 'the Muslims of Limassol'. Queen Victoria sent a telegram of sympathy. Sendall was anxious to use the army of workers that had been gathered for relief and cleaning up, for flood protection work and needed funds to pay them. The inhabitants of Limassol were clearly very anxious, having seen the consequences of the failure to act after the 1881 flood, that this time adequate preventive work be undertaken. 'They had', the high commissioner emphasized, 'assembled en masse' in the centre of the town while he was there, to press the point.[43] At the beginning of December, he moved back to Limassol and based himself there, the better to cope with the situation. He wanted to divert the Garrylis river to a canal, which would avoid the town and channel the water towards the sea directly. This proposal was rejected in London. He then moved on to a scheme proposed after the 1881 flood by Samuel Brown, on the grounds that the main problem was not the Garrylis river, but the water pouring down the Phylia ravine further inland. The proposal was to dam the river higher up and use the water for irrigation purposes. Sir Walter personally rode up to the Phylia valley to inspect the possibilities for himself. His dispatch emphasizes the narrowness of the ravine and the abundance of stone at hand for

---

40.   Sendall to Ripon, 2 December 1894, CO67/88. The Mosque had been built by one of Limassol's wealthiest Muslim benefactors, Köprülüzade Hadji Ibrahim Ağa, as was the wooden bridge that was swept away by the flood. Köprülüzade's son, Hadji Huseyin Ağa, was a member of the Limassol municipal council during the flood. Tuncer Bağışkan, *Ottoman, Islamic and Islamised Monuments in Cyprus*, (Nicosia 2009), p.288.
41.   Local contributions were published in the *Cyprus Gazette*, and local press to ensure that all the money would go to the sufferers. The Sendalls' name was at the top of the list with the largest contribution. *The Owl*, 24 November 1894.
42.   Sendall to Ripon, 4 December 1894, CO67/88, NA.
43.   Sendall to Ripon, 24 November 1894, CO67/88, NA.

19. The Djami Jedit mosque in Limassol before the 1894 flood

20. The minaret of the same mosque demolished by bluejackets from the *HMS Arethusa*

the dam. Again he was turned down by London. Cyprus was not a place where money was to be spent on 'grandiose schemes'. Although this was patently a public works, rather than a municipal project, the Treasury would go no further than to authorize, if the legislative council agreed, a modest interest-free loan from the local locust tax surplus fund. [44]

Lady Sendall joined her husband in Limassol for three weeks over the Christmas period. No doubt she too busied herself organising relief work. This high-level support for the people of Limassol in their hour of need was much appreciated. 'The name of Sendall towers above all', reported *The Owl*. The town council sent him a letter saying that his personal solicitude could 'never be forgotten'. The Limassol paper *Salpinx* was effusive. 'If his noble and generous deeds were silenced, the very stones would resound them....No other High Commissioner has *narrowed the gap between government and people*. No other has raised their hopes...as much as Sir Walter Sendall'. The paper then linked his beneficence to another issue: 'If it depended on him', it opined, 'he would abolish the [wine] tax'.[45] The paper was right, but the high commissioner's hopes in this direction had been dashed, while he was staying in Limassol, by the response received from the secretary of state - a response rushed off on 13 November, the day news was received of the Limassol flood. Perhaps, the matter was taken from the bottom of the pile and dealt with speedily, in order to ensure that no pressure was applied to abolish the tax as a result of the natural disaster. Lord Ripon instructed Sir Walter to inform the memorialists that the secretary of state was unable to meet their wishes. To do so, he was told, would be to set a precedent for other aggrieved sectors which would be difficult to dispute. A disheartened Sendall, struggling to cope with the flood devastation without any financial assistance from London, observed wrily that since it was impossible for the government to take wine tithes (in kind), they would from now on be systematically bankrupting the wine-growers and killing the wine industry, so greatly expanded during British rule.

All hoped and believed that the tragic events in Limassol would delay the departure of the Connaught Rangers for Malta. 'The maintenance [of the

---

44. Sendall to Ripon, 4 December 1894 and reply, Ripon to Sendall, 21 February 1895, CO67/88.
45. *The Owl*, 24 December 1894, Σάλπιγξ, 19 November 1894.

garrison] at not less than its present strength for a time longer', pleaded Sir Walter, 'will greatly contribute to the recovery of the town .... and would be a measure gratefully recognized and appreciated throughout the island.' [46]

21. The bridge over the river Garrylis built immediately after the flood

---

46.   Sendall to Ripon, 4 December 1894, CO67/88.

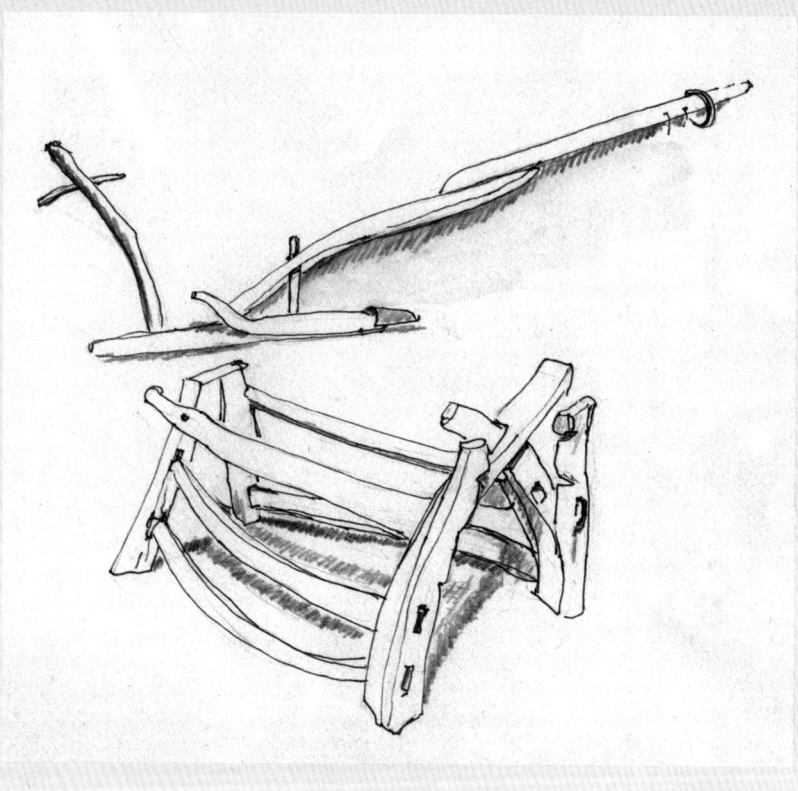

Αλέτρι (plough) and *στρατούρι* (wooden frame for pack animals)

1895

Troop Withdrawal, Uncertainty about the Future, An Island Abandoned? Political Agitation, Home Leave, Gennadius and Gennadius, A Governor in Bondage

The pleas fell on deaf ears. The reinforcement of the garrison in Malta would not be delayed. Allowing the forces to go on hanging around uselessly in Cyprus when they were needed elsewhere, was not on the cards. The needs of the little town of Limassol did not feature in the broader scheme of things being mapped out in London. The sterling relief work, so willingly carried out by the Connaught Rangers in the aftermath of the flood, had endeared them to the Limassolians, who flocked down to the roadstead to see them off as they boarded the troopship *Jumna* on 13 February.[1] An editorial in *The Owl*, dwelling nostalgically on 'the strong division of three brigades of 1878', considered the departure of the remaining thousand men 'the first act in the evacuation of Cyprus'.[2] With them went the last vestiges of any concept of the island of Cyprus as a strategic military base. The token company of 100 men, left behind temporarily to clear up, was less than reassuring. Sendall, contemplating his first home leave, inquired with more than a hint of irony, if, as had been

22. SS *Jumna* (builder's model)

---

1. *The Owl*, 19 February 1895. See also Σάλπιγξ, 12 November/26 November 1894 and Sendall to Ripon, 16 February 1895, CO67/90, NA.
2. *The Owl*, 19 February 1895.

the procedure in the past, the commanding officer of the company of sixty men now remaining, a lowly lieutenant, would be taking over the administration of Cyprus in his absence.³

The rumours that the British would soon leave Cyprus altogether, a nagging fear the previous year, now came to the fore. It was reinforced by the debate in the House of Commons on 8 March when the government sought ratification of the grant-in-aid budgeted for the island. The cleavage within the Liberal party was displayed prominently in this debate and may have tinged the tone of the chancellor of the exchequer's response. Led by Charles Dilke, by now a confirmed Unionist, speaker after speaker questioned the value of the possession. Far from defending the British acquisition of the island, Jumbo, as William Harcourt, the portly but fiery chancellor was fondly nicknamed, vented Liberal spleen against 'the impolicy of the acquisition of Cyprus', which was 'not on the way to anywhere' and of no use either to the navy or the army. It was not even any use as a sanatorium and the garrison had been withdrawn. Britain had been lumbered with 'a very squalid possession'. Pressed to explain if this meant that he was about to announce a withdrawal, he demurred. The subsequent proposal by the well-informed Member for Warrington that the Porte should be paid a lump sum to commute the Tribute, elicited the telling response, 'and who would pay the bondholders?'⁴

Harcourt had not indicated any intention of withdrawal from the island, but his strong denunciation of its acquisition when the mood of members on his own side of the House clearly was to be shot of it, exacerbated the disquiet created by the departure of the Connaught Rangers. The chief source of anxiety was the slant put on the story by *Nea Imera*, a paper published by the cosmopolitan Greek shipping community in Trieste, and reproduced widely in the local press, even before the high commissioner had been informed by Whitehall of the debate. The attitude of the chancellor of the exchequer 'and other powerful politicians' was considered a sure sign that Britain was about to pull out of Cyprus, lock, stock and barrel.⁵ The sense of Britain's abandonment was stimulated

---

3.   Private letter, Sendall to Ripon, 17 March 1894, Add 43564, f., Ripon Papers, British Library (BL).
4.   Hansard, 58 Victoriae, Vol.XXXI, 683-698, Cyprus - Grant-in-Aid, 8 March 1895 and 19 March, 1387-1410.
5.   See translation of *Imera* article in Sendall to Ripon, 7 April 1895, CO67/90, NA.

by the absence of any understanding response from London over the depressed wine industry and the Limassol flood.

The sentiments expressed by the chancellor of the exchequer in the House of Commons were to have something of the catalytic effect that would attend the word 'never' chosen by the under-secretary for the colonies half a century later, to dispel any idea that the British would relinquish the island. But in 1895, the Greek Christians *feared* their departure, convinced that retrocession to Turkey would follow. This was a fate even worse than being annually fleeced by the English. On 25 March, the anniversary of the Greek revolt against the Ottoman Empire, the pancyprian demonstrations were intended to underline the islanders' Hellenic, rather than Ottoman, identity. Sir Walter warned that bigger public meetings were being planned for April.[6]

It was not the new radicals, but the established politicians of a generally moderate and collaborative disposition that began planning a dynamic reaction. The fact that it was Achilleas Liassides, one of Sendall's closest associates, who led the revolt within the legislative council, was an indication of how catholic the protest was. Liassides urged the council to reject the budget soon to be laid before it, with the avowed object of bringing things to crisis point. He was aware that the Cypriot legislature could be bypassed by order-in-council, but in this case the people might refuse to pay their taxes. What was the point in paying them when they were not spent for the benefit of the taxpayers? He highlighted the fact that the Treasury had just reduced the public works vote, from the modest £12,000 sought by the Cyprus government to £10,000, and declared that the elected members had nothing but the responsibility of passing bills of which they disapproved, without possessing any effective control over them whatsoever.[7]

23. Achilleas Liassides

---

6. Sendall to Ripon, 7 April 1895, CO67/90, NA.
7. Ibid.

The resolution was adopted, after which the council adjourned for the Easter break. During the break, public meetings were to be organised in all the main towns. The purpose of the meetings was to protest against taxes and the Tribute and to demonstrate the will of the people to be united with Greece, should the British leave.

A deputation of leading Muslims, headed by the *mufti*, urged Sendall to prohibit the meetings. The change of administration had brought about 'excessive liberty and moved the Christian population to a lot of nonsensical thoughts. The rights of Muslims on the island are prior to all others', they declared, 'but they are overlooked and disregarded'. Between the end of March when they were announced and 15 April when the Greek Christian demonstrations took place, the Cypriot Muslims did their best to prevent them by threatening intercommunal disturbances, a tactic that would continue into modern colonial times and spill over disastrously into the early years of the Republic of Cyprus. The intention was to inhibit any possibility of union with Greece. This Christian agitation should not be allowed to grow. They called for immediate tough suppression. 'When the ant is winged,' opined *Kibris*, 'its end is near at hand'.[8] Their case was bolstered by rumours of provocative Christian behaviour. A judge with a special interest in *Evkaf* affairs, M.B. Seager, had been informed by Muslim sources that Greek Christian schoolchildren had marched through Tacktakala, a Muslim neighbourhood, on 25 March singing songs about slaughtering the hated Turks and that religious riots were in the offing. Neither Sendall, nor even the principals in the Colonial Office, were inclined to take the latter very seriously. Fairfield described Seager as 'a particularly inept person' and attached 'no importance to his views'.[9]

Nevertheless, there is no doubt that the concern over the future status of Cyprus, created by the withdrawal of the garrison, had introduced a new polarisation of interest. This would manifest itself in the summer of 1895, as it would some fifty years later, in municipal affairs. The failure of some of the elected councils created by the municipal law of 1883 to raise the funds required to carry out minimum municipal services had resulted in

---

8.   *Kibris*, 15 April 1895.
9.   Sendall to Ripon, 22 April 1895. See also enclosure and minutes, CO67/91. Captain Seager had, it seems, been absorbed into the more corrupt ways of the system he had been studying since his arrival on the island in 1878. Nevertheless, he made a valuable contribution to the examination of Ottoman Law on Foundations and Endowments and its implementation in practice.

an amendment to that law in 1884, allowing the government to annul such councils and create appointed municipal commissions. These constituted an equal number of Christian and Muslim members and a British president. Sendall had been much impressed in 1894 by the efficiency and popularity of the elected council in Limassol, with whom he had collaborated closely after the flood, in contrast to the sluggishness and unpopularity of the appointed Nicosia commission. The district commissioner, usually appointed as president of such commissions, had little time or energy to attend to the town's needs. The high commissioner was therefore anxious to reintroduce an elected council in Nicosia. Elections were at any rate due in July of that year.[10] When they took place, no doubt as a consequence of the Christian agitation in the spring of 1895, the Muslim councillors in Nicosia resigned as soon as they were elected and thus deprived the council of the quorum required by law for it to elect a mayor. In so doing, they forced the government to appoint a new municipal commission. The government was not amused and proceeded to appoint Achilleas Liassides, who had won the election, as its president. Muslim protests and demands for an English president met with a curt response.

> *This is a duty that the government has found from experience, can no longer be fairly imposed on an English official, for the time of every English official is so fully occupied with the work of his own post that he cannot devote that attention to municipal affairs which his appointment as President of the Municipal Commission would require....In selecting Mr. Liassides as President, the government considers that it has acted in the best interests of the town and the [Muslim] community. I am directed to add that it was in consequence of the action of the Mohammedan gentlemen who were lately elected members of the Municipal Council and their subsequent resignation that compelled the government to appoint a Commission in order to carry out the affairs of the municipality.*[11]

Moreover, the new polarization was, as it was to be in the future, part and parcel of an expression of broader Turkish concern at the turn of events on the island. It is no coincidence that there was a markedly more

---

10.   See Order by H.E. the High Commissioner in Council No.247 in *The Cyprus Gazette*, 26 June 1895. This order-in-council provides for municipal elections to take place on 18 July 1895.
11.   See correspondence and minutes in file SA1: 1458/95, CSA.

aggressive attitude by the Ottoman Porte to its rights in Cyprus in the winter of 1894-1895. The rumours of a British withdrawal would not have escaped Constantinople. While always underlining the Ottoman status of the island, the Porte now displayed a new assertiveness. In January 1895, the Constantinople *Evkaf* overruled the Cypriot *Evkaf*'s choice of trustee for the ancient Aziziye Tekke in Nicosia by recognizing the *ilam* of the chief *cadi*.[12] There followed a contretemps over who had the right to appoint the chief *cadi* of Cyprus, there being two rival contestants. In replying firmly to the Porte on 15 May 1895, Lord Salisbury stated that Her Majesty's government recognized no right of the Sultan to appoint offices in the island. He stressed that the Porte, in practice, had accepted this view for years.[13] A parallel can be drawn here with Ottoman tactics used after the withdrawal of European forces from autonomous Crete in 1907. The Porte would once again attempt to use the appointment of *cadis* as part of a campaign to reassert sovereignty over that island, which, like Cyprus, was still, in law, within the Ottoman Empire.[14]

An indication of the new explicitly enotist trends becoming discernible in a more confident and assertive Greek Christian community was its behaviour towards the Hellenic consul, Georgos Philemon. The Greek diplomat 'allowed himself to be publicly received and feted as the representative of what the Cypriote newspapers describe as "our king" '. It was the custom in Cyprus at this time to honour a particularly esteemed visitor by meeting him on the outskirts of the town and accompanying him to the centre. Just such a greeting had met the Greek consul on his arrival in Limassol for the celebration of 25 March anniversary of the Greek Revolt against the Turks. Sendall described his behaviour generally as unfriendly to the Ottoman government and likely to give offence to the Ottoman population of the country to which he was accredited. In an interesting reflection on the peculiar state of things in Cyprus, Sendall asked Whitehall to make representations because 'the foreign consuls all reside in Larnaca and it is only occasionally that I see any of them'.[15] Public

---

12. Sendall to Ripon, 28 January 1895, enclosing a letter to the Chief Cadi from the Sheikh-al-Islam informing that he has issued a *berat* appointing Salahi Effendi, the grandson of an earlier trustee, as the new trustee of the Aziziye Tekke. For more on the Aziziye Tekke, see Tuncer Bağışkan, (2009), 26-28.
13. Ripon to Sendall, 15 May 1895 CO67/90, NA.
14. See Robert Holland and Diana Markides, *The British and the Hellenes: Struggles for Mastery in the Eastern Mediterranean 1859-1960*, (Oxford 2006), 152.
15. Sendall to Ripon, 22 April 1895, CO67/91, NA.

demonstrations of the desire of the Greek Christians of the island to be united with Greece were as yet rare, especially in conservative Nicosia, but with the growing rivalry between the old style gradualists and the new more radical politicians, public manifestations of Hellenic sentiment were inevitably on the rise.

The high commissioner decided against prohibiting the protest meetings, not, since the departure of the Connaught Rangers, having any substantial force with which to back such a prohibition. Moreover, he believed any official ban would be more likely to cause a breach of the peace than the meetings themselves. He intended to allow them to take place, but to put the responsibility for maintaining law and order squarely on the shoulders of the organisers.[16] He and his principals in London considered the object of the demonstrations reasonable enough. 'There [did] not appear to be any real protest against the British occupation…The only danger in the situation lay in the chance of a fight between Muslims and Christians.' A message was sent from the secretary of state to the Muslim leaders explaining that 'the liberty of public meeting [was] the same for all, whether in Cyprus or elsewhere'. But they were reassured that the civil and personal rights of the Muslims would be safeguarded.[17] Sendall telegraphed the secretary of state for a new official confirmation that there was no plan for a British withdrawal. He received a statement two days before the demonstrations were due to take place, but only after it had been modified at Fairfield's suggestion. 'We must be careful about the wording', he minuted. 'Some day the Foreign Office might want to surrender [the island] as part of a deal in the Levant. Therefore I should not use the word "England" which binds the country in perpetuity. We need only say "Her Majesty's Government has no intention of leaving Cyprus" and reiterate that it "remains Ottoman therefore the status is not for discussion between the British Government and the Cypriots". This statement was immediately telegraphed to all district commissioners to be distributed to the community leaders in each district. Sir Walter held special meetings of the executive council to work out a plan of action. A letter was sent to the organisers, stressing their responsibility to maintain law and order. The police were put on the alert, but in spite of Muslim assertions that there would be trouble and that ammunition had been imported into the island,

---

16. Report on Meeting of the Executive Council, 22 April 1895. SA1: C226/1895, CSA.
17. Ripon to Sendall, 12 June 1895, CO67/91, NA.

24. Limassol demonstration in April 1895

the district commissioners were confident that the demonstrations would go off peacefully, as indeed they did. Meetings took place in all the main towns except Famagusta on 4 April. All went smoothly and quietly. Not surprisingly, given the views of the leaders in each area, the emphasis in the Limassol and Larnaca area was focused on the demand for union with Greece, while in Nicosia and the east of the island, the emphasis was against taxes and the Tribute. Nevertheless, it was in this latter area that the Muslim community reacted most strongly to the Greek Christian efforts.

In Nicosia, on the day of the meeting, a crowd of a few hundred people had already gathered on the Karbi Ismail (D'Avila) Bastion by mid-morning. Liassides and other members of the organising committee clambered up on to a pulpit that had been erected in the space, but 'His Beatitude and his reverent companions remained seated in their carriage'. The Archbishop was an old man, but perhaps he also felt safer secluded thus from the proceedings. He was among those who had warned Sendall that the Turks were planning trouble. By midday numbers had grown to several hundred. After the speeches, the demonstrators began moving up the dusty road to Government House to deliver a resolution, as they had done in 1887. As they walked, the crowd was swollen by people arriving from the outlying villages of Ayios Omoloyites and Strovolos to about 3,000. Young noted the 'tender age' of most participants. The crowd, led by the Archbishop, presumably still in his carriage, trudged on up the dusty drive to Government House. Sir Walter came out in front of the house to greet them and addressed a few carefully chosen words.[18] The crowd dispersed peacefully, the gentle harbinger of an angrier mob, which would pick up the threads of this popular expression of discontent in the more combustible atmosphere created thirty-five years later.

The Famagusta meeting did not take place until a few weeks later. In the intervening period, Liassides had toured the Karpass villages, drumming up support for the pancyprian demonstration, perhaps dangling prospects of the lucrative cultivation of tobacco, if tax reform could be pressed through. In later years the Karpass was to become a tobacco-growing area. Subsequent reports that during this tour Christians had been supplied with guns and ammunition by a certain Hadjinicola, a schoolmaster in

---

18. King to Chief Secretary, 29 April 1895, SA1:C266/1895, CSA.

Vatilli, were not taken seriously by the authorities. 'I know Hadjinicola well', Travers, the district commissioner, reported. 'He is quiet and the last man that I imagine capable of doing that of which he is accused – especially as many of the Turks are hugely indebted to him. One man who supported this story, Hasan Hamaza, by name, is one of the worst characters in the village.'[19] The demonstration, when it finally took place, was as peaceful as all the others.

It is interesting that Famagusta lagged behind the other areas, even Paphos, in the organisation of this demonstration. Was it that the church had no bishop to coordinate things in the area or was it that the Sendalls chose to visit Famagusta during the Easter break? Lady Sendall's levees and Sir Walter's receptions, by now expected features of the couple's district tours, would create an uncomfortable environment for the organisation of political demonstrations. Liassides' visit to Famagusta may have been delayed for that reason alone. The town had been a backwater since the beginning of Ottoman rule. In the heady days of 1878, its port was advertised as having the potential to challenge Valetta. Two decades later, the tiny Venetian harbour was still so silted as to afford shelter only to vessels with the shallowest draught. The island's trade remained concentrated on the southern roadsteads of Larnaca and Limassol. The malarial boggy flats that surrounded the derelict medieval city deterred interest in the area. The Greek name for the town was Ammochostos – 'buried in sand' and, indeed, the Lewises encountered a great deal of it when they stayed in the southern Greek Christian suburb of Varosha.[20] But the land around Varosha was extremely fertile with abundant subterranean water. Gardens of lemons and pomegranates provided the basis of a budding trade with Syria.

In 1895 British investors began tentative enquiries into reviving the idea of railway construction in the island. An entrepreneur long interested in Cyprus, Charles Provende, proposed an ambitious joint venture with the government for a railway connecting Nicosia to Larnaca and combining this with a modern farming enterprise. The local administration responded very positively, but angled for more. They pressed for Famagusta to be included in the project. This jewel in the crown of the flourishing

---

19. Benjamin Travers, District Commissioner of Famagusta, to Chief Secretary, 9 May 1895, SA1:C266/1895, CSA.
20. Lewis, 283.

25. Silted Famagusta port, ca.1897

crusader kingdom of Cyprus had a special allure for the colonial government. The mirage of the city restored to its former glory hovered over the mundane reality of an administration strapped for cash. This elusive chimera of renaissance, significance and glamour underpinned a sense that it had been cheated of a legitimate *raison d'être*. In arguing for a branch line from Kondea to Famagusta, a report by Young, the chief secretary, who knew Famagusta well and obviously had a soft spot for it, stressed that although the old city was derelict, the port, once dredged, did have potential. By the 1890s the new Famagusta suburb of Varosha was coming to life. According to the 1891 census, it had a higher rate of growth than any other town on the island. By 1893 Famagusta had 'the best' racecourse in Cyprus to which, according to *The Owl*, 'thousands of people from the outlying villages flocked in their gorgeous and picturesque attire....to witness an event unprecedented in Messarian (sic) sporting annals'.[21]

Sendall was all for investment in the island, but he urged that investment should be government-led. Using taxes to lend money to infrastructural enterprises which the government could not control was an unnecessarily risky enterprise. The government itself should borrow money to invest in infrastructure. What better indication to other investors that the British were here to stay? As early as 1892, he had formally expressed the opinion that

> *If the Government is ever to be relieved of contributing towards the expenses of Cyprus, it will, in my opinion, be by treating the island as (what indeed it is) an improvable property and spending money on it with a view to a return.*[22]

The Colonial Office rejected Provende's railway proposal, without even referring it to the Treasury because of 'the present financial situation on the island'.[23] Fairfield's 'do nothing policy' died hard. But whose fault was the 'present financial situation on the island'? With a finger pointed firmly at the Treasury, Sendall retorted that this was 'hardly the Cypriots' fault'. Since he had first taken formal stock of the island in 1893, he had come

---

21. *The Owl*, 27 May 1893.
22. Sendall to Ripon, 14 February 1893, CO67/79, NA.
23. Fairfield to Provende, 28 May 1895, CO67/90, NA.

to the conclusion that 'Cyprus will never be able to pay its way until its natural resources are developed'.[24] He would take the opportunity of his forthcoming home leave to press the point in London as strongly as possible. The ideas set forth in the correspondence between the Colonial Office and Sendall, set off by Provende's desire to invest in the island, provide an interesting insight into the extent to which the intervention in Cyprus was part of a broader capitalist enterprise. The substance of the interchanges between Whitehall and the high commissioner were about how best to secure the return on that capital.

The legislative council resumed its session after the Easter break. One of its first acts was to vote unanimously, Muslims and Christians all, against a gratuity of £200 sought by the government for the retiring commissioner of Kyrenia, Robert Fisher. Since there was no money for public utilities, none could be spared for perks. The protest meetings had resolved to send a memorial to London and a committee had been formed to draw it up, most of them legislative councillors. Meanwhile the session continued to work normally, enacting the first substantial piece of legislation on educational reform since the British occupation. The 1895 Education Act provided for two pancyprian boards of education - one Muslim and one Christian - whose task would be to supervise and regulate village school committees. The chief secretary of the government would be the chairman of both boards, the chief *cadi*, *mufti* and Archbishop being members ex-officio. The other salient provision of the new act was for the proper qualification of teachers, both in male and female educational establishments. This would be greatly facilitated by the teacher training system established in the Pancyprian gymnasium.

The extraordinary rapport within the legislative council, between Sir Walter and the elected members, that facilitated the enactment of this legislation, is all the more remarkable for being in the midst of a major protest against current taxation. Sendall admitted that he took

---

24. See Sendall's draft report for 1893-1894, explaining at length why and in which direction the island should be developed. The remarks were removed in their entirety from the report before it was published. See private letter to Ripon, 14 February 1893 and enclosed draft report CO67/79, NA. In his private letter too, hoping to convince the new secretary of state, he stresses the need to put the revenue on 'a more secure footing' through investment. He stresses that 'Cyprus is a highly improvable property, and from a merely business point of view, it is a question whether we are acting quite wisely in meeting every suggestion for improvement, which involves spending money with a simple 'non possumus'.

26. Ayios Loukas fair at Famagusta, 18 October 1898

'a considerable personal share' in debating the legislation and reported to London 'the reasonable and conciliatory spirit displayed throughout the debate by the elected members of the council in whose hands the ultimate decision upon every point practically lay'. He believed the new legislation would 'place the schools upon a secure footing' and that if it worked as he hoped it would, it could not fail 'to produce a lasting effect upon the character and condition of the people'.[25] The legislative council was now working constructively on substantial reforming legislation and acting as a check on government. The distinguished archaeologist, David Hogarth, who was visiting Cyprus in 1895, was clearly impressed.

> *Nothing strikes a stranger who may chance to attend a meeting of the Legislative Council more than the demeanour of the Greek members. They have a programme, an argumentation behind it and a mastery of sure method of free debate which might excite the envy of the Irish nationalists.*[26]

The programme of the Greek Christian elected members, moreover, extended beyond the council meetings, to organised demonstrations of protest at street level most effectively (in Parapedi in October 1894 and the Pancyprian protests of April and May 1895). The council was still sitting in June when complaints were made by elected members against two district judges, the weak and indolent Seager and the notoriously corrupt Grigsby. Unqualified to practise law, the latter had nevertheless been appointed as a district judge in Paphos, where he proved to be hiding from charges for fraud in England. Both complaints were found by the administration in Cyprus to be totally justified and resulted in the two judges' removal. Grigsby was accused of 'intemperate habits leading to systematic neglect of work'. Seager was accused of allowing the court registrar to conduct himself in a manner incompatible with the due administration of justice. Seager was heavily in debt to the registrar, a certain Kyriakides. He allowed him 'to interfere in the proceedings of the court, putting questions to the witnesses and interpreting evidence in cases in which he was personally and pecuniarily interested'.[27] 'It is much to be regretted',

---

25. Sendall to Ripon, 5 June 1895, CO67/92 NA. For full text of the Education Act see 'A Law to Provide for the Establishment and Management of Elementary Schools in Cyprus' enacted 3 June 1895, *The Cyprus Gazette,* Supplement, 4 July 1895.
26. David Hogarth, *A Wandering Scholar in the Levant,* (London 1896), 193.
27. Sendall to Ripon, 18 June 1895, CO67/92, NA.

commented Sendall, 'that in a single session of the Legislative Council, complaints should have been proffered against the administration of justice in two district courts. In each of which case, enquiries have proved complaints justified.' [28]

After the closing of another marathon session of the legislative council, the Sendalls began to prepare for their first home leave after three years on the island. Sir Walter had put some drive and efficiency into the listless, shambling regime he had inherited. By juggling his officers around the island to the administration's best advantage, and by keeping a close check on each officer, he got the best out of them. He had, for example, instituted a system of diaries, records of work which all senior officials were obliged to keep daily.[29] These records were sent up to Government House for review on a regular three-monthly basis. District officers were being made accountable.

Merton King, the commissioner of Nicosia, who had failed to contribute to the Blue Book for the second year running in 1893, on the grounds that there was 'nothing new to report', submitted a careful account of the year's work in 1894. He had by then been relieved of the additional burden of responsibility for Nicosia town by the appointment of Liassides, who was in a position to be more effective as president of the municipal commission. In combination with Sendall's exhaustive tours of inspection and the new level of committee work within the legislature, this close interest taken by the high commissioner in the administration of the towns, as well as remote rural areas, produced results. The Cypriots at last found themselves with a governor, who not only worked, but who wanted to work *with them* for the island.

The Limassolians demonstrated their special appreciation by organising a civic welcome for the Sendalls as they entered the port on the first stage of their journey home.[30] It is very likely that it was on this occasion that the poet, Vassilis Michaelides, composed a poem in honour of the high commissioner.

---

28. Sendall to Ripon, 8 July 1895, CO67/92, NA.
29. The commissioners were a little indignant and somewhat reluctant but they did conform. See 'Keeping of Diaries by Commissioners', SA1:713/1896, CSA.
30. Sendall to Ripon, 19 June 1895, CO67/92, NA.

"Όπου κ᾿ ἰ᾿ ἂν πᾶς, οἱ στράτες σου
νἂν δάφνη κ᾿ αἰ μερσίνι(ν)·
κ᾿᾿ ὅπου πατᾶς νὰ πλάσκουνται
τριαντάφυλλα κ᾿ αἰ κρίνοι.

(Wherever you go, let the way
Be strewn with daphne and laurel,
And where you tread let there be
Roses and lilies.) [31]

The council requested a portrait of Sir Walter to hang in the town hall.

Nevertheless, he returned to London depressed and worn down. He was clearly distressed by a fact that he could now no longer deny. The Treasury had been allowed to purloin the island's wealth for its own purposes, presiding over an iniquitous tax regime that *he* was obliged to impose. Moreover, the arrogance with which their Lordships curtailed not only the basic expenditure of the island but *every* financially related action of the administration, had become intolerable to him - not least the obstruction of his new practical method of collecting arrears, coming so soon after the total absence of support during the flood and the abandonment of the island by the military. They had also recently reduced the public works budget by the £2,000 they had themselves admitted they owed the Cypriot taxpayers. In that sum lay the difference between being limited to minor maintenance jobs and embarking on new construction. He would not remain silent. If there was no adequate response, he would resign. Bar a short holiday in Ireland, the Sendalls spent their five-month leave at 26 Eaton Square. Their time at this conveniently situated London residence was taken up largely in lobbying for Cyprus - in Westminster, in the press, in the Colonial Office.

It was during the couple's journey home to England that a general election, fought chiefly over Home Rule for Ireland, which had split the Liberal party, returned a Conservative government to power in coalition with the radical Liberal Unionists under Joseph Chamberlain. A grateful Lord Salisbury offered Chamberlain more or less any ministry he wanted. He took

---

31. Vassilis Michaelides, *Ποιήματα*, (Limassol), 1972, p.63. For full poem and translation, see appendix 1.

the unprecedented step of *choosing* the Colonial Office. It was a dingy, gloomy sub-office in Whitehall still lit by candlelight and, until then, considered an office of last resort. Chamberlain took the building, as he intended to take the empire, by storm. Cobwebs and candles were swept away. Each dusty nook and cranny was now exposed to the full glare of modern electricity. 'It was a total transformation...Everyone in the department felt it, and presently everyone in the colonial service felt it,' wrote Flora Shaw in *The Times*, 'to the furthest corners and the loneliest outposts of the Queen's dominions'.[32]

For Sendall, the arrival of Chamberlain in the Colonial Office could not have come at a more opportune moment. He sought an appointment with him as soon as he arrived in London and received one almost immediately - at last a secretary of state who spoke the same language. Speaking in the House of Commons a few days after his meeting with Sir Walter, Chamberlain echoed the high commissioner's sentiments. 'I regard many of our colonies as being in the condition of undeveloped estates which can never be developed without imperial assistance'.[33] But the new secretary of state's approach to the occupation of Egypt also coloured his approach to Cyprus. Chamberlain had felt uncomfortable about the motivation behind the occupation of Egypt in 1882 and the way it was subsequently being administered. Attacking Granville's policy, he had accused the Liberal government of making 'finance and creditors the keynote of policy' and of 'sacrificing the liberty and independence of Egypt to the security of the bondholders'.[34] In a letter written in October 1892 to his close colleague Sir Charles Dilke, who took a special interest in Egypt and Cyprus, Chamberlain had stressed the importance of 'snubbing the bondholders' in the radicals' schemes to reorganise the Liberal party.[35] Dilke had visited Barbados when Sendall was governor there, just before his Cyprus posting. Their correspondence indicates a cordial relationship, which would have been useful in gaining a speedy audience with Chamberlain.[36] It is not beyond the bounds of possibility that Dilke, who was also known to

---

32. J.L. Garvin, *Life of Joseph Chamberlain,* Vol. III, (London 1934), 10-11.
33. Ibid.
34. Joseph Chamberlain to Charles Dilke, 9 October 1892, JC5/24/1-554, Vol. 2, Birmingham University Library, (henceforth BUL).
35. Joseph Chamberlain to Charles Dilke, 9 October 1892, JC 5/24/1-554, Joseph Chamberlain Collection (JCC), BUL.
36. Dilke to Sendall and Sendall to Dilke, 3 and 6 November 1890, Dilke papers, Add.43914.f.164, BL.

Robert Herbert, was instrumental in Sendall being sent to Cyprus in 1892. Robert Herbert was brought back to the Colonial Office as permanent secretary for a short spell immediately after Chamberlain took over. The concentration of these powerful figures with some knowledge of the island's affairs around the new secretary of state would have lent weight to Sendall's case.

The secretary of state did not turn a deaf ear to Sir Walter's distress at the use to which Cyprus was being put by its colonial masters. Immediately after their meeting, Chamberlain began enquiring about the Cyprus Tribute. He wrote a private letter to Lord Selborne asking for information. Selborne replied that for at least two years before the occupation of Cyprus, the British and French governments had had to pay the interest on the Turkish loan to the bondholders out of their own pockets. A private note from Fairfield corroborated this information. 'Between 1855 and the Russo-Turkish War (1877) the Turks provided for the service of the debt out of their own revenue. At the time of the Russo-Turkish war they went bankrupt all along the line.'[37] Fairfield warned that attempts to commute the loan had come up against Foreign Office objections. France had to be kept happy in order to maintain the British ascendancy in Egypt. The Treasury also displayed a reluctance to pay the 2% interest on the loan that would be needed to pay off the Turks. In a tell-tale footnote, Fairfield hinted that the powerful bondholders, who were pocketing an annual dividend of 4% on their shares, would try to resist such a proceeding, each bond being now worth a tidy £118 per year.[38]

During his meeting with Chamberlain, Sendall had underlined the fact that because of the annual haemorrhage of the Tribute, very little money had been spent since the British occupation on infrastructure. The public works vote was hardly enough to maintain existing roads, let alone build new ones. He focused on the lack of bridges 'which were always left until last and were badly needed if continuous traffic throughout the year were to be provided for and productivity improved'. He cited the example of the itinerant threshing machine that had been recently introduced to the

---

37. Selborne to Chamberlain, 4 August 1895, JC9/3/1/2 and Fairfield private note for Chamberlain dated 1 August 1895, JC9/3/1/4, JCC. Chamberlain Papers, BUL.
38. Ibid. See also table in *The Investor's Monthly Manual*, 30 December 1899, Paul Mauro, Nathan Sussman, Yishay Yafeh, *Emerging Markets and Financial Globalism, Sovereign Bond Spreads in 1879-1913 and Today*, (Oxford 2007), 17.

27. Joseph Chamberlain's related political and imperial ambitions

island which 'owing to the want of roads and bridges, its field of operations could not admit of success'. But the key to greater productivity was irrigation. Wherever it had been introduced in a small way on the island, it had made a phenomenal difference in terms of the quality and quantity of produce. Water must be massively stored and distributed. The deep narrow valleys which formed the beds of the winter torrents, and open on to the plains on all sides, lent themselves to the building of dams. Moreover, there was plenty of stone to be found on the spot. He had had experience of seeing the distribution of water from such dams in Ceylon with success and he was confident that the results in Cyprus would be equally good.[39]

A third infrastructural project could be the building of a railway. Private investors had lately shown an interest in the latter. But Sendall was all for investment by the British government because:

> *The mere intimation of an intention on the part of Her Majesty's Government to sanction a loan for works of improvement and development in Cyprus, would have such an immediate effect in improving confidence in the stability of our hold over the country*

---

39.   Sendall to Ripon, 18 August 1895. This was Sendall's response to Chamberlain's request for 'observations upon the subject of capital expenditure as applicable to the development of the natural resources of Cyprus', CO67/96.

> and its resources, which is the real question at issue, that the capitalists who are now shy of embarking on any enterprise in the island would readily come forward and could safely be trusted to discover for themselves in what direction capital might be invested to their own great advantage and to the lasting benefit of the people and the government.[40]

Markets would be opened up by the improvement of communications from the area of production to the ports and from the ports to Egypt. For the latter, Sendall advocated a government subsidy for a regular steamer service. In addition, shipping generally should be encouraged to call at more than one port in Cyprus, by being obliged to pay harbour dues only at the first port of call.[41]

Fairfield was clearly put out by this new dynamism. He grumbled that dams would be far too expensive and might burst with tragic consequences, while the problem of distribution was insurmountably costly. Introducing a lot more water to the Mesaoria would create a malarial swamp. Wouldn't it be better if the Cyprus government just drilled a few artesian wells? But times had changed. Chamberlain insisted on immediate action. He wanted an irrigation expert in Cyprus within the following three months. A railway expert was also to be found.[42]

During his leave in Eaton Square, Sir Walter continued to lobby against the Tribute and for Cyprus. The Archbishop sent the memorial resulting from the April demonstrations not directly to the British government, but to Sendall, confident that it would thus be handed over in the most favourable way. In 1887, the same memorialists had bypassed their governor, Henry Bulwer, and travelled to London at great expense in the belief that it was the only way their case would be heard. During their stay in London, Bulwer had skulked in Germany on yet another leave of absence from his island charge. Now, the memorial, sent by Young to Sendall, was carefully checked for translation defects and passed on to the secretary of state with lengthy comments and observations from both Young and the high commissioner.

---

40. Ibid.
41. Ibid.
42. See attached Fairfield and Chamberlain minutes.

Sendall could have been aided in checking the translation by his new acquaintance, Ioannis Gennadius. This wealthy Greek intellectual and diplomat resided in London. He was very active in promoting Greek issues in Britain. No doubt the introductions would have been made by his brother Panayiotis. Panayiotis Gennadius was an eminent botanist, who had served as minister of agriculture in Greece, and the previous year, had been in Cyprus on a three-month mission of enquiry into the state of agriculture on the island.⁴³ His subsequent report on the state of the island's agriculture had been warmly endorsed by no lesser an authority than the director of Kew Gardens, William Turner Thistleton-Dyer. ⁴⁴ Ioannis Gennadius was extremely well connected. He had created the Greek Committee in London, which had included several leading Liberal politicians, not least Chamberlain and Dilke, among its members.⁴⁵ The Sendalls would also have discussed the Cyprus Tribute with Gennadius. He had his own experiences to contribute, having personally worked on settling the Greek Debt of 1824. In doing so, he had become aware of the influence of major bondholders in its management.⁴⁶

A veritable lobby for Cyprus was evolving at Eaton Square. Sendall was in touch with Charles Christian, the Levantine director of the Imperial Ottoman Bank in Larnaca and also with the Member of Parliament for Warrington, Robert Pierpoint. The latter had spoken with knowledge and vehemence on the financial complexities of the Tribute in the March debate in the House of Commons that had caused such a stir. He now tabled new questions on the affairs of Cyprus.⁴⁷ The Sendalls' friendship with Pierpoint resulted in the Liberal politician joining Lady Sophia in fundraising in London to fulfill the passionate desire of the lepers in Nicosia to worship in their own church instead of the 'old dilapidated room' which had served the purpose until then.⁴⁸ He had taken up their invitation to visit them in Cyprus the following February. It would be an

---

43. Ibid. The Gennadius mission had been Sendall's response to a long-standing demand of the members of the legislative council for scientific advice to the Cypriots for the development of agriculture.
44. Thistleton-Dyer to Ripon, 10 September 1895, CO67/96, NA.
45. Lord Rosebery was the chairman of the Greek Committee. William Harcourt, now chancellor of the exchequer, was also a member. Paper entitled 'Autobiographical Notes', Box 11, folder 11.1, John Gennadius Archive, Gennadion Library, Athens (henceforth GL).
46. Ibid.
47. Parliamentary debate on grant-in-aid of £35,000, proposed by the government for Cyprus for 1895, published in *The Times*, 28 August 1895.
48. *Cyprus: Annual Report 1897*, 98.

opportunity to see the situation for himself and enjoy the island at its springtime best.⁴⁹

Backing new proposals by Charles Christian for the Tribute's commutation, Sir Walter took the unusual, but very effective step of countering the Treasury's arguments that the bondholders could not be paid off, by sending an actual bond to the Colonial Office on the back of which one of the regulations clearly stipulated that it *could* be paid off after twenty years, in other words after 1879, with or without the consent of the bondholders.⁵⁰ Questions in the House, no doubt primed from Eaton Square, were countered with evasive answers, in which the problem of satisfying the French government predominated.⁵¹ The government, pressed by this new assault by the Cypriots and their high commissioner, and threatened with a new debate on the administration of Cyprus, was indeed dusting down the old proposals for commutation of the Crimean War loan. What emerges from the minutes is the major obstacle of upsetting the French government, for so many years free of the pressure and financial drain of appeasing their bondholders. Being nice to the French was vital to Britain's dominating presence in Egypt. A telling minute observed that

> *If we reduced the whole, we should disassociate ourselves from France and thereby lose (quantam valeat) the hold we have over Egypt. For under the present arrangement, we save the French Government £75,000 a year.*⁵²

Chamberlain's enquiries had revealed the extent to which the issue of the Tribute was entangled in questions of high policy and high finance. He pursued its commutation with the support even of the most conservative of politicians who had just returned to the Treasury, Sir Michael Hicks Beach. Nevertheless, the project would take time. Meanwhile, he attacked on another front. On writing to the Treasury about the 'unsatisfactory state' of relations between Cyprus and the United Kingdom which had

---

49. Filios Zanettos, Ιστορία της Νήσου Κύπρου, Vol. II, (Larnaca 1911), 914.
50. File 14361 headed 'Turkish Loan of 1855', private letter from Sendall to Lord Campbell, 16 August 1895, CO67/96, NA. See also attached copy of 'the conditions of issue' printed on the back of the bonds of the 1855 loan, and a letter from Charles Christian to Sir Edward Hamilton, permanent assistant secretary to the Treasury dated 18 March 1895. The letter proposes a scheme for paying off the bondholders, which Sendall has already proposed to Chamberlain.
51. *The Times,* 28 August 1895.
52. Minute signed by Meade, dated 21 August 1895, in File 14361 headed 'Turkish Loan of 1858', CO67/96, NA.

received his special attention since coming to office, Chamberlain urged the immediate arrangement of an annual grant-in-aid for the island to be fixed at £40,000, the sum that was gained annually by the British taxpayer from Cypriot revenue. In view of the circumstances of the acquisition of the island, he observed, it would be hardly creditable to continue the present arrangement. His three predecessors had all sought fixed grants-in-aid, but had been denied on the grounds that the prevailing (financial) circumstances were inopportune. In arguing that now things had changed, Chamberlain was creating in Cyprus something of a pilot scheme for his new concept of empire.

> *But now that Her Majesty's Government are seeking to base their relations with the dependencies, not on consideration of temporary expediency, but upon lasting and clearly defensible principles, Mr. Chamberlain has no doubt that their lordships [of the Treasury] will agree with them.*[53]

Chamberlain was sweeping away entrenched excuses for inaction with the thoroughness with which he had once bulldozed highways through the slums of Birmingham.

Just before this letter was sent to the Treasury, Sendall had signalled his unwillingness to return to Cyprus. He passed on the word through Robert Meade, who had taken over from Robert Herbert as permanent secretary and was the man he trusted most, because he had 'known him throughout'. Sir Walter expressed the desire to be appointed elsewhere, even the Isle of Man, until somewhere else became available. He explained the need he felt to cut short his present appointment.

> *The Government of Cyprus is an interesting post, but it has many drawbacks, not the least of which is that, **owing to the bondage under which we live to the Treasury, the position of the Governor is most disheartening, and, in a sense, humiliating.** This is strong language, but I am quite prepared to justify it, and it is a subject upon which I could say a good deal if it were wished that I should do so.*[54]

---

53. Buxton writing on Chamberlain's behalf to the secretary to the Treasury, 6 September 1895, CO67/96, NA.
54. Private letter from Sendall to Meade, 10 September 1895, CO67/96, NA

We do not know whether he was given an opportunity to expand on this subject, but one can imagine it quite likely that he would have been, perhaps over lunch, with Robert Meade. Rumours were circulating in Cyprus based on a confidence divulged to *The Owl* by a reliable source, that 'the High Commissioner [did] not intend resuming office unless he succeed[ed] in bringing with him some measure of relief for Cyprus'.[55] Sendall's private letter has the feel of genuine anguish, rather than manipulative pressure tactics. He applied for a new posting again in November, from Tipperary. This time he wrote directly to Chamberlain for the governorship of Jamaica that had just become vacant. Chamberlain insisted on him returning to Cyprus. He was to be sent back, not exactly with a firm new policy, but with promises that such a policy was in the pipeline. Sir Walter would be the ideal person to implement it.

As part of his campaign for Cyprus in London, Sir Walter had given an interview to the *Westminster Budget*. In it he had stressed that the government was unable to improve productivity on the island, the Tribute payment leaving them just enough for the bare minimum of expenses. He illustrated the primitive methods of ploughing and threshing on the island, by displaying little carved wooden models of Cypriot ploughs and threshing boards. In pressing the absence of development, he cited the great strides in this direction being taken in Egypt, 'If only we could *Egypt* Cyprus',[56] he told the *Budget*. In other words, instead of pursuing a policy of minimum expenditure on the island in order to pay the bondholders, how much better it would be to follow the success story of Egypt, a country in exactly the same predicament, and spend money on the development of the island, the better to pay the debt.

Sendall had similarly expressed a desire to 'Egypt Cyprus' in his annual report to parliament in 1894.[57] Egypt's notorious debt crisis had resulted in increasing Anglo-French involvement in its administration, Egyptian products were fetching the same low prices now afflicting Cyprus, but, under Lord Cromer's indirect but firm administration, it had continued to increase its annual revenue by increasing productivity. The key was irrigation. Sir Walter simply sought a little of the leeway given to Cromer

---

55. *The Owl*, 27 September 1895.
56. Interview given by Sendall to *The Westminster Budget*, reproduced in *The Owl*, 12 September 1895.
57. *Cyprus: Annual Report 1894*.

in his administration of the country, the acquisition of which had resulted in the abandonment of any interest in government investment of any kind in Cyprus. No doubt he had read Alfred Milner's best-selling book, *England in Egypt*, and also *Egyptian Irrigation*, written by the engineer, William Wilcocks.[58] It must have seemed to him that the potential would be greatly increased once the island was freed from the humiliating and hopelessly restricting bondage to the accountants in the Treasury. But beyond the appointment by Chamberlain of an expert from India to enquire into and report on irrigation possibilities for the island, Sir Walter returned to Cyprus only with promises.

28. Portrait of Sir Walter Sendall (etching in *Westminster Budget*)

---

58. Alfred Milner's somewhat propagandistic account, of British achievements in Egypt, was published in 1892 and was into its eleventh edition by 1904.

Red polished ware excavated in Cyprus

1896

A Warm Welcome Back, Money in Hand, A Start in Tax Reform, 'Natives' in the Executive Council, Fraud in the Public Works Department, Archaeological Activity, Vakoufs and Cadis, Tennis in Troodos, Rebellion in Crete

On a cold January morning the Sendalls stepped off the deck of the French *Messagerie* steamer that had brought them from Alexandria, down the rickety gangplank and into the Larnaca customs boat that would take them to dry land. The steamer was anchored too far offshore for the couple to be aware of the stir that their arrival had caused in the little town. But as they neared the coast, they heard and saw the buzz of expectant activity. The word 'WELCOME' was inscribed in large letters on an arch at the end of the pier. A Union Jack fluttered above the centre of the arch and on either side, the Greek and Turkish flags. The pier was strewn with myrtle, but most impressive and extraordinary was 'the great concourse of people' all along the beach on both sides, with overcrowded rowing boats bobbing precariously on the shallows as their passengers craned for a better view.

As Sir Walter helped his wife across the heaving gap between the customs boat and the bottom step of the pier, Young and Cobham moved forward to greet them. They were accompanied by the Larnaca mayor and the town notables, clerical and lay. The mayor and member of the legislative council, Nicolaos Rossos, delivered a welcoming speech in Greek and then presented Lady Sendall with a bouquet of flowers. Sendall himself was presented with a posy by Eleni Loizou, the assistant to the mistress of the Larnaca girls' school. She then 'delivered in a clear and courageous voice the most appropriate address'. All the speeches delivered in Greek were translated into English by a Mr. Demetrios Karageorghiades. 'The disturbed eyes of the High Commissioner marked the emotion aroused by the welcome accorded him, while Lady Sendall, whose most affable smile and face generally denoted extreme good-heartedness, seemed moved to tears.'[1]

After shaking hands with the people standing there, Sir Walter gave his arm to Lady Sendall and began to make his way slowly through the space opened for him by the crowd. The people surged around not only on

---

1. Ένωσις, 3 January 1896.

the sea front, but in the square in front of the law courts. As the high commissioner and his wife walked along, the schoolboys, who were drawn up in rows, sang God Save the Queen, then the *zaptiehs* presented arms. Sir Walter and Lady Sendall went upstairs to the government offices and there exchanged greetings with the many prominent citizens who had gathered. At about 11 o'clock they set off for the capital.

The welcoming greetings did not end in Larnaca. As their carriage approached Nicosia, the Sendalls became aware that the horses had been reined in to a walk. Through the window they could see people gathered on either side of the road. The crowd grew larger as they approached Nicosia. Citizens, summoned by the toll of church bells, had gathered on the outskirts of the town to greet the returning high commissioner. Liassides, now mayor, and the Archbishop were there. Schoolboys had been allowed, indeed encouraged, to leave their lessons to join in the civic welcome, a move that created a backlash of disapproval in radical circles. The chief objector was the Peloponnesian radical, Nicolaos Katalanos, but even he admitted that citizens had left their jobs to come and meet the 'foreign άρχοντα'.[2] The popular enthusiasm for Sir Walter was unprecedented. High commissioners were wont to come and go undisturbed by any local interest. This one had touched a chord, but with that respect and warmth came great expectations. Had the Cypriot memorial been considered favourably? 'Sweet words are not enough', opined the Nicosia paper, *Φωνή της Κύπρου*, in an editorial Sendall chose to send to London.

> For eighteen years we have been hearing of Her Majesty's interest in the Cypriots. No occasion was ever presented nor the least document exchanged without mention being made of the lively interest of the Government in the Cypriot people... ...They threaten to abandon us and at the same time they say they are greatly interested. We ask for a suspension of taxes and as they proceed more energetically in the collection thereof, they tell us that Her Majesty's Government is greatly interested in Cyprus....We make demands and they refuse us everything, without, of course, omitting the assurance that Her Majesty's Government is greatly interested in the Cypriots.[3]

---

2. Nicolaos Katalanos, *Ο Ζήνων*, (Nicosia 1914), 102.
3. *Φωνή της Κύπρου*, 3 January, enclosed in Sendall to Chamberlain, 6 January 1896, CO67/97, NA.

Φωνή της Κύπρου, reported the high commissioner, reflected the general cynicism about Her Majesty's government 'with force and accuracy'. He stressed the importance of being allowed to include in his opening speech in the legislative council in early March, 'some indication of [Whitehall's] intentions respecting measures to be adopted for developing the resources of the island and the amelioration of its condition'. He suggested pointedly that, in fact, this occasion would be 'the most convenient form in which to convey to the people, the reply of Her Majesty's Government to the memorial which was sent to England last autumn'.[4]

London did not produce anything for him to offer during his opening speech. The Colonial Office had not even passed on his letter to the Treasury at the beginning of March, when the legislature assembled for the new session. The predicament of the high commissioner was their least concern. Chamberlain was waiting for the results of his efforts towards commuting the Tribute before replying to the Cypriot memorial and the Treasury fretted over the steep increase in expenditure on the island during Sendall's high commissionership.[5] Sir Walter would have to disappoint his councillors.

He made the most of the only practical indicator of changing attitudes in London. The irrigation engineer from India, J.H. Medlicott, had arrived promptly in February and had wasted no time in getting down to work. His arrival could be presented as a token of the British government's new commitment to investment in harnessing the natural resources of the island. In his speech Sendall tried to make up for the absence of a clear statement of policy by playing the investment card for all it was worth. It had been a year of rock bottom prices for wheat and even for carobs, the crop that had proved a life-saver the previous year, ameliorating the slump created by the low price of cereals. Addressing the newly convened council, he homed in on the gloom resulting from the low prices to underline the need for a new approach. Neither the Cyprus government, nor the Cypriot people, he observed, could influence prices, but they could, by investment in irrigation, massively increase productivity. Once more he turned to the example of Egypt, 'where the loss of income through falling prices, estimated at three million sterling [had] been more than compensated for by

---

4. Sendall to Chamberlain, 6 January 1896, CO67/97, NA.
5. Treasury to Colonial Office, 30 January 1896, CO67/102, NA.

greater out-turn (sic) of the produce which the cultivator has been enabled to raise'. The fact that Her Majesty's government was fully alive to its importance was indicated, he maintained, by the speed of Medlicott's arrival. In the same vein, he went on to stress the importance of improved communications, better roads and more bridges, and a frequent steamer service to Alexandria, all of which were targeted by the Cyprus government for 1896. They would facilitate the expansion of the already lucrative trade in livestock, fruit and market garden produce to Egypt.[6]

The legislative council was not impressed by these constructive words because they were backed by

> *No definite assurance. The solicitude of the government in developing resources has so far been proved solely by expression of sympathy wherein a marked contrast is offered to the more than solicitude displayed when the question is one touching the collection of revenue.*[7]

They pointed out that the government had not even offered the position of director of agriculture to Panayiotis Gennadius, whose three-month mission to Cyprus the previous year had been very productive, but much too short. The council earnestly hoped that the efforts of the government would not be restricted to the compiling of reports, but that such works as [His] Excellency had referred to might actually be taken in hand. They went on to praise the anti-flood works in Limassol, underlining the absence of assistance from London in this regard. The works were carried out at Sir Walter's insistence and had been completed with exclusively local funds. The elected members rounded off their reply with the annual protest against the Tribute and the continued absence of Cypriots in the executive council, both major issues that Sendall had tried hard to remedy.[8]

The councillors also complained that too much money had been spent on law and order, but they could not deny that this year, in contrast to those

---

6. Speech of the high commissioner, delivered to the legislative council at the opening of the session, on Wednesday, 4 March 1896, enclosed in Sendall to Chamberlain, 14 March 1896, CO67/98, NA.
7. Address of the legislative council in reply to the high commissioner at the opening session on 4 March 1896, enclosed in Sendall to Chamberlain, 14 March 1896, CO67/98, NA.
8. Ibid.

that went before, the police were to be congratulated, for they had finally run down the Hasanpouli bandits, the last of whom had been rounded up in the village of Kedasi in February. They had run riot in the western part of the island throughout 1895. Murder, rape and a highway robbery perpetrated on no less a carriage than that of Mr. Williamson of the Cyprus Company, had halved the wheeled traffic on the roads. *The Owl* observed that the brigands had become

> *Lords of the hills. They sleep on village threshing floors where the villagers supply them with food and drink and keep guard. In the morning they are wakened, their satchels charged with food and they go on their way rejoicing.*[9]

The special police force, composed of local Paphos men, formed to deal with the bandit problem, had failed, the villagers being no more prepared to cooperate with them than with ordinary *zaptiehs*. It had therefore been disbanded. Sendall put down the capture of the bandits to the increase in and better manning of village police stations and particularly to the out-law legislation insisted upon by Young, in Sendall's absence, approved by the elected members and enacted at a special session of the legislative council the previous November. As a result of the new law, villagers were imprisoned even on suspicion of giving the fugitives shelter.[10]

The Hasanpouli brothers, Mehmet Ahmet and Hasan Ahmet, were escaped convicts who had been at large for over twelve months. During that time they were known to have committed eleven murders, five acts of abduction and rape, nine of shooting and wounding and numerous acts of highway robbery. These elusive bravados have been much romanticized.[11] No doubt their behaviour was, in part, a result of unrelenting and oppressive tax collection, a defective penal code and inadequate prison accommodation. They were by no means champions of the oppressed masses against the tyranny of the urban-based moneylenders and legislators, as they are sometimes made out to be. Most of their victims were

---

9. *The Owl*, 12 September 1895.
10. Sendall to Chamberlain, 28 February 1896 and enclosures, CO67/97, NA.
11. Paul Sant Cassia, 'Better Occasional Murders than Frequent Adulteries': Discourses on Banditry, Violence, and Sacrifice in the Mediterranean in Fernando, Shuski and Arbor, *States of Violence*, (Michigan 2006), 219-268. Katsiaounis, (1996), 154-157 and Rebecca Bryant, (1998), 67-69. In a more fictional vein, Bill MacFarlan, *The Hunt for the Hasamboulia*, (Nicosia 2007).

peasants, and rape and disembowelment were among the punishments meted out to families who were suspected of turning against them. The inhabitants of the areas they frequented were caught between the fear of the consequences of defying the government and the more immediate fear of defying the bandits. Nevertheless, the bandits were certainly held in awe for their daring and defiance of a much hated tax regime. 'Their appeal [was] not that of agents of justice, but of men who prove that even the poor and weak can be terrible.'[12] They were popular enough for the government to bury the hanged bandits within the prison yard for fear that a funeral would cause a riot.[13]

The penal code was being rewritten by the chief justice, Sir William Smith. Prison building and reform were nearing completion in 1896, helped by the fact that the prison population had been reduced considerably in Sendall's time.[14] This meant that the third long-term prison block in the new central prison in Nicosia, planned by Bulwer, could be scrapped for a short-term prison block built apart from the other two. By making this move and ruling that prisoners with a two-year prison sentence were short-term, the high commissioner secured a more substantial convict labour force for public works and was able to move the prisoners out of the Büyük Khan, which had served as an inadequate and unsuitably placed prison since the beginning of the occupation. They were now housed 'on the job' in a purpose-built prison.

Finally, the long-awaited telegram arrived. Chamberlain had at last squeezed most of the required additional sums from a reluctant Treasury. At the beginning of April, the high commissioner was able to inform the legislative council that £19,000 had been approved for the public works vote – Sendall had asked for £20,000 for 1896, double the maximum vote for that department laid down in 1883. A new engineer would join the staff to head an enlarged department, a move that reflected a determination to improve communications as part of the drive to increase productivity. The island was also granted an extra £500 for the education vote to facilitate grants for the growing number of village elementary schools. Sir Walter had asked for £1,000. The elected members replied promptly,

---

12. Hobsbawm, *Bandits*, (London 1972), 58, cited in Katsiaounis, (1996)155.
13. Katsiaounis, (1998), 168.
14. Murders were reduced by 50% between 1890 and 1897: 97 murders in 1890, 49 murders islandwide in 1897. See *Cyprus: Annual Report for 1897–1898*, [c.-92887].

expressing 'their unfeigned pleasure and gratification'. Here was further proof, they noted, of Chamberlain's interest in the island. They hoped that 'this day [would] mark the dawn of the era of development and progress that has been so long and so eagerly prayed for by this country'. There was no doubt in their minds as to whom they had to thank for this new turn of events. It was 'in great measure due to the continued representations made by Your Excellency for the welfare of Cyprus and its people'. The council underlined 'its keen appreciation of the feeling that has prompted these efforts and its satisfaction at the happy result'.[15]

With the new money in hand, the high commissioner embarked on a public works programme whose immediate focus was the improvement of communications. Bridge-building had been repeatedly set aside since the occupation for want of funds. As a result, large areas of the road network were generally dangerous and useless for wheeled traffic for much of the year. Sendall's earnest and detailed dispatches on the most effective method of bridge-building which required the crown agents' cooperation were clearly boring for at least one of his principals. While Sendall

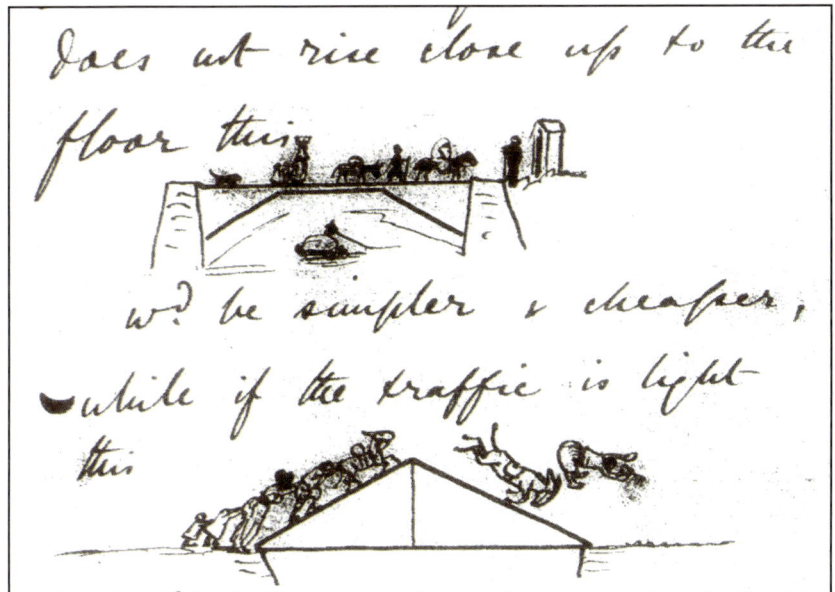

29. Doodle composed by Edward Fairfield while responding to Sendall's urgent requests for bridge-building material (see note 16)

---

15.   Members' response included in Sendall to Chamberlain, 22 April 1896, CO67/98, NA.

telegraphed an urgent message for the dispatch of bridge materials from London so the work on Peristerona bridge could be completed before the rainy season, Fairfield doodled his way through a draft reply.[16] Sendall stressed that the masonry was already in the process of construction, the pier being extended by stone arches where the riverbed was exceptionally wide, but that it must be completed before the rainy season.

To remedy the unreliable steamer connections with Egypt, he picked up the negotiations already started by Young the previous year with various shipping companies, for a regular mail service. In November that year, he was able to announce that the government had entered into a contract with Bell's Asia Minor Steamship Company 'for the establishment of a weekly service between Cyprus and Egypt'.[17] This would take effect from 1 January 1897 and be funded largely by the surplus on the revenue collected for the Field Watchman's tax.[18] This British, rather than Ottoman, tax was imposed in 1892 for the appointment of a field watchman ($αγρο$-$φύλακας$) in each village as a deterrent against theft or the destruction of crops by grazing animals. Like the locust tax, it was not charged to general revenue, but kept in a special fund in Cyprus. At the same time, in cooperation with the legislative council, Sir Walter worked on modernizing the antiquated fiscal regime.

The evaluation of property had been envisaged since the early days of the British occupation as a basis for doing away with tithes. Indeed, the major land survey for which Kitchener had been employed in 1879 had been initially intended for this purpose. Trying to define boundaries of individual ownership had proved too complicated. Some progress had been made since, particularly in the delimitation of forests, but the complexities of hereditary arrangements in the Ottoman system, the undefined boundaries of ecclesiastical properties, the vagaries of the *vakoufs*, together with the extent of land mortgaged and remortgaged, hindered the surveyors. The attempt had been abandoned a few years earlier. Sendall now sought to reintroduce a land evaluation bill. In preparation, he first drafted a bill

---

16. Sendall to Chamberlain, 22 June 1896 and attached minutes and drafts including doodled cartoon of bridges, CO67/99, NA. Fairfield was apparently in the habit of illustrating his minutes when bored. See Elizabeth Longford, *Jameson's Raid: The Prelude to the Boer War*, (London, 1982), 26.
17. Albert T. Madella, *The Cyprus Sea Post Office 1906-1932*, (Limassol, (no date), 3-4.
18. Sendall to Chamberlain, 13 October 1896, CO67/101, NA.

141

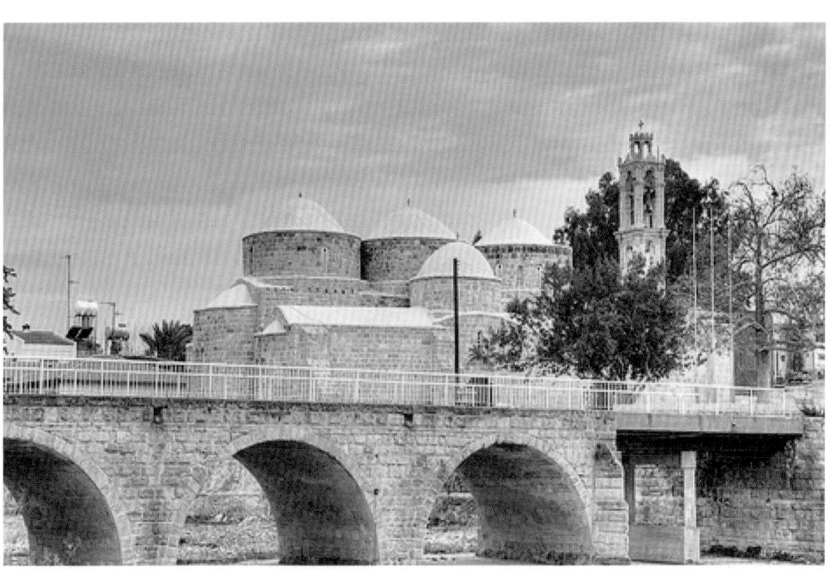

30. Peristerona bridge (completed in 1897)

'to make temporary provision to protect the claims of ecclesiastical corporations to certain properties in Cyprus'. This euphemistic title was intended to encourage the ecclesiastical community to register the considerable extent of the island which they owned and thus lead the way to comprehensive registration. According to the bill, the claim could only be protected if it was delineated and registered.[19] Sendall clearly saw this law as a way of beginning to take stock of property ownership. The bill drafted in 1895 for the evaluation of property was subsequently reintroduced.

At the same time, a first step was proposed in the direction of doing away with the remaining irksome and unproductive minor tithes that were hangovers of the antiquated Ottoman fiscal regime. On this matter, as on the matter of reducing wine excise, the high commissioner had had 'frequent discussion at the Colonial Office' while he was on leave in London the previous year. Now having, at last, 'some command of money beyond an irreducible minimum of expenditure', he proposed to reduce the wine excise by 2% and, at the same time, to do away with the tithes on such articles as figs, honey, potatoes, onions, other garden produce and all citrus 'the collection of which is very costly to the government and extremely vexatious to the cultivator'. The total loss of revenue would amount to £4,680, which would be amply made up for by alternative taxes: chiefly by introducing an import duty on petroleum and tobacco, but also by a surtax of 2¼ piastres on 22,000 goats. £1,035 would be saved by not having to collect the tithes on market garden produce. Sir Walter emphasised that the bill had been agreed upon only after *repeated* conferences with elected members. He now asked for any objections made to the bill in London - and he did not really expect any - to be conveyed by telegraph as soon as possible because the petroleum duty would have to be collected immediately to prevent stockpiling.[20]

To his dismay, there was considerable opposition in London to both the vital reforming bills, the initial objector being in both cases, Edward Fairfield. The architect of the 'do nothing' policy, pursued with such alacrity in the previous years, he was clearly put out by the energy

---

19. Sendall to Chamberlain, 6 April 1896, and report by Queen's Advocate, attached, CO67/98, NA.
20. Sendall to Chamberlain, 18 April 1896, CO67/98, NA.

143

displayed by Sendall in undoing it. He sought every opportunity to put him down. Sir Walter managed to push on with his reforms with difficulty and, in spite of the Colonial Office and the Treasury, only because of Chamberlain's support, but Chamberlain could not be minutely involved in the affairs of Cyprus. Fairfield still wielded considerable influence as regards the island in the Colonial Office. In the case of the 'suspension of tithes' bill, his objections were quibbling. Why should the government give up tithes on figs and citrus just when they had begun to show an increasing yield? Fairfield refused to take into account that the marginally increased yield was due to a greater efficiency in collection that itself cost money. Moreover, he argued shortsightedly that Sendall was exaggerating the likelihood of increasing imports of petroleum.[21] Thus primed, the Treasury added its disapproval of clauses five and six which gave the high commissioner the power to raise, lower or suspend the dues provided to replace the tithes if the yield was not the expected one. Was control slipping out of their hands? Sir Walter explained that these clauses were included for reasons of political expediency – in order to persuade the elected members to pass the bill. The clauses were, in effect, superfluous, since the government was confident that the new taxes would easily recoup the funds lost by the suspension of the tithes, but

> *It was an article of faith with the elected members of the council that if the proceeds of taxation as a whole cannot be allowed to be reduced, so neither can it be allowed to be increased, and I expect there would be difficulty in passing the bill if these provisions, the object of which is to maintain the proceeds of taxation at a uniform level, are to be eliminated.*[22]

Sendall pointed out that the same kind of clauses had been included by the elected members in the evaluation of property bill for the same reasons.

Nothing if not tenacious, the high commissioner embarked on intensive discussions with the elected members to find a formula that London would accept. The Treasury turned down the legislative council's compromise proposal that clauses five and six could be removed if all surplus

---

21. Ibid. See attached minute signed by Fairfield.
22. Sendall to Chamberlain, 18 May 1896, CO67/99, NA.

revenue from this tax was placed in a fund for agricultural development on the island. Sendall had backed this suggestion, pointing out that the very small sums for agricultural development spent so far were gleaned from the surplus of the locust tax, not charged to the general revenue. Therefore no money at all had been spent on agricultural development from general revenue since 1878.[23] After another week's discussion, he had got the elected members to agree that half of any surplus would continue to go to the Sinking Fund of the 1855 Crimean War loan in London. He assumed the Teasury would accept this further concession to their demands for a share of any surplus, and once again sought urgent ratification by telegram so that the two bills could be enacted before the legislative council adjourned for the summer. In doing so, he underlined the absurdity of trying to continue to collect the tithes in question. They were very unpopular and produced 'a low yield from a peasantry which borrows at usury to pay them'. Not only were they troublesome to assess and recover, but they were in chronic arrears. He hinted that the present attitude of his principals was contrary to the new atmosphere he had encountered while in London.

> *Even had I not been encouraged to hope that the introduction of reforms in our fiscal system might at the present time be regarded with favour and as harmonizing with our general policy of progressive development, I should still, at no distant date, have brought under your consideration the advisability of abolishing these particular tithes and replacing them with less objectionable modes of raising revenue.*[24]

Fairfield admitted the legitimacy of the elected members' complaints about the absence of a budget for agricultural development, but fended off the need to respond positively by pointing to the alternative facility of the fixed grant-in-aid 'now under discussion', which would prevent these situations arising. He was subsequently backed by his superiors in refusing to allow Her Majesty's government 'to be dictated to' by the Cypriot legislature.[25] This increasingly heated contretemps between the high commissioner and his principals indicates the extent to which reform initiated in Cyprus was being resisted in London.

---

23. Sendall to Chamberlain, 20 May 1896, CO67/99, NA.
24. Sendall to Chamberlain, 6 June 1896, CO67/99, NA.
25. Lengthy minute signed by Fairfield, 12 June 1896, CO67/99, NA.

The high commissioner was curtly instructed to stall the procedure and 'recast his proposals'. Terrified of jeopardizing the fixed grant-in-aid by being too forthright, he ate humble pie. 'I recognize that it is important to give full explanations to Her Majesty's Government and I have withdrawn the bill for the present.'[26] It seems that in spite of the optimism created by his interview with Chamberlain the previous summer, and the more impassioned protest to Robert Meade against his humiliating state of bondage, he was still to be exposed by his principals in London in full view of his Cypriot subjects. Neither the legislative council, nor the high commissioner were to be allowed to decide on the best disposal of part of the hypothetical surplus arising from the taxation. The legislative council was adjourned without either bill being enacted. Nevertheless, still unable to believe that this was more than a temporary hitch, Sir Walter accepted the 'very public spirited' invitation of the Abbot of Kykko to offer hospitality to the entire legislative council for a special session to be held at his ancient monastery high in the Paphos Forest. This would enable the bills to be enacted as soon as ratification was received from London. By offering accommodation, the abbot had met 'the chief difficulty of holding sittings of the Council during the residence of the government at its summer quarters.'[27]

The annual migration of the administration to Troodos provided some relief, not only from the heat, but from the unpleasant realities with which the administration was daily confronted.[28] The jottings in the diary of a young subaltern, also encamped in Troodos for the summer, provide us with an insight into the diversions and entertainments of that year. Riding, target practice, cricket and reading novels helped the days go by for Frederick Alexander Breul, but social interest was focused on the ongoing tennis tournament that took place in the garden of Government Cottage and at the dances and musical evenings that followed. Here female company, even young female company, could be counted on. 'Mrs Kenny and I were determined to win at all costs', he observed, 'and did viz (4-6) (6-4) (6-4)'.

---

26. Sendall to Chamberlain, 27 May 1896, CO67/99, NA.
27. Sendall to Chamberlain, 1 June 1896, CO67/99, NA.
28. Tabitha Morgan, *Sweet and Bitter Island: A History of the British in Cyprus*, (London, 2010), 25-32.

31. Tennis in the garden at Government Cottage, Troodos

> *September 27th Sunday:* Owing to the fearful fuss Miss Ferguson made, she was presented with a prize which I conclude should have gone to me as I won. They told me they never intended giving the gentlemen anything. Of course, not giving me a prize did not matter but the least I did expect was to be congratulated on winning the tournament. Not a bit of it. Only 3 people congratulated me, and all the others went so far as to clap any strokes that either Mrs Kenny or I hit into the net, and Ashmore insulted me by saying I played a mean game because I returned a few more balls to Miss Ferguson than to Bertie as if she couldn't take care of herself. It was hardly Ashmore's place to tell me anything, having practically been hissed himself for sending very short balls over the net to ladies whom he was playing against in previous tournaments.[29]

Breul was clearly a favourite at Government Cottage, attending dinner and participating in musical evenings there frequently. Lady Sendall took a special interest in him. 'Fetched my songs away from Government House,' he noted on one occasion. 'These Lady Sendall had bound for me some days before.' A typical evening at the Sendalls is recorded as follows:

> *July 17th Friday:* Went to the Governors to dinner. The Tysers, Potts, Lascelles, Ashmore and ourselves were there. The table was jolly badly arranged. I took in nobody and sat between Stayner and Mrs Potts. Potts made a damned fool of himself and took upon himself to lead the show. Lady Sendall sang 3 or 4 songs. Miss Shaw with the mandolin, Mrs Tyser with the violin and Lady Sendall on the piano played a trio. Afterwards Miss Shaw and Lady Sendall played a duet. The Spencer girls came in after dinner and the elder one sang two songs. I sang "Ho Holly Jenkins" and 'Oh Honey my Honey". Miss Shaw was looking awfully pretty and exceedingly saucy. On the whole the evening was a very jolly one.[30]

The hot summer months came and went and no ratification of the two bills arrived from London. With the wine harvest approaching, the lucrative French market still blocked and no reduction on wine excise in spite

---

29. Unpublished diary of Frederick Alexander Breul, a young subaltern with the company of Gloucesters garrisoned at Polemedia, courtesy of his grandson, David Dew.
30. Ibid.

of the dramatic Troodos demonstration two years earlier, Sendall needed to make a gesture. He decided to go ahead and sign a subsidiary bill 'to amend the tithe ordinance' which had been passed by all the elected members, Muslim and Christian, unanimously. This amendment facilitated farmers and wine merchants to appeal against arbitrary assessments of the value of their product, one of the main complaints in the wine-growers' memorial of 1894, and offered a token support to a deeply distressed district in the absence of any rebate on excise. A report by the Limassol commissioner, in itself an appeal for leniency in tax collecting, is an eye-opener into the continuing problems in the area. These were further exacerbated by an earthquake in July. There were no fatalities but there was damage, fear and disruption. The distance between the London view and those servants of the Queen battling with realities in Cyprus is nowhere clearer than in the minutes attending Sendall's dispatch on the amended tithe ordinance. Fairfield advised that Sir Walter should be 'chided gently' for getting a law enacted without London having given the go-ahead, especially a law which would make wine excise revenue more difficult to collect.[31] The men on the spot knew that most of it was uncollectible.

Instead of receiving ratification of the two fiscal bills in November, Sendall was subjected to further questioning and more demands for modification. He would not take no for an answer. He would reintroduce the taxation bill, which he described as '*the most beneficial bill ever introduced*' into the Cyprus legislature and questioned his principals' understanding of the modifications he had made in consultation with the elected members after the first Treasury objections to the bill. The provisions of the bill no longer limited the amount of revenue at the disposal of the government, but were 'intended to secure that a portion of that surplus would be at the disposal of the government for a particular purpose, namely the operations of the agricultural board'. Moreover, he took the secretary of state to task once more for suggesting that the legislature in Cyprus enjoyed 'practically complete control over the allocation of revenue'.

> *There is no other country under British administration in which such taxes are imposed which it is the object of this measure to get rid of and there is, I think, no other dependency of the*

---

31. See minute signed by Fairfield attached to Chamberlain to Sendall, 2 September 1896, CO67/100, NA.

Crown in which the power of assessing economic reforms through legislation has been so completely taken out of the hands of the local government.[32]

Sendall had an additional reason to be aggravated by his principals in London in 1896. At the end of 1895, the Treasury had uncovered a case of chronic embezzlement of funds held in the public works department account. As Sir Walter argued convincingly from the start, there was no way either he or the chief secretary could have discovered the fraud, because the Treasury itself had insisted in 1891 that the audit carried out by them was to be totally independent of the Cyprus government. W.H. Griffin, the fraudulent bookkeeper whom Bulwer had appointed in 1889 at a greatly reduced rate, had been pocketing small amounts on a regular basis. In the same year Cunningham, a 'practical' engineer, better suited to the job of superintendent of works which had brought him to the island, had 'lapsed' into the position of head of the biggest spending department in the government, again at a much reduced salary, when Bulwer got rid of Samuel Brown and his assistant Foley – 'the Alexandria (spending) ring'. The inadequacy of the public works department staff generally had already been pressed upon Chamberlain by Sendall the previous summer. The corruption was one of the consequences of the shoddy state to which the administration had been reduced by Sir Henry's 'economies' – the half-hearted attempts of a gentleman of leisure to implement Fairfield's policy. The high commissioner was able to demonstrate that 'the arrears in the audit [began] in the year 1891-92, and [had] been accumulating ever since' and that the Treasury must have been or should have been aware of them. Sir Walter's principals had finally to admit that the present government of the island could not, under the circumstances, be held responsible. It was, on the contrary, the Treasury which had failed in its supervision. But Sendall could not forgive Fairfield. 'How could you,' he wrote in a personal letter, 'shift on to your own officer, the responsibility for the shortcomings of the Exchequer and Audit Department?'[33] Fairfield had been quite gleeful at the opportunity to cast aspersions on the high commissioner, who, together with the secretary of state, was making his life increasingly uncomfortable. A few months later he would make sour comments about the 'immaculate' nature of Sir Walter's administration.

---

32. Sendall to Chamberlain, 18 May 1896, CO67/99.
33. Sendall to Fairfield, private letter, 9 August 1896, CO67/103, NA.

> *Sir W. Sendall is so convinced that his administration is immaculate that the least hint to the contrary drives him into fury and makes him relieve his feelings at interminable length and a tremendous cost of paper and ink.*[34]

But Fairfield had, at that time, greater cause for anxiety. He was embroiled in the scandal created by allegations that Chamberlain and the Colonial Office were complicit in the Jameson raid carried out on the Transvaal Republic on 29 December 1895, as a high official supposedly involved. In November 1896 he would succumb to a series of strokes, leading to his death in April 1897.[35] Griffin's trial more or less coincided with the sensational trial of Jameson and other officers at the High Court in London. In Cyprus, the fraudulent accountant in the public works department was found guilty of embezzlement. He was sentenced to eighteen months hard labour, which he served in the island.

Griffin would have carried out at least some of his sentence in the new short-term prison block then under construction. He would be serving in a penal system on the move. As well as the new prison building, there was a new penal code and a new concept of prison administration. The prison would no longer be run on the side by an overworked police commandant. Sendall had sought a specially appointed prison director, who would have under him two English prison wardens. In the end, Walter Giles, who was already serving as warden in the central prison in Nicosia, was promoted to the job of director, but his jurisdiction was restricted to administration and discipline. Three judges were in charge of prison policy.[36]

Sendall clearly thought highly of Giles. Earlier in the year he had been most honourably involved in preventing the escape of three convicts, one of whom was a Hasanpouli. Giles chased the convicts, who took flight along the Pedeios riverbed. He shot two dead and arrested the survivor. The warden had recently applied to leave the island, being unable to keep his large family on his meagre salary, but the high commissioner was very anxious to retain his services. Giles's letter to the chief secretary is an

---

34. Minute signed by Fairfield, 8 August 1896, CO67/100.
35. Thomas Packenham, *The Boer War*, (London 1979), 29-30 and Elizabeth Longford, (1982), 217-247. Fairfield's death a few months later of a heart attack was widely attributed to the strain created by his embroilment in the Jameson affair. See Robert Kubicek, *The Administration of Imperialism: Joseph Chamberlain at the Colonial* Office, (Durham, N.C, 1969), 19.
36. Sendall to Chamberlain, 30 September 1896, and enclosure, CO67/101, NA.

eye-opener into the life of a lower paid English civil servant on the island. Neither he nor his large family would be able to join the summer exodus to the Troodos mountains. They would spend the whole summer in their house close to the Nicosia prison, some distance from the town. He had tried to send his elder daughter to school in Beirut, but his savings ran out. Now he could not afford to send any of his five children to school at all - even in Nicosia. He had asked to be transferred to another colony or back to England. The timely promotion allowed Giles and his family a better quality of life and secured a conscientious and experienced director for the prison.[37]

The completion of the new prison would release public works funds for another large project that Sir Walter was already planning. Fairfield's 1883 report refers to the 'commodious public offices' in Nicosia.[38] In fact, the only public office constructed by the British in the capital since 1878 was the secretariat on the road to Government House. This building had been designed as a barracks for the Cyprus Pioneer Force, but was converted

North-east corner of the central prison, Nicosia

---

37. Ibid.
38. Papers relating to the Administration and Finances of Cyprus, June 1883, C.3661, 26.

for bureaucratic use in 1879.[39] The other public offices and courts were currently housed in the most unsuitable rented accommodation all over Nicosia. Both Muslim and Christian citizens complained about the inconvenience this caused.[40] The high commissioner had a vision of purpose-built offices in close proximity to each other in the centre of the old city and had gone as far as having plans drawn up. The current situation he described as 'a disgrace'. The rented Supreme Court rooms were so badly arranged as to cause the maximum inconvenience to all. There was also 'a third room [in the building], the size of a good cupboard in which the judges [sat] when not actually involved in hearing a case'. The District Court was housed in a 'mean hired hovel'. The building rented for the use of the district commissioner was 'an old dirty and rickety dwelling house of two storeys'. The land registry office was larger, but expensively rented and much too far from the district office and the courts. Since the majority of cases brought to court involved disputes over land, the courts and the registry office should be near each other. At the same time, the district commissioner also served as coroner and sheriff of his district. He kept the chest in which the money of suitors was deposited and received the daily revenue collection of the receiver general. It followed that both the district commissioner's and receiver general's office should also be in close proximity to each other and the courts. An excellent site, large enough to accommodate all these offices, was to be found in the centre of Nicosia, 'namely that on which stood the Turkish *konak* at the time of the occupation'. Sendall goes on to describe the *konak* as follows:

> *The old range of buildings in which were located the various Turkish offices was ill-built, the structure has fallen into complete decay and in its present condition is an eyesore and a reproach to the local government. The site provides sufficient space to accommodate all the offices required. It is approached by a good road and has in front of it the largest open space in Nicosia and behind it an excellent garden. The old building will provide a small amount of material capable of being worked into the new. The selection of this place will be, for sentimental reasons, grateful (sic) to the Turkish population and is not objected to by the Greek Christians.*[41]

---

39. Schaar, Given and Theocharous, (1995), 115-226.
40. *The Owl*, 19 July 1893.
41. Sendall to Chamberlain, 30 September 1896, CO67/100, NA.

Sir Walter remained silent on the historic nature of the site. Did he not consider the fact worth mentioning, or was he deliberately downplaying its significance in order to secure approval for the demolition? His depiction of 'an eyesore in an advanced state of decay' was no doubt true. Most of the *konak* consisted of rickety Ottoman structures incorporated into the Lusignan, but one suspects that he was playing down the medieval element. It was imperative to build new offices and this was the obvious site. The Cyprus government was living on a shoestring. Whether or not it was the Lusignan palace, there were undoubtedly Gothic elements in the architecture and one can imagine the issue being discussed at the high commissioner's dinner table by knowledgeable guests. Camille Enlart, the French medievalist, was actually in the island for the first half of 1896 on a research mission for the French government. He was obviously on cordial terms with senior British officials, regardless of the passion with which he depicted a specifically French medieval heritage. In his book,

32. Entrance to the Konak or Serai as drawn by Camille Enlart, 1896

written in 1897, he describes the condition of the Serai, to some extent reinforcing the doubts raised regarding its candidacy as palace of the Lusignan kings:

> *The old Serai of the Pasha and the Venetian Governors of Nicosia, today half-ruined and abandoned, is also situated in the lower part of the town, on the square and near the Paphos Gate. It also has an entrance gateway on the square with an open loggia over it....The entrance gate of this palace dates from the fourteenth century...it is only on the side opposite this that there survives a lower, stone-built portico which may go back to the fourteenth or fifteenth century. The other buildings are in a wretched state of decay or in ruins and the porticos attached to them are of wood..... The buildings that I have been describing have neither the amplitude nor the magnificence that must have characterized the old royal palace of Cyprus but their plan appears to correspond fairly well.*[42]

Sendall was anxious not to wait until the public works funds were freed by the completion of the central prison before starting on the new government offices. To bridge the gap, he proposed borrowing on the by now proverbial surplus locust tax, currently being invested by the Crown Agents in Australian development funds. Thus, another new concept was launched – that of a local development fund. The high commissioner argued strongly for the funds to be invested in Cyprus.

> *The money is the savings of the people of the country. The crying want of the island is capital, a fact in no small degree due to the annual depletion of the Treasury chest for the payment of the Tribute, and it is anomalous that savings from taxation on its inhabitants should be invested, not in Cyprus which has saved the money and to which the money would be of inestimable value as a source of employment and so of the promotion of the prosperity of its people, but in the development of Australia.*[43]

---

42. Camille Enlart (translated and edited by David Hunt), *Gothic Art and the Renaissance in Cyprus*, Trigraph, London 1987 after the original *L'Art Gothique et la Renaissance en Chypre*, (Ernest Leroux, Paris, 1899), 395-399. Sendall must have been on friendly terms with Enlart, going to the trouble of obtaining a copy of the plans of the Kyrenia fortress for him. See ibid., 29 and Sendall to Chamberlain, 1 June 1896, CO67/99, NA.
43. Sendall to Chamberlain, 30 September 1896, CO67/100, NA. Fairfield has scrawled in the margin here 'Stuff! They get the interest.'

Sendall was assuming the 'permanent character' of the locust tax, which had less and less to do with the catching of locusts, a devastating plague which had by now been most successfully restricted. The locust tax was jealously kept in being by the local government for their local use. The transfer of the funds to London may have been an attempt by the Treasury to reduce the Cyprus government's leverage in view of the high commissioner's energetic spending tendencies. Chamberlain's response was not negative. He agreed that the locust tax fund should be invested locally but he urged moderation. He considered the loan proposed was too big in view of the short supply of capital. 'Some honey should be left in the pot.' He asked Sendall to revise the estimates for the project and draw up new plans excluding the agriculture and forestry department. The Serai was demolished in 1897 but the building of the new offices did not get underway until after Sendall's departure. The only new government office constructed in Nicosia during his term was the small government printing office opposite the secretariat. An efficient local printing establishment was a key factor in reducing dependence on London and speeding up administrative and legislative procedure. Cartright, the new government engineer, described the building as 'well arranged'. 'The Superintendent of the Printing office may be congratulated', he observed, 'on the possession of the best offices of any department in the island.'[44]

Chamberlain also excluded the new *Evkaf* office proposed by Sendall from the construction plans. *Evkaf*, he argued, should either go on hiring offices or build their own.[45] The always ambiguous status of *Evkaf* continued to create complications. It reflected the uncomfortable way British administrative methods cohabited with the traditional ways of an Ottoman province. The subtext of this grating relationship was undeclared competition between the Porte's attempts to reintroduce some substance into the Sultan's sovereignty over the island for the long term and a British reluctance to concede any more authority than necessary to the Porte's agents. Turkish dissatisfaction arose from the fact that one of the few attributes of the Ottoman status of the island which the British enforced assiduously – but to their own advantage – was the collection of the Tribute. In almost every other aspect of administration, Ottoman

---

44. Report on Public Works in *Cyprus: Annual Report 1897-1898*, 51. The same building, with ugly, patchy extensions, still houses the government printing office today.
45. Chamberlain to Sendall, 14 September 1896, CO67/100, NA

Government Printing Office completed in 1896

attempts to retain a stake in what was, after all, still proclaimed to be an Ottoman province, came up against the hard rock of British determination to administer the island without interference. These conflicting tendencies came to the fore in incidents affecting Anglo-Turkish relations at the international level, for example over Yiallouris's extradition and the disposal of Cypriot salt. Differences over how the chief *cadi* should be appointed had emerged in the wake of rumours of British withdrawal. The chief *cadi* who was finally appointed at the end of 1895, Mehmet Attaoullah Pasha, was a congenial, educated, literary and cooperative individual, who helped to smooth over difficulties arising from the ambivalent status of the island.

Although the Muslim delegates in the legislature cooperated with their Greek Christian counterparts to challenge the government in matters of taxation and expenditure, they preferred not to raise issues concerning purely Muslim affairs within the largely Christian legislature. A series of complaints against the absence of Muslim consensus on decisions in *Evkaf*, on the handling of *vakouf* lands and, particularly, in the disposal of *vakouf* incomes, were made directly to the high commissioner. These issues continued to create problems within the Muslim community and in Muslim/British relations. Mehmet Attaoullah took a more constructive and conciliatory attitude to the recurring issue of the extent of British involvement in the administration of *Evkaf*. Sendall decided to postpone a new law regulating the appointment of trustees of *vakoufs*. He did not want to damage his good relations with the new chief *cadi* by ignoring Muslim reluctance to have the affair raised in the legislature. Attaoullah's help was needed particularly in the reform of Muslim education, which lagged sadly behind.[46] It became clear, however, in the course of the year that a certain faction within the Muslim community would continue to attack the present administration of *Evkaf* in spite of the high commissioner's attempts at conciliation.

The attack on the administration of *Evkaf* was led by Tuccarbasi Hadji Ahmet Derviş Pasha, the owner of *Zaman* newspaper. Among his closest allies was Hadji Hafız Effendi, the intellectual, but ineffective, headmaster of the Rusty'e (Muslim boys' junior high school) and elected member of the legislative council.[47] For the previous two years, the school building having collapsed from the absence of maintenance, lessons, such as they were, had taken place in rented premises, during which time enrolment had dropped from 141 boys (1891) to 80 in 1895. This was in marked contrast to the steep rise in attendance at Christian schools at both primary and senior level. Indeed some leading Cypriot Turks chose to send their children to The Pancyprian Gymnasium to secure a good secondary education.[48] Concerned by the deteriorating state of Muslim education, Sir Walter demanded a complete reform of the school that would bring it in line with reformed schools of the Ottoman Empire. A new building was constructed and the reforms carried out with the enthusiastic support of the *mufti* so that the school was raised from the status of *rusty'e* to *i'dade*, (senior high school) following the Ottoman prototype, except that the Greek language had priority over French. In these efforts Attaoullah was clearly Sendall's guide and collaborator. It was left to him to find a suitable man to be appointed principal of the reformed school while he

---

46. Sendall to Chamberlain, 16 January 1896, CO67/97, NA.
47. See Hadji Hafız Ziyai, MLC, to Sendall, 3 July 1897, SA1/1736/1897
48. Rebecca Bryant, (2004), 114.

was on leave in Istanbul. The *mufti* too, was as appreciative as the Archbishop regarding Sendall's 'kind and education-inducing assistance'. The high commissioner had 'built the new school, brought new masters and put the curriculum in a perfect condition'.⁴⁹ But Ahmet Derviş's faction remained disgruntled.

Perhaps the leaders of the opposition to the *Evkaf* administration resented, among other things, the amount of *Evkaf* money spent on maintaining and restoring medieval monuments, the most spectacular of which remained under its auspices as mosques.⁵⁰ There was less Muslim interest and involvement in the more ancient monuments and remains. The Cyprus Exploration Fund, founded in 1887, has been described as initiating the scientific era in archaeological exploration on the island, but by 1892 it was running out of money.⁵¹ The British Museum then used money

Entrance to *Rustye i'dade* school, Nicosia

---

49. Ibid.,112. See more generally, Part II Chapter IV for the differences within the Muslim community.
50. Despina Pilides, (Nicosia 2009), Vol. II, 417.
51. Robert Merrillees, 'A Summing up' in Tatton-Brown ed. *Fact, Fancy and Fiction*, 277-278.

bequeathed by Emma Tourner Turner to finance a series of excavations on the island between 1893 and 1896. The British Museum's agents in Cyprus at this time were two businessmen, Charles Christian, who lobbied for the commutation of the Tribute, and his friend John Williamson of the Cyprus Company in Limassol. Both showed a keen interest in the development of Cyprus generally. They were bidding, for example, to invest in and manage the new irrigation project currently being planned by Medlicott. They also took an interest in the island's ancient past.[52] This was not necessarily purely scholarly interest.

In the nineteenth century, selling artifacts was very much part of the archaeological scene. Archaeologists, such as Max and Magda Ohnefalsch-Richter expected to sell to eke out their income.[53] Sir Walter's predecessor, Sir Henry Bulwer, a man of considerable means and taste, took a notable hoard home with him in 1892. His collection is now housed in the Fitzwilliam Museum in Cambridge. There is also the Bulwer Tablet, on which the Greek language is etched in Cypro-syllabic script. The British Museum picked it up in Sir Henry's home county of Norfolk as late as 1950 and it has since been the subject of much scholarly interest. [54]

By the end of the 1890s, there was an increasing awareness of the need to protect antiquities and promote scientific discovery, but by regulating rather than banning the trade. The British Museum excavations were directed by Arthur Smith, Alexander Murray and Henry Walters. Their excavations in Amathus, Kourion and Enkomi contributed significantly to establishing a link between Late Bronze Age Cyprus and the Mycenean world.[55] John Myres of New College, Oxford, who was also involved, had already taken on a broader role in promoting Cypriot antiquities by combining with Max Richter in cataloguing the objects of the Cyprus museum in Nicosia. The museum had moved in December 1889 from a room in the secretariat to a house in Victoria Street.[56]

---

52. Veronica Tatton-Brown, 'Excavations in ancient Cyprus: Original Manuscripts and Correspondence in the British Museum', in Veronica Tatton-Brown ed., *Cyprus in the Nineteenth Century: Fact, Fancy and Fiction* (Oxford 2001),169, and Haggard, (1926),124-140.
53. R.S. Merrillees 'Summing up...' in Veronica Tatton-Brown ed., (2001), 278.
54. For more on the Bulwer Tablet, see T.B. Mitford, 'The Bulwer Tablet', BICS supplement 10 (1961), and information provided by M.B. Hatzopoulos in 'Chypre de la Multiplicité des Royaumes à L'Unité de la Province Lagide: Transition et Adaptation' (forthcoming).
55. Louise Steel, 'The British Museum and the Invention of the Cypriot Late Bronze Age' in Tatton-Brown (2001), 160-161.
56. Robert S. Merrillees, *The First Cyprus Museum*, (Nicosia 2005), 6-7.

The Sendall administration now proposed a new legal structure for antiquities generally, and the museum in particular. In January 1896, no doubt egged on by Myres, who did not remain silent on the official neglect of the island's archaeological heritage, the high commissioner asked London to allow a Cyprus government subsidy of £100 per annum, so that the museum might be better managed and the objects properly cared for, catalogued and exhibited. 'The government', he noted, 'hands over to the museum the antiquities which fall to its share, but this appears a somewhat doubtful boon, unless at the same time, the government helps towards the maintenance of the museum'. Sir Walter sought also to boost the museum's budget by increasing the fine for illicit digging which, he argued was not, as it stood, large enough to be any kind of deterrent.[57] The secretary of state stalled on this plea to ratify funding until, at Nicosia's insistence, the government bill was finally given the go-ahead, by telegram from London in May of that year.

Presenting the bill in the legislative council, Sendall urged the members not to obstruct it, by introducing new elements. He stressed the necessity of putting the museum on a legal corporate footing, in view of the fact that 'the collection, though small is quite unique'. He noted that 'this opinion [had] been confirmed quite recently by one of the greatest of archaeological authorities, Dr. Murray of the British Museum'.[58]

The elected members reacted to what appeared to be an attempt to slip the museum bill past at the close of the session together with other minor matters. The preservation of Cypriot antiquities, they argued, was a very serious matter and the bill should not be rushed through. In the course of the debate that followed, the Greek Christian councillors showed a lively interest in the prevention of the export of Cypriot antiquities and proposed prohibitions that the government feared would be suicidal for the bill that London was already reluctant to sanction. The ex-officio members did, however, bow to the elected members' insistence on a review of the bill by a select committee representing all parties in the house. It was during the brief deliberations within that select committee the same afternoon that a provision was introduced to the museum bill allowing 'no object of antiquity [to] be exported unless a similar object [was] already in the

---

57. Sendall to Chamberlain, 17 January 1896, CO67/97, NA.
58. Minutes of 26 May 1896, Minutes of the Legislative Council, 1896, 269, Library of the House of Representatives of the Republic of Cyprus (MHR).

possession of the Cyprus museum'. The amendment was agreed to by the government members and the law was enacted by the legislative council on 27 May 1896.[59] It put the museum on a corporate footing and provided that the existing objects and all future objects in the museum would be held in trust for the community of Cyprus. The high commissioner was to preside over a management committee that would consist of six ex-officio members which he appointed, and three members elected by the subscribers to the museum. At the same time, the penalty for illicit digging would be hiked up from five to fifty Turkish lira, the amount recovered being devoted to museum funds.[60] News of the enactment of this legislation had reached the British Museum within three weeks. On 25 June 1896, Edward Maunde Thompson, the museum's secretary and principal librarian, wrote to Sir Robert Meade seeking a veto,

> We have heard that a new law has been passed in Cyprus to regulate excavation which is a useful measure. But there is a proposal to prohibit the exportation from the island of any object that is not a duplicate(sic) in the Cyprus Museum. This is serious and the Trustees of the British Museum would find it very inconvenient. At the present moment we are carrying on excavations in Cyprus and have just hit upon a most important series of tombs containing antiquities of great interest and value. It would be a serious matter if we were hampered by the proposed regulations: and I hope that Mr. Chamberlain will put his veto on it.[61]

A month later, the Cypriot public was informed by an official notice in *The Cyprus Gazette* that Her Majesty had disallowed the law.[62]

The sequence of events during a second attempt by the Sendall government to reintroduce the legislation the following year, also indicates a reluctance in London to comply. In 1897 the same draft 'Museum Law' was reintroduced together with a bill 'To amend the existing Law with

---

59. Minutes of 26 and 27 May, Minutes of the Legislative Council 1896, 267–270 (MHR). The members of the Select Committee which completed its report on the afternoon of 26 May, were the Chief Secretary, Merton King, the Nicosia commissioner, Hafiz Effendi, Georgos Pavlides, the Abbot of Kykko and Achilleas Liassides.
60. Sendall to Chamberlain, 17 January 1896, CO67/97 and Sendall to Chamberlain, 5 July 1896, CO67/99, NA.
61. Maunde Thompson to Meade, 25 June 1896, Cf. Minutes 4 July, Letter Book General, No. 6, British Museum, General Archives (BMGA).
62. Notice by high commissioner dated 28 August 1896 in *The Cyprus Gazette*, August 28 1896.

33. Carting antiquities away from Idalion

regard to the Discovery of Antiquities'. This was intended to prevent the flight of important archaeological finds from the island by reducing the time allowed for payment of the fine. The notice in the *Gazette* declared that 'This Law may be cited as the Antiquities Law 1897 and shall come into force on a day to be notified by the high commissioner'.[63] But that day never dawned. It is clear from the official minutes that the expense involved in supporting the 'unimpressive' Cyprus Museum was a cause for London's stalling on the new legislation on antiquities, but opinion was split between those in the Colonial Office who believed that 'the Cypriots [were] beginning to set a value on their antiquities and must be allowed to place some restriction on their export' and the view that

> There is not the remotest chance of the museum paying its way within the next generation. No one in Cyprus has interest enough even to visit it much less subscribe towards its expenses. It is a sheer waste trying to keep it up. The H.C. should sell enough [artifacts] to repay the Govt. and store the rest in some government building till a new generation arises or, at any rate, until Cyprus ceases to be an annual burden on the British taxpayer.[64]

The official stinginess with regard to Cyprus died hard, but by 1897 the idea that the Cypriots deserved to have access to their antiquities was taking hold. Sendall even suggested that the Cyprus Museum should carry out its own 'small' excavations. One therefore cannot rule out the influence of the British Museum in putting the brakes on this first attempt to protect and to keep important finds in the island. The proposed restrictions on antiquities leaving Cyprus was clearly regarded with some misgiving in those quarters. Maunde Thompson once again sought Chamberlain's intervention, this time for exceptions to be made in the law specifically for the British Museum.[65] Chamberlain's response to this appeal for favourable discrimination was not positive, but the legislation was not enacted until 1905 – eight years later.[66] It is clear that the original initiative to protect

---

63. See *The Cyprus Gazette*, 5 May 1897, for the legislation reintroduced in 1897 and assented to by the legislative council, together with an amendment to the existing law with regard to the discovery of antiquities. 'Final article 27: This Law may be cited as the Antiquities Law 1897 and shall come into force on a date to be notified by the High Commissioner'.
64. Minute, M. Graham, 14 October 1897, CO67/110, NA.
65. Private letter from Maunde Thompson to Anderson, 5 July 1897, CO67/110, NA.
66. Draft letter from Chamberlain to Maunde Thompson, 16 July 1897, CO67/110, NA.

and promote Cypriot antiquities within the island was taken by Sendall's government in 1896 and 1897 and was supported by the Cypriot legislators. The reluctance to move forward was due, as in the case of political and financial reform, to London's reluctance to disturb the conveniently anomalous status quo. Nevertheless, the laws governing Cypriot antiquities, introduced and ratified locally in the Sendall years, laid the foundations for a watershed in the 'transition from looting to learning' that characterised archaeological excavations in the last decade of the nineteenth century.[67] Imperial tendencies regarding the island's antiquities were shifting from arbitrary 'possession' to 'curator'. These tendencies were driven, not least by the new Cypriot awareness of the need to protect their ancient heritage, especially as it was reflected in debates within the Cypriot legislature.[68]

The archaeological finds linking Bronze Age Cyprus to Mycenae emerged just as a new national awareness began gradually to erode the timid *raya* temperament, so characteristic of the Christian *millets* of the Ottoman Empire. The vehicle was education, which was beginning to forge a Hellenic consciousness in all Ottoman cities where Greek Orthodox communities flourished, from Salonika to Alexandretta.[69] In Macedonia the struggle was spiked by competing nationalisms laying claim to minds and territory. Far from cushioning the Cypriots against such influences, the political awakening encouraged by British rule had quickened and activated the trend in Cyprus. The impetus provided by electoral politics and a free press was complemented by the steep rise in literacy. More young Cypriots proceeded to further education in Athens and Alexandria. The church too was, as it had always been, in touch with the broader Greek Orthodox world. In 1895 as part of an ecumenical campaign, Archbishop Sofronios had sent a message of solidarity to the Greek Orthodox bishops in Macedonia, protesting against the absorption of more bishoprics by the Bulgarian exarchate. In the Balkan mountains rival guerrilla groups were forming and in July 1896 revolt against Ottoman rule broke out once more in Crete.[70]

---

67. Merrillees, 'A Summing up' in Tatton-Brown ed. (2001), 278.
68. Minutes of 26 and 27 May, Minutes of the Legislative Council 1896, 267-270 (MLC).
69. See generally Paschalis Kitromilides, 'Greek Irridentism in Asia Minor and Cyprus', *Middle Eastern Studies*, 26:1 (January 1990).
70. Douglas Dakin, *The Unification of Greece*, (London 1972), 161-163.

The Cretan revolt did not make a great impact in Cyprus, nor did it leave the Christian community there unmoved. Fund-raising took place on an ad hoc basis, the Archbishop resisting the exhortations of the more radical press to lead the way. The district commissioners all reported that fund-raising was going on, but there was none of the excited 'war fever' that would grip the towns the following year and, even more, during the Balkan Wars in 1912.[71] A move in Nicosia to organise young Cypriots to join the rebels in Crete was met with less equanimity by the authorities. A neutrality order-in-council enacted that summer made recruiting volunteers an offence and it soon petered out. The effort had not been widespread. In fact it was attributed by the authorities largely to the efforts of one man. Nicolaos Katalanos was the editor of the more radical Nicosia newspaper *Evagoras*, which sought to cultivate a Hellenic consciousness and promote the concept of *enosis* (the union of the island with Greece). Katalanos was a Peloponnesian by birth. He had settled in Cyprus in 1893 after studying at the Greek School in Smyrna and the University of Athens. He had taught mathematics at the Pancyprian Gymnasium until January 1896 when he had been sacked. The immediate cause was his refusal to allow his pupils to leave the classroom to join the welcome for Sendall organised by the Archbishop on the outskirts of Nicosia on his return from leave, but that act of insubordination simply punctuated more chronic differences with his employers. After his rejection by the establishment, he became a leading light among the new nationalist radicals, using *Evagoras* to launch increasingly scathing attacks on the more gradualist and collaborative approach of the Archbishop.

Similar divisions were now apparent in all the main towns in the island. Middle-class electoral politics had arrived, not least in urban Cyprus, by 1896. In November of that year the number of voters participating in elections for the legislature doubled.[72] In the following years electoral fever would spread to municipal elections.[73] In the first decade of the twentieth century, this political cleavage in middle-class society was to become engrained in the chronic struggle for the archiepiscopal throne that followed the death of Sofronios. Radical politics really began to take off in 1897,

---

71. District commissioners' reports in file headed 'Cretan Disturbances', SA1:1259/1896, CSA. See also Petros Papapolyviou, (2001), 89-113.
72. See election statistics in *Cyprus: Annual Report for 1896*.
73. Diana Markides, 'Nicosia under British Rule' in Demetrios Michaelides ed. *Historic Nicosia*, Nicosia, 2012.

but the new politicians were already beginning to make some impact in 1896. In that year, the dynamic Katalanos took over the editorship of *Evagoras*, and then defeated Liassides in elections for the presidency of *Agapi tou Laou* (Love of the People), the most prominent of the working men's clubs. During the November elections, Theofanis Theodotou and his brother-in-law, Kyrillos Papadopoulos, the radical bishop of Kition, gained a seat in the legislature.[74]

The background of the brothers Theodotou provides an insight into the social and political mobility in Cypriot society at the end of the nineteenth century. Theofanis Theodotou and his brother, Antonios, were new arrivals in Nicosia. They were both born and brought up in the tiny village of Phini in the Troodos mountains. They both went to university in Athens and Paris; Theofanis, the politician, studied law, and Antonios, medicine. Their acceptance in the capital would have been facilitated by the sophistication acquired through their education in Europe. Almost certainly, that education and their acceptability were also due, not least, to their uncle, Archbishop Sofronios. Nevertheless, their familial link to the establishment did not prevent them pursuing radical policies. Leading lights in the promotion of education generally and athletics in particular, they became generous benefactors.[75] Sendall displayed no great discomfort at the election result, simply recording the new members in his report for Chamberlain.[76] After all, Liassides and Constantinides, labelled 'unconscionable rabble rousers' by Bulwer, as leaders of the 1889 memorial, were found by Sendall to be the most effective and cooperative members of legislative council and had already been marked up as prospective permanent 'native' members of the executive council. This was in spite of the fact that Liassides had headed the Pancyprian demonstrations of April 1895.

In 1897 Sir Walter would begin to express greater concern as to the extent to which the new members would collaborate in enacting the two key reform bills. As the division between the old and new members in the legislative council became more confrontational, Liassides and Constantinides would be denigrated by the radicals as Sendall's

---

74. Aristides Coudounaris, *Βιογραφικόν Λεξικόν Κυπρίων*, Nicosia 2005, 123.
75. Coudounaris, (2001) 177-179 and *Ο Φιλελεύθερος, Σελίδες της Κύπρου: Μεγάλοι Κύπριοι*, 12-16.
76. Sendall to Chamberlain, 18 November 1896, CO67/101, NA.

'favourites'.[77] This tactic would become more entrenched in the years following Sir Walter's departure, making it more and more difficult for the British administration and the elected members to work together constructively.

---

77. Zanettos, (1911), 967-968. Filios Zanettos was a radical politician who became prominent in the following twenty years, and took a radical's view of the growing political division within Greek Cypriot society.

Dr Heidenstam at Leper Farm, 1906

34. Dr. Carl von Heidenstam in front of the church built for the leper colony with funds raised by Lady Sendall

Φύτη (Phyti) embroidery (detail)

1897

An Unfortunate War in Thessaly, Repercussions in Cyprus, Two Key Tax Bills, Queen Victoria's Diamond Jubilee, The Legislative Council Meets at Kykko Monastery, Irrigation Project Set To Go, Enlightening Women, A Moving Farewell

It was early in 1897 that the *Ethniki Etairia* made a furtive appearance in Cyprus. This Athens-based nationalist society was already being planned in 1895 'for the rekindling of a national conscience ... and the preparation of enslaved Greeks for the liberation'. It was now drumming up support for a militant expansionist agenda. The campaign was carried out, not only within the state of Greece, but among Greek communities throughout the Eastern Mediterranean.[1] By 1897 it had become extremely powerful. Nationalist tendencies whipped up in Athens during the Cretan revolt were already colouring the work of correspondents of Cypriot papers reporting from the metropole, most of whom were Cypriot students at university there.[2] In January 1897 Demetris Metaxas, a doctor in the Greek army, came to Cyprus on a two-month secret mission to set up a Cyprus branch of the *Ethniki Etairia*. His cover story was that he had come to visit his sister who had settled in Limassol and was married to a Dr. Thomides. He was a leading light in the burgeoning athletics scene in Limassol so intimately connected with nationalist tendencies. The two champions of the Pancyprian Games of 1896, for example, were high-profile volunteers for the Greek-Turkish war of 1897.[3] Other personalities who may have been involved in the *Etairia* and who were also active in the organisation of athletics were Nicolaos Katalanos in Nicosia and Dr. Filios Zanettos in Larnaca.

The two latter-named were Greek nationals. Their involvement in nationalist activities in Cyprus has been used to portray the *enotist* movement there as artificial or implanted.[4] By far the majority of nationalist leaders were Cypriots but it was not remarkable that some Greek nationals lived in the island. There is an exceptional fluidity among Greek-speaking populations of the Eastern Mediterranean, engendered by commerce,

---

1. See generally, Dakin, (1972), 139-140 and Yiannis Yiannoulopoulos, *Η Ευγενής μας Τύφλωσις*, (Athens 1999), 156-161.
2. Papapolyviou, (2001), 43.
3. They were Charalambos Nicolaides from Nicosia and Anastasis Andreou from Limassol. See ibid., 100.
4. For example, Andrekos Varnava, (2009), 163-164.

36. Athletes who participated in the Pancyprian Games in Limassol in 1897

ambition and the fortunes of war. Many Cypriots had and have family links within the Greek state, in the Aegean islands and in the great commercial ports of the Eastern seaboard. The president of the Cyprus branch of the *Ethniki Etairia* was a Cypriot, the newly-elected member of the legislative council, Bishop Kyrillos of Kition. Another two members of the legislative council cited on the same list as being involved were both Cypriot – Theofanis Theodotou and Ioannis Kyriakides. The latter had been one of the organisers of the wine demonstration at Parapedi. The activities of the *Etairia* in Cyprus do not seem to have amounted to much more than fund-raising, nor do its activities seem to have extended far beyond Limassol.[5] Nevertheless, the fact that the island had been included in the society's area of activity would have reinforced the feeling among those approached of belonging to a broader struggle.

An existing network with a nationalist bent had already been established in Cyprus with the founding of the first Greek Masonic lodge, *Zenon,* in Limassol in 1893. An overspill from the existing English lodge, St. Paul's, created by officers of the British garrison in 1888 under the aegis of the Great Lodge of England, the Greek lodge, true to the nationalist traditions of its master lodge in Athens, attracted the more radical and dynamic elements in middle-class society and would become increasingly related to their politics.[6]

Cypriot fund-raising, initially, was for the support of Cretan refugees and was not limited to the efforts of the *Etairia* or the Masonic lodges. Sofronios, who was not involved in either, spearheaded a highly organised effort to arrange accommodation for Christian refugees now pouring out of Crete. Indeed, he asked for the help of the high commissioner in arranging for some of the refugees to be diverted to Cyprus. With the approval of his principals in London, Sendall sought help from the Royal Navy, whose vessels were already carrying refugees from Crete to islands within the state of Greece. He was told that there were no ships available to sail east. Cypriot efforts to arrange for the use of a merchant ship from Piraeus in the end failed, perhaps, as a result of the refugees themselves not wanting to come as far from home as Cyprus, according to material found by Petros Papapolyviou.[7]

---

5. Papapolyviou, (2001), 89-92.
6. Katsiaounis, (1996), 189-191.
7. Papapolyviou, (2001), 65.

A more serious problem arose when the network and funds created for the relief of refugees were diverted. They would be used for organising the passage of Cypriot volunteers for the war against Turkey that was anticipated with such enthusiasm and impatience in Athens. The hostilities on Greece's northern frontiers were to a large extent the sad consequence of pressure on the Hellenic government and monarchy, created by nationalist frenzy whipped up in Athens. The pressure resulted in a popular but foolhardy move: the dispatch of a Greek military detachment to assist the rebels in Crete and after that the high-profile participation of the King's son and heir, Constantine, in the subsequent war in Thrace. Both were desperate attempts by a beleaguered monarchy to regain popularity.

The dispatch of Greek soldiers to Crete was a move which intensified nationalist emotions in Cyprus, as it did in the rest of the Greek world – Archbishop Sofronios, who could by no means be described as a radical or a warmonger, had himself sent a telegram to King George of the Hellenes, congratulating him on the brave move.[8] Ripples of the war fever raging in Athens reverberated across the Eastern Mediterranean and the Cypriots followed the Alexandrine Greeks in organising the passage of volunteers for the war. The Greek consul, Georgos Philemon, was not uninvolved in these efforts. He could with full legitimacy call up Greek nationals, and had a tendency to fudge the distinction between these and Cypriots who were, in fact, still subjects of the Sultan. His activities in this connection were not dissimilar to the activities of Greek consuls in Egypt, Salonika and other fringe areas. Consuls in these places worked at a popular, as well as official, level. At the former level, in areas under the direct rule of the Sultan their 'revolutionary' activities were clandestine.[9] There was nothing clandestine in the approach of the Greek consul in Cyprus.

It was indeed the call-up for Greek nationals announced by Philemon in the Cypriot papers on 11 March that triggered a wave of Cypriot volunteers, a move the Greek consul clearly encouraged. Before boarding Greek-owned vessels especially commissioned from Smyrna, the young men paraded in the streets to the loud appreciation of the townsfolk in the ports. The volunteers included pupils of the Pancyprian Gymnasium,

---

8.   Ibid., 50. The telegram was sent in the wake of a meeting of the Archbishop with some Members of the Hellenic Parliament who were visiting Cyprus. Papapolyviou found the telegram in the Archbishopric Archive, Β/Φακ., ΚΖ, Εθνικά.
9.   Douglas Dakin, *The Greek Struggle in Macedonia, 1897-1913*, (Thessaloniki 1969), 119-204.

priests from the archbishopric and monks from Kykko monastery, but also ordinary peasants from villages as far-flung as Trikomo, Karavas and Morphou.[10] The Greek consul addressed the young men before they sailed.

> *We live on the fringes of Hellenism, but let no one say, as from today, that the Cypriots are the least of the Hellenes....Fight with your brothers for Macedonia, as your ancestors fought with Alexander when he passed by here on his way to conquer Asia.*[11]

These rousing words were greeted with great gusto and the symbolic flinging of fezzes into the sea. By the end of March, Philemon was reporting to Athens that 760 Cypriot volunteers had left for Piraeus.[12]

Sendall informed London that an attempt to prevent the volunteers leaving by force would be counter-productive and that anyway he did not have the means to do so. Once war broke out in Thessaly, 'the island's inhabitants became more excited'. Telegrams arriving 'daily from the seat of war, [were] eagerly discussed in every town and every village in the island'. Their population was 'in a fever of excitement' about the present and apprehensive about the future. The local repercussions of the Greek-Turkish crisis highlighted the lapsed state of imperial security on the island. The mixed force of *zaptiehs*, 'who were normally adequate', could not now be relied on, while the forces of The Crown consisted of 'a single company of a line regiment, quartered at a distance of three days routine march from the seat of government. The captain (and therefore officer in command) and the senior subalterns [were] on the sick list, the former with a serious fracture of the elbow sustained at polo, which [was] likely to incapacitate him for some weeks. The naval squadron [had] not lately been in this part of the Mediterranean and no British Man-of-War [had] visited Cyprus for twelve months'.[13]

---

10. See detailed catalogue in Petros Papapolyviou, (2001), 314-367. See also Sendall to Chamberlain, 7 April 1897, CO67/105, NA.
11. Ibid., (author's translation), 228.
12. Ibid., 229. Fezzes were perceived to be a symbol of *raya* status. Similar scenes took place in Alexandria. See the fascinating diary of the young Cypriot, Savvas Tzerkezis, who volunteered to join the Greek army while he was in Alexandria, as a result of boredom and want of cash. See Savvas Tserkezis, *Ημερολόγιον του Βίου μου*, (Nicosia 2007), 51-52.
13. Sendall to Chamberlain, 23 April 1897, CO67/105, NA.

37. Evelthon Schizas, a Cypriot volunteer in the 1897 Greek-Turkish War

The island had long since been defined as not worth defending and problems had clearly not been envisaged with internal security. The new tensions between Muslim and Christian on the island did not as yet amount to much. Refusing to sit at the same cafes in some places, an example supplied by Sir Walter, indicated rather the everyday intimacy of the various sections of the population and the mildness of the present tensions. Nevertheless, they worried Sendall, and when these concerns were relayed to the secretary of state, he found them, in combination with the vulnerable state of the Cyprus government, 'extremely disquieting'. Issuing an order of neutrality in this case, the island being in law Ottoman territory, was highly complicated and led to lengthy exchanges within Whitehall and enquiries in Vienna about Bosnia, whose status, also a product of the Congress of Berlin, could be compared to that of Cyprus. The Balkan province was under Austrian occupation, while remaining technically under the sovereignty of the Sultan.[14] The high commissioner limited the official government reaction to a proclamation warning the population

> *To abstain from any meetings, assemblies or processions to the disturbance of public peace, and from giving cause for provocation tending to a breach of the public peace by means of any act, writing, word or gesture as they will answer to the contrary at their peril.*[15]

Sir Walter immediately visited Limassol and Larnaca, the most likely trouble spots. The Porte had not, as yet, complained of the activities in Cyprus, but if there were complaints, the recruiting of Cypriots at least would have to be suppressed. This could create a violent reaction against the *zaptiehs* and riots. The dilemma was resolved by the speedy end to hostilities in Thessaly in the middle of May, after an easy Turkish victory.

Even before the end of the war, Sendall was able to report, on returning to the capital, that 'the most perfect tranquillity prevail[ed] everywhere'. He was satisfied that 'there [was] a sincere desire among responsible people to preserve the peace and to avoid all occasion for friction or collision between the two races during the prevalence of hostilities [in Thessaly]'.

---

14. See file Cyprus 8399, 'Recruiting for the Greek army' in which advice is sought by Chamberlain from Foreign Office on this complex issue, CO67/110, NA.
15. 'A proclamation by the High Commissioner', dated 23 April 1897 on the cover page of *The Cyprus Gazette*, No. 548, 23 April 1897, CO67/105.

An alarming explosion in an Easter bonfire at Varosha had proved to have no political motivation, while in Larnaca, where the bishop, the radical Kyrillos, had the good sense to suppress the Judas bonfires, Easter passed off peacefully.[16] In Limassol, there had been some excitement because a Turkish policemen wandered into a church smoking a pipe, but the affair only had significance within that parish. The high commissioner turned down the offer of a gunboat that the War Office was scrambling to send to Cyprus waters.[17]

His decision not to attempt to intervene to prevent the volunteers leaving had allowed an outlet for passions that might otherwise have been unleashed within the island. The authorities must have been particularly pleased to see Nicolaos Katalanos, the most rumbustious of the Nicosia radicals, depart for the front in Thessaly. The Peloponnesian activist would almost certainly have led a reaction to any attempt to stop the volunteers. This lesson would be noted and repeated by Sendall's successor, Sir William Haynes Smith, during the Balkan Wars of the next decade. In the first half of 1897 a new sense of resentment against Britain had been created by the leading part of the British navy in the bombardment of the Suda Bay peninsular, *Akrotiri*, in Crete, by the European powers in February. The high commissioner had warned London that because of this resentment and the growing Greek-Turkish tension, he was not planning to organise high-profile festivities for Queen Victoria's Diamond Jubilee. But after the Greek defeat, when it was learnt that it was Queen Victoria with Tsar Nicholas II, who had dissuaded the Sultan from ordering his forces to march on down the open road to Athens, all antipathy was focused on Germany whose attitude had been particularly hostile to the Greeks. Britain and France, much to Katalanos's irritation, became, in the eyes of the Greek Christians, 'the Protectors of Liberty'.[18]

In contrast to the Athenians, the Cypriots refrained from blaming the Greek monarchy for the defeat of the Greek army. They always had a soft spot for the Greek royal family, who offered a counterpoint to obligatory respect due to the British queen. The Hellenic monarchy provided them

---

16. For the Easter bonfire incident at Famagusta, see File 8703, 25 April 1897, CO67/105. It is interesting that Bishop Kyrillos Papadopoulos of Kition, sometimes described as a depraved nationalist, had behaved so responsibly as to reduce the likelihood of disturbances in Larnaca.
17. Minutes attached to Sendall to Chamberlain, 23 April 1897, CO67/105.
18. Papapolyviou, (2001), 212.

with a royal family they liked to call their own, much to the irritation of the British in Cyprus. Once Prince George of the Hellenes was installed by the European powers as high commissioner of Crete in the aftermath of the war, his portrait decorated many middle-class Cypriot parlours.[19] There *was* much Cypriot criticism, however, of the short-sighted policies of the Greek government and the paralysis of the highly politicised Greek civil service. This was compared unfavourably with the 'permanent' British civil service in Cyprus, which was not affected by changes of government in London.[20]

In spite of the dramatic regional developments and the inevitable repercussions within the island, Cypriot relations with the British administration were growing daily more collaborative and more productive. The informal consultation already taking place at the executive level was, in June 1897, institutionalized by the modification in the Queen's Instructions that Sendall had asked for. The first 'native' executive councillors were formally appointed. Sendall had argued successfully that the previous instructions allowing for 'natives' to be summoned only on very special occasions were quite inadequate. It was now 'desirable that members should be regularly and systematically consulted upon large questions and administrative questions' for which the royal instructions failed to make adequate provision. From now on they could be summoned as 'additional members, whenever the High Commissioner judged it advisable'. The first 'Additional Members' of the executive council, as they were formally termed, were Achilleas Liassides, Paschalis Constantinides, and the chief *cadi*, Mehmet Attaoullah. The latter left the island shortly afterwards to become chief *cadi* in Beirut.[21] Sendall had become close to Attaoullah through their successful collaboration in bringing about much needed reform in the Muslim High School in Nicosia, and in working with him, had found an unaccustomed flexibililty regarding the thorny Anglo-Turkish issues over *Evkaf* and *vakouf* properties. The chief *cadi* had been involved too in the care of Muslim monuments. A poem in praise of Abdulhamid and his gift of water for the Hala Sultan Tekke in Larnaca, inscribed on a fountain in its grounds in 1895, was attributed to 'Attaoullah'.[22]

---

19. Basil Stewart, *My Experiences of Cyprus*, (New York, 1908), 100-101.
20. Papapolyviou, (2001), 125.
21. Sendall to Chamberlain, 7 May 1897, CO67/106, NA.
22. Tuncer Bağışkan, (2009), 59-60.

The growing perception of themselves as 'Greek' and 'Turk' rather than 'Christian' and 'Muslim', did not prevent the Cypriots combining against the colonial administration in matters of appointment and taxation. The appointment of more Cypriots to high office was not moving as fast as the legislative council would have wished, although Sendall was as anxious as they were to increase the Cypriot element in the civil service. He would not have disagreed with the bishop of Kition who, arguing against a decision to appoint a new chief clerk in England, had insisted that a Cypriot be appointed 'in order that there should be one foreigner less in the civil service'. In doing so, he coined the phrase, to be picked up many years later in quite a different context, 'Cyprus for the Cypriots'.[23] The elected members were particularly anxious to see the appointment of Cypriot judges. Their case was put formally in the elected members' reply to the high commissioner's inauguration speech in the legislative council in March 1897.

> *The chief obstacle, it is understood, to the fulfillment of the expressed desire of the people, is the danger of jealousy arising from the different elements of which the island's population is composed. The Council confidently assures the Secretary of State that such an obstacle exists only as a creature of the imagination, and as conclusive evidence of its non existence in fact, the Council desires to instance the fraternal harmony that has ever governed the relations of the two sections of the community both before and since the occupation.*[24]

This united Cypriot front displayed so firmly by the elected representatives for their mutual benefit is important, coming at a time of growing Greek-Turkish tension within the region. The elected members' reply to the high commissioner was considered to be the formal Cypriot reaction to the government's performance and policy in the previous year. It was not as appreciative as London and Sendall would have expected in view of the radical change in approach, especially regarding financial policy, since the arrival of Chamberlain in the Colonial Office. On the contrary, it was harsher than that of the previous year. By 1897, Sir Walter's efforts were clearly bearing fruit. On 30 January the Cyprus government had at last been able to announce officially the intention of Her Majesty's

---

23. Bishop of Kition's speech in legislative council, quoted in Sendall to Chamberlain, 20 May 1897, CO67/106, NA.
24. Elected members' reply to the high commissioner's opening speech to the legislative council signed 11 March 1897, enclosed in Sendall to Chamberlain, 14 March, CO67/105.

Government to apply to Parliament for a loan of £60,000 from Imperial Funds at a low rate of interest for the purpose of carrying out a considerable experiment in irrigation in Cyprus.[25] In his inaugural speech to the legislative council, the high commissioner was careful to present that investment as a confirmation of the British government's intention of remaining in Cyprus and thus to end the uncertainty about the island's future status which had so deterred foreign capital. He was also able to point to other areas in which the labours of his four-year term were beginning to bear fruit. Among other things, thirty-four bridges had been built the previous year, and the road from Limassol to Paphos, delayed for so many years, was all but completed. There was finally a weekly mail service to Egypt, reinforcing a lucrative commercial interaction. The export of livestock particularly had shot up:

1891 - 190 oxen 151 sheep
1895 - 936 oxen 231 sheep
1897 - 3054 oxen 4992 sheep[26]

The Cypriots were in a position to take advantage in 1897 of an Egyptian ban on livestock from Syria and in so doing created a valuable niche.

While indicating some appreciation for these improvements, and most especially Sendall's 'personal efforts' in connection with the 1895 Education law, there was a sting in the tail of every response in the elected members' reply. In education, a more liberal allowance was required in order to make the law effective. The improved communications would provide a great impulse to trade, but only if the 'very heavy' harbour and lighterage dues were reduced and the mail service extended to the other coastal towns. The irrigation loan itself would have to be carefully supervised in order not to 'prove fruitless and barren'. But the bitterest attack was against the taxation system itself, the amendment of which, Chamberlain had just rejected. The elected members referred to the tax system as 'an exercise of the greatest ingenuity' which had 'achieved an augmentation of taxation to the extent of at least one third, the great proportion of which had been introduced under the name of duties'. They argued that if the country was to be taxed so heavily, the country demanded that it 'be accorded the

---

25. *The Cyprus Gazette*, No. 537, 30 January 1897.
26. Table enclosed in Sendall to Chamberlain, 10 December 1897, CO67/108.

benefits of the taxation imposed' and also reduction of taxation in relation to the ability of the resources to produce. They insisted that any deficit from whatever cause (including the Tribute) should be 'provided for by those who derive political advantage from the occupation'.[27]

Baffled by this harsh reaction to all the government's efforts and concerned by news of Chamberlain's own consternation at the Cypriots' response, Sendall and Young sought an explanation privately from a group of elected members. The cause was to be found in a single paragraph in the secretary of state's reply to the 1895 memorial. He had not replied until a year after he received it. The delay had been due to his attempts, in the intervening period, to have the Tribute commuted, a fact that could not be divulged to the memorialists. In his reply, Chamberlain had said that 'the feelings of the people [had] somewhat changed' since the memorial had been written, because of the various improvements in administration and development that were taking place. This was an accurate statement, but the Cypriot elected members feared that the gratitude expressed to Chamberlain in February 1896, in response to tidings of the new public works and education grants, had been taken to infer that they, the Cypriots, were gradually becoming contented with the burden of the Tribute – that their needs had now been satisfied. They feared that any new compliments made would be used against them. They were therefore 'compelled to avoid all language of gratitude' in their recent address to the high commissioner.

In a meeting with Young on the subject, the elected members present, who were all Greek Christian, stressed that their main resentment continued to be against payment of the Tribute. 'Why', they asked, 'were Bosnia under Austrian administration and Algeria under the French, both still like Cyprus, remaining under Ottoman sovereignty, not required to make the same payments? When the Cypriots saw how Bosnia had prospered under Austria and how much the French had done for Algeria in irrigation works and railways from the very commencement of the occupation, they thought England should have done more for them.' Sendall, anxious not to deter Chamberlain from his present positive attitude to the Cypriots, explained to the secretary of state that the members needed to be seen

---

27. Members' Reply, 11 March 1897, enclosed in Sendall to Chamberlain, 26 March 1897, CO67/105.

to be hammering away against the tax system, especially in view of the rejection of the 'tithe substitution' and 'property revaluation' bills in London.[28]

Tax reform became even more urgent with the imminent launching of the irrigation project. The elected members insisted that the loan for this project would not be serviced by the locust tax fund as London would have wished, but from general revenue. In order to pressure both the elected members and London to reach agreement on the formula for the 'revaluation of property' bill, Sendall took the unusual step in March 1897 of enacting the new 'tithe substitution' bill by order-in-council. He needed the revenue the new system was expected to produce, to pay the interest on the irrigation loan. On the one hand, his efforts were being held up by the long-drawn-out procedures in London – the tax bill had not even been sent from the Colonial Office to the Treasury when Sendall went ahead and enacted it arbitrarily. On the other hand, he foresaw that the enactment of bills in the Cypriot legislature would henceforth be further complicated by political differences within the Christian community. The new harsh tone in the members' reply to his opening speech in February augured cracks in the constructive spirit in which bills had been hammered out recently. The members newly elected the previous November, Theofanis Theodotou and the Bishop of Kition, could not be relied upon to agree with Liassides and Constantinides as their predecessors could.[29] We have here the first inkling that the divide in middle-class politics within the Greek Christian community of Cyprus, stimulated by electoral politics and a free press, was now discernible within the legislature.

Laws pertaining to water rights, also required before the irrigation project could be started, were likewise being delayed endlessly in London. The bills were not returned to the island in time to be enacted before the adjournment of the legislature at the end of May. The high commissioner, therefore, once more planned to take up the hospitality offered by the Abbot of Kykko for an extraordinary meeting at his ancient monastery deep in the Paphos forest. He hoped that by then, Medlicott, the conceiver of the project, who was about to take up employment on the island as its supervising engineer, would be there to advise. Sendall also took the

---

28. Private letter Sendall to Wingfield, 4 June 1897, CO67/105, NA.
29. Sendall to Chamberlain, 5 April 1897, CO67/105, NA.

precaution of ensuring that Panayiotis Gennadius, appointed to the great satisfaction of all, that year, as director of agriculture, would be an ex-officio member of the legislative council. His presence would encourage the elected members to take on board the new necessary modifications to water rights that would have to be in place before the irrigation project could be embarked upon.

This time a meeting did take place at Kykko Monastery in the first fortnight in August, to debate and enact the irrigation legislation. The property revaluation bill was stuck in London, but Sendall's preemptive enactment of the taxation reform bill had secured a means of financing the project. The legislative council and the government were united in wanting the work to start on the major irrigation experiment as soon as possible. What an extraordinary session it must have been – a 'Legco' outing. The elected members converged from their various constituencies on the bleak Byzantine monastery perched high on a stony crag in the Paphos forest and settled as best they could into tiny monks' cells, while Sir Walter with his retinue of civil servants and assorted official members rode down from Troodos to set up camp in the monastery grounds. Would they all have sat around the abbot's table that evening and drunk the abbot's wine? – Muslim Turks, Christian Greeks and official English with the medley of ex-officio members, Heidenstam, Gennadius among them, blurring the edges. It was a unique occasion, symptomatic of Sendall's adminstration. Government and elected representatives went out of their way to meet together to prepare the way for this first development project in which so much hope for future prosperity was invested. It was twenty years since the first high commissioner had been welcomed at the Nicosia branch of the monastery, a time full of hope and expectations that had until the last few years remained unrealized. This new encampment in the monastery's mountain base signalled a new optimism, a new willingness, both by governed and governor, to collaborate. Sir Walter was more than happy to have the meeting in such an uncolonial setting. It was for him a practical solution to the problem of carrying on legislative business in the hot summer months when the central government moved up to Troodos. But this was an unusual approach - not one that Sir Henry Bulwer would ever have contemplated. Nor was Sendall's example taken up by subsequent high commissioners, while the new elected members would need little prompting to become obstructionist.

There is an eerie silence about the legislature's session at Kykko in Colonial Office correspondence. Did Sendall sense official disapproval and remain silent on the details or were his reports withdrawn from the official correspondence? The minutes of the legislative council record the detailed debate and the local newspapers offer us a colourful coverage of the occasion. They depict the quiet monastery transformed into a bustle of activity. Messengers hurried back and forth between the white tents among the trees where the high officials and, in some cases, their wives, were encamped.

Lady Sendall and Lady Evelyne Young were certainly there, busying themselves with meetings of the Nicosia hospital committee.[30] It was, in fact, due to their exertions that the Cyprus branch of the Royal British Nurses' Association was formed that year. The Association, formed in 1888, had only received its charter in 1893. The concept remained controversial for some years, provoking the formidable opposition of the aging Florence Nightingale. She was convinced that it would erode the vocational ethos of the nursing profession.[31] That Lady Sendall was involved enough to create a Cyprus branch at this time once again reflects her progressive attitude to female education and employment.

The presence of such an illustrious gathering in so remote a region could not but raise the curiosity and expectations of its inhabitants, largely goatherds and charcoal burners, who were deeply affected by the colonial government's stringent measures to protect the forest. Petitioners from the Tylliria area on the remote west coast at the foot of the Paphos forest, made the arduous journey to the monastery on foot to complain personally to Sir Walter about the severe restrictions on their grazing and woodcutting rights. The negative impact of these measures on individuals trying to eke out a living from the forest was, to some extent, softened by new forestry initiatives. Sendall, together with the Greek director of agriculture, Gennadius, was able to urge them to take advantage of the free grafting of olive and carob trees now encouraged by the government within the forest areas that covered this region.[32] At the same time, they could point out that a small government-run forest industry in

---

30. Φωνή της Κύπρου, 29 August 1897.
31. *Cyprus: Annual Report 1903* and information derived from the website of the Royal British Nurses Association.
32. Ibid.

38. Kykko Monastery

the Paphos area was selling ready-cut roof beams and ploughs, a popular enterprise set up by the Paphos district commissioner.[33]

The serious business of the day took place in the monastery's great hall (*synodiko*) beneath 'a magnificent icon of the virgin framed in gold'. The hall was lit by antique lamps and chandeliers. At the end nearest the ancient library, at long tables, sat the members of the public, clerical and lay, who had made the journey up the mountain to listen to the proceedings. The proceedings were 'lively' and sometimes 'stormy', as article after article of the new water rights legislation was scrutinized day after day. Most of the councillors were seated, but a few stood about the hall and some took time out to wander around the dimly lit corridors of the monastery. The labours of the council were rewarded by a great feast on the penultimate evening. The following day, the bill was finally voted through. Before the council was prorogued, it was the new radical member, Theofanis Theodotou, who proposed that a telegram be sent from the council to Queen Victoria on the occasion of her Diamond Jubilee anniversary. Before departing, the members, official and elected, gathered at the entrance of the monastery for a group photograph.[34]

If a salient event in regional terms that impinged on Cyprus affairs in 1897 was the war between Greece and Turkey, another was Sultan Abdul Hamid's punitive pogrom against the Armenians. This was a bloody attempt at quashing the new 'plague' of nationalism. Nationalist movements had, for years, been threatening the Ottoman grip on the Balkans. More recently, nationalist passions had begun stirring in the Turkish heartlands of Asia Minor. The subsequent massacres of Armenians, following on from the Bulgarian massacres so lethally exploited by Gladstone in his Midlothian campaign, found a great deal of sympathy in Europe, not least with the prime minister, Lord Salisbury, whose abandoned policy of British-supervised reform in Asia Minor had so raised the political expectations of the minorities in the region.[35] In practical terms, there

---

33. Sendall to Ripon, 8 May 1894, enclosing letter from G. Smith, Commissioner of Paphos to the principal Forest Officer, CO67/106, NA.
34. Αλήθεια (Alithia), 19 August 1897. See also Minutes of the legislative council of Cyprus, Session 1897, (MHR). The first session of the legislative council at Kykko Monastery: Council met on 2 August 1897. It was adjourned for informal discussions, then reconvened for another fourteen days to debate and enact the legislation.
35. W.N. Medlicott, 'The Gladstone Government and the Cyprus Convention, 1880-1885', *The Journal of Modern History*, Vol. XII, June 1940, 187-208.

arose the question of how the expected flood of refugees would be dealt with, a problem exacerbated by exaggerated rumours about the numbers likely to make for Cyprus. But there were also oblique reverberations affecting the island's financial condition. Negotiations had been taking place with the Sultan, who appeared in 1897 to be prepared to commute the Cypriot Tribute for a lump sum, as he had done with the Bosnian Tribute, for much needed cash for his treasury. The matter was shelved in 1897 by Salisbury, in part because of the political impropriety of being seen to hand over a large sum of money to the Sultan, when he was once more causing havoc in Armenia and Crete.

On the island itself, fear of an invasion of refugees was exacerbated by an epidemic of smallpox in Asia Minor. Sendall had still not managed to acquire the coasting vessel he had sought for all manner of purposes, including picking up illegal and possibly diseased immigrants. Now he tried, but failed, to gain London's assent to a proclamation prohibiting the landing of refugees on the island. The government in London, already accused of not having done enough to save the Armenians, could not make itself vulnerable to further attack. Moreover, charitable organisations were encroaching with all kinds of unhelpful ideas about how and where such people should be settled on the island. The government's pleas that there was not a penny to spend on destitute Cypriots, let alone newcomers, were ignored. The island did not in the end attract much Armenian interest, being overshadowed, as ever, by the magnet of Alexandria. Those who did come were somehow catered for, Sendall himself encouraging an Armenian industrial weaving project in Larnaca. Textiles manufactured in Larnaca were to be exported to Turkey.[36]

Overall, these upheavals which, together with the deteriorating situation in Macedonia, had such a destabilizing effect on the Eastern Mediterranean, made little immediate impact on the island. Through 1897 the administration was able to continue to create the physical and intellectual infrastructure for a more productive island. Sendall characteristically focused on education as the key to stimulating the productive process. The desire for education was itself stimulated by the *fin de siècle* blossoming

---

36. Sendall to Chamberlain, 11 June 1897, CO67/106, NA. While the cultivation of silk worms and the manufacture of silk and '*aladja* (cotton/silk cloth)' continued as a cottage industry well into the twentieth century, efforts made at the end of the nineteenth century to expand the cultivation of silk in the island met with little success.

of Greek irredentism and in turn fed into it. It had been taken for granted since Kimberly's decision not 'to make English a general vehicle of education', that it would be a communal affair. The 1895 Education Act had set in process the creation of a 'normal school' for training teachers in the Pancyprian Gymnasium and, by awarding conditional grants, created a stimulus for schools to have qualified teachers. The response among the Greek Cypriot population had been massive. There had been a 40 per cent rise since 1896 in the school population (5,476 boys and 759 girls in 1896 to 8,864 boys and 1,369 girls in 1897). Village after village began building a schoolhouse and applying for qualified teachers and a government grant. One hundred and twenty-two new village schools now existed, in addition to the 179 registered the previous year. Sir Walter estimated that at least 60 of these would qualify for aid in the coming year. Heads were shaken in disbelief in Whitehall at the figures offered by Sendall, explaining the need for a substantial increase in the education grant. 'Surely all this is not in one year!'[37] Chamberlain refused to increase the grant until the overall revenue for the year had been assessed, but he approved doubling the money given to the Pancyprian Gymnasium's 'normal school' to facilitate the qualification of more teachers.[38] Sir Walter had impressed upon him the excellence of the work undertaken at the Pancyprian Gymnasium.

> *I recommend that this establishment that I know well from personal observation, be given this sum which, having regard to the character of the school and the exertions which are made by the people to maintain it, cannot be regarded as an excessive contribution from the Government, as long as the free examination of teachers is made a condition of the grant.*[39]

Nineteen of the government-aided Christian elementary schools were girls' schools. The inspector of schools, Josiah Spencer, noted in the annual report of 1897, 'an increased willingness on the part of the villagers to send their girls to school'. Meanwhile, the Phaneromeni girls' school in Nicosia, in whose hall Lady Sendall organised fund-raising concerts, had had several new classrooms built, to which the government

---
37. Sendall to Chamberlain, 6 May 1897 and attached minutes, CO67/106, NA.
38. The subsidy was enshrined in the Education Amendment Act 1897. Five per cent of education tax collected from each Greek Christian taxpayer went to the Pancyprian Gymnasium.
39. Sendall to Chamberlain, 6 May 1897, CO67/106, NA.

contributed £30. It was attended by 395 girls and the mistresses were aided in their work by some of the masters from the Pancyprian Gymnasium who gave lessons on special subjects to the higher classes. The school was becoming useful as a training school for mistresses in the island's girls' schools.[40]

The Sendalls' own liberal intellectual environment would have lent itself to promoting the education of women. When Elizabeth Lewis came to Cyprus, she had already published an article in the journal *The Nineteenth Century* on 'A Reformation of Domestic Service', the main purpose of which was to allow 'ladies as well as servants' to 'beat their wings for higher intellectual heights'.[41] She and other friends had been involved in promoting education in Cyprus long before the arrival of the Sendalls. Her name, together with those of George Bowen and Ioannis Gennadius, appears in the list of members of The Cyprus Society, formed in London in the 1880s for the promotion of education and health in Cyprus.[42]

The Sendalls' Nicosia friends too were linked to female enlightenment and education. Achilleas Liassides and his betrothed, Theano Paroudi, were pioneers in promoting amateur theatre, while Theano was headmistress of Phaneromeni girls' school.[43] It was her prodigy, Eleni Christou, a bright pupil from the village of Kythrea, whom Sir Walter recommended for the Queen Victoria Jubilee Scholarship. This scholarship was Sir Walter's personal initiative, funded out of his own pocket. The interest from the capital he deposited would provide an annual scholarship for a girl from the school to pursue further education abroad and return to teach in Cyprus. This award is interesting, not only because it promoted female education, which Sir Walter might have considered an unnecessary luxury in such a penny-pinched island. It is not one that would have been considered by earlier administrations for the 'men and lads' (let alone the women) whose 'healthy appearance ..... seemed to show that their calling [was] sufficiently remunerative to provide them with all their needs'.

---

40. *Cyprus: Annual Report for the Year 1896-1897*, 58.
41. Elizabeth Alicia M. Lewis, 'A Reformation of Domestic Service', *The Nineteenth Century*, Vol. XXXIII, January-June 1893, 127-138. In this extraordinarily modern article, Elizabeth Lewis suggests, among other things, Take Aways on street corners, to allow housewives and servants more time for mental activity.
42. See list of members of The Cyprus Society in Andrekos Varnava, (2009), Appendix X, 297-299.
43. See Coudounaris, 187.

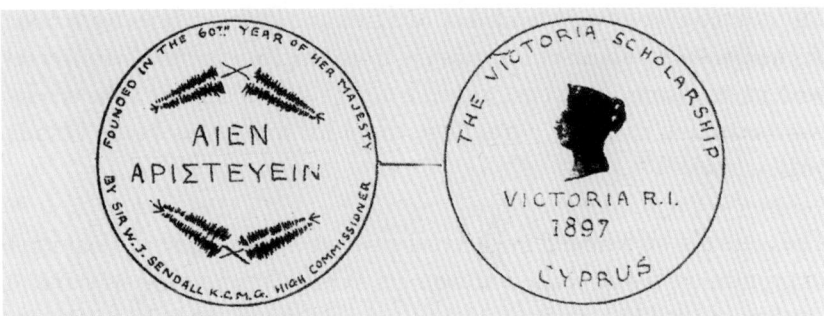

39. Sketch of the Victoria Scholarship medal, drawn by Sir Walter Sendall

The scholarship was a willing response to a need that *was* felt and expressed. The number of girls receiving a basic education in the island, though minimal in relation to the number of boys, reflected a surprisingly progressive outlook among the local population to female education. Sir Walter's award is also interesting in that the scholarship neither stipulated that further education should take place in Britain, nor did it exclude Athens. In fact, Eleni Christou was already at the *Arsakeion* girls' school in Athens, and clearly in financial difficulties, when she was presented with the scholarship by the British ambassador.[44] The medallion for the Sendall Scholarship depicted Queen Victoria on one side. There had been considerable correspondence on this matter, the Queen having taken a dislike to the original portrait. Final approval was given by Her Majesty at Osborne on 10 January 1897.[45] On completing her course at the *Arsakeion*, Eleni Christou spent two years in Lausanne. In 1901, when Theano resigned her post as headmistress to marry Achilleas Liassides, Eleni returned to Nicosia and took over as headmistress of Phaneromeni school, where she was equipped to enthuse her pupils with her own passion for education. In later years, true to the cause of promoting women's involvement in public affairs, she founded, together with Theano Liassides, the first and most prestigious women's association, Ένωσις Ελληνίδων.[46] Later in life she would found and run a boarding school, H Ακαδημία Θηλέων, (Academy for Young Ladies), where older girls would receive language tuition and be taught domestic science, typing and shorthand. She retired in 1959, but the academy was still functioning in the 1970s.[47]

---

44. Σάλπιγξ, 9 December 1897, citing a letter from Edwin Egerton, British Ambassador at Athens to the principal of the *Arsakeion* school for girls, 1 December 1897.
45. Private letter, Osborne to Wilson, Colonial Office, 10 January 1897, CO67/103, NA.
46. Coudounaris, (2001), for Eleni Christou, 668-669, and for Theano Liassides, 307.
47. 'Ακαδημία Θηλέων', Ο Φιλελεύθερος, Βιβλιοθήκη, No. 49, January 2011.

Sir Walter's scholarship for Phaneromeni was balanced by a scholarship for a pupil of the *I'dade*, the Muslim High School, whose 'complete reform' he had supervised personally. He was able to announce the scholarships during his speech closing the legislative council session in June 1897. He planned very little else by way of clebrating Queen Victoria's Diamond Jubilee within the island. The Greek-Turkish War was not over when preparations began in earnest in England and the situation in the Eastern Mediterranean remained uncertain. A small detachment of mounted *zaptiehs* went to London to take part in the stunning ceremonies there. The high commissioner was anxious that they take their own horses, in spite of the extra expense, 'so that the Cypriot *zaptiehs* would be shown to the best advantage'.[48] But in Cyprus the celebrations would be minimal. He said as much to the members of the legislative council, but 'expressed a confidant expectation that those marks of respectful devotion which had always been spontaneously evinced whenever Her Majesty's name was brought before the people of the country, would not be wanting on this occasion'. His consideration was much appreciated. What actually occurred on Jubilee Day in Cyprus was another extraordinary expression of sympathy and solidarity of the Cypriots with their high commissioner. 'I must confess', Sendall reported to Chamberlain, 'that I was not prepared for the universal and spontaneous outburst of loyalty which took place on the 22nd of June, and which will make that day a memorable one in the history of Cyprus'.

> At the service in the morning the Phaneromeni church and the adjacent streets were filled to overflowing. The English National Anthem was sung to Greek words, and the service concluded with enthusiastic Vivats for Her Majesty. I drove through the streets in an open carriage and nothing could exceed the enthusiasm of the orderly crowds by which they were thronged.

The celebrations were not limited to the capital. Judging from the absence of Cypriot jubilation at past and future royal anniversaries, this was a tribute to Sendall himself and a message to the government he represented. Rumours abounded now of his impending departure and this occasion

---

48. Sendall to Chamberlain, 9 April 1897, CO67/105, NA. See also Basil Stewart 259. The author relates an anecdote referring to the reaction of the Duke of Cambridge, on seeing the Cypriot *zaptiehs* parading with other Imperial Forces at the Agricultural Hall, Islington. 'You don't mean to tell me these people are white!'

marked the beginning of an unprecedented and comprehensive attempt by the Cypriots to keep him on the island. On the occasion of Her Majesty's Diamond Jubilee, a memorial, signed jointly by the archbishop, the *mufti* and other Christian and Muslim notables, was addressed to Queen Victoria. It stressed that

> *the just and impartial administration of Sir Walter Sendall, and his earnest endeavours for the welfare and prosperity of Cyprus have gained our deepest gratitude. We earnestly pray that Your Majesty may be pleased to permit Sir Walter Sendall to remain as our High Commissioner beyond the time of the customary period. We are fully confident that the news that Sir Walter Sendall, who has endeared himself to all, has been granted a second period as High Commissioner of the island of Cyprus, will be gratefully received by the whole population without distinction of creed or race, and that this will be supreme evidence of the high interest taken by Her Majesty in this island.*[49]

There followed a steady flow of petitions from every town and most villages in Cyprus. Between July and November 1897, memorials bearing pages and pages of signatures in Greek and Ottoman Arabic characters, mayors' seals, *mukhtars*' stamps and flowery pleas for Sendall to stay in the island were all to no avail. The Secretary of State was glad, came the reply, to hear of the esteem in which Sir Walter Sendall was held, but there was no question of acceding to the Cypriots' request. The Colonial Office was impervious. 'Sir Walter Sendall is 64 years of age', noted one minute, 'and there are too many waiting for his removal to allow this request to be granted.'[50] It is clear that the petitions so laboriously organised by the Cypriots bore no weight in Whitehall. Robert Meade indicates that Sir Walter was seeking a first-class posting to round off his career in order to increase his pension – a posting he should have received long ago.[51] The consensus was that he should be given that chance now. Certainly Sendall

---

49. File Cyprus No.16141, Original Greek and Turkish, and translation of the memorial, 15 July 1897, CO67/107, NA. The official translation is 'additional'[evidence] but the Greek phraseology is stronger than this - a little dig perhaps at the British government's protestations of interest in the Cypriots' welfare. which were 'as a brass cymbal'.
50. Minute on the Memorial by Edward Wingfield, dated 16 July 1897, File Cyprus 16141, CO67/107, NA.
51. Minute on package of petitions from Cypriot villages, by Robert Meade, attached to Sendall to Chamberlain, 14 October 1897, CO67/107, NA.

40. *Zaptiehs* participating in Jubilee celebrations in London, 1897 (etching in *The Illustrated London News*)

was not given the option of staying on in Cyprus if he chose, so we shall never know what his reply would have been. If, as it seems, he was seeking an increased pension, that was the one expense the Cypriots would almost certainly willingly have borne to keep him on the island longer. But they were not going to be asked. Their wishes in this matter were not a priority. In November, Sendall was offered the governorship of British Guiana, a first-class posting.

Correspondence in the National Archive indicates that, whereas initially the high commissioner was to have stayed on the island until March to prepare the following year's budget, for some personal family reason he suddenly requested an urgent departure on one of the warships currently stationed at Marmaris on the Turkish coast.[52] He was refused a ride on one of Her Majesty's ships, the request clearly being considered rather brash in Whitehall, but he and Lady Sophia caught the next mail boat to Egypt on 1 January 1898.

The Sendalls chose to set off on the journey home from the port of Limassol, disembarking at Larnaca only for the formal swearing in of Arthur Young who would take over until the arrival of the new high commissioner. Nicolaos Katalanos, who wrote as sourly of anything

---

52. Telegram: Sendall to Chamberlain, 26 December 1897, CO67/108, NA.

Πρὸς τὴν Αὐτῆς Ἐξοχωτάτην Μεγαλειότητα τὴν Ἄνασσαν.

Μεγαλειοτάτη,

Ἐπὶ τῇ εὐκαιρίᾳ τοῦ πανηγυρισμοῦ τῆς εὐκλεοῦς Ὑμῶν βασιλείας οἱ ὑποσημειούμενοι, Ἀρχιεπίσκοπος Κύπρου, Μουφτῆς Κύπρου καὶ Αἰδετὰ Μέγη τοῦ Κεντρικοῦ Μετζελισίου Ἰεραί, ταπεινῶς προσερχόμεθα, ὅπως ἐκφράσωμεν Ὑμῖν τὰς ἐγκαρδίους ἡμῶν εὐχαριστίας ἐπὶ τῇ συνετῇ ἐκλογῇ, ἣν ἡ Ὑμετέρα Μεγαλειότης ἐποιήσατο, διορίσασα τὸν Σὶρ Οὐῶλτερ Σένδαλ ὅπως ἀντιπροσωπεύῃ Αὐτὴν ὡς Μέγας Ἁρμοστὴς ἐν τῇ Νήσῳ ταύτῃ.

Ἡ δικαία καὶ ἀμερόληπτος διοίκησις τοῦ Σὶρ Οὐῶλτερ Σένδαλ καὶ αἱ διαρκεῖς καὶ ἀκάματοι αὐτοῦ προσπάθειαι ὑπὲρ τῆς εὐκλαρίας καὶ εὐδαιμονίας τῆς Κύπρου ἐπεσπάσαντο τὴν μεγίστην ἡμῶν εὐγνωμοσύνην· διὸ καὶ διακαῶς ἱκετεύομεν τὴν Ὑμετέραν Μεγαλειότητα, ἵνα Αὐτὴ εὐδοκοῦσα, ἐπιτρέψῃ εἰς τὸν Σὶρ Οὐῶλτερ Σένδαλ νὰ παραμείνῃ ὡς Μέγας ἡμῶν Ἁρμοστὴς καὶ μετὰ τὸ πέρας τῆς νενομισμένης περιόδου, ἐπὶ μίαν ἔτι ἑξαετίαν.

Εἴμεθα πάντῃ πεπεισμένοι ὅτι τὸ ἄγγελμα, ὅτι ὁ Σὶρ Οὐῶλτερ Σένδαλ, ὅσον κατόπιν προσφιλὴς τοῖς πᾶσιν, ἐνεγράφη δευτέραν περίοδον ὡς Μέγας Ἁρμοστὴς τῆς Νήσου Κύπρου, θέλει εὐχαρίστως ἀκουσθῇ ὑφ' ἁπάξαπαντος τοῦ πληθυσμοῦ τῆς Νήσου, ἄνευ διακρίσεως πίστεως ἢ φυλῆς καὶ ὅτι τὸ τοιοῦτον θέλει θεωρηθῇ ὡς μία ἔτι ἀπόδειξις τοῦ ὑπὲρ τῆς Νήσου ταύτης ὑψίστου ἐνδιαφέροντος τῆς Ὑμετέρας Μεγαλειότητος.

Ἐν Λευκωσίᾳ Κύπρου, τῇ 19ῃ Ἰουνίου 1897.

† Ὁ Ἀρχιεπίσκοπος Κύπρου Σωφρόνιος

Μουφτεύς Θεοσίδης
Ἀρχιδοῦκας Γ. Μιχαηλίδης

41. Petition to Queen Victoria in Greek and Ottoman Turkish script by Christian and Muslim leaders, asking for Sir Walter Sendall to be granted a second term as High Commissioner

عتبۀ علیای حضرت قضا البجیه

معروضه چاکرانه لریدر

بر قبیل بغضی وباسمه بفویم ادارۀ مجلس مرکزیۀ اعضای منتخبی بندگانه صداقت مدآب سیر والئزه-سندل، ال اشتوجریره داخلنده وکالت همت ماپیدنه نصب و تعیین طرف درسریف نامجاد ریزنده وقوع بوله نخاشیکماه ذه قولودی خاکیای معلا اعضای سیاریه دوسرطنت جدلت غایات همت بناهیده به راسمه تذکر و نکوبی مناسبنده بالكمال خضوع عرض محمدت جرئت ایدرز.

والئ شایالهم سین (والنزه-سندل)، بخلاصۀ ادارۀ عادل و بطرفانۀ سی جیب الکومرته شكلاه چاکرانزك قنائمه اولفنه شایرلیهلك مدت معادره توقفنده اولار ده جنده سنه بمدت دها مقام ولوئزه ایفاسی خصوصه مسعده محاسبه عالیۀ همت سکماندبنك لطفاً برسریع وارزاده بوالمئى كمال نجوح وثنیقله نضرع ایدرز.

نك حب و درداری محبح احرازنجمه اول شایالم (والنزه-سندل)، بیله ایبنك ایجنج بردست ملوی بیل قربی داپیلكده ایعقا بویرجعى تنببیلك عاصه له نك ذبیۀ مذهب وقومت بالمجموم اهالى جزیره لرفنده بغنت شناسان نفقی واردۀ اشتوجریره خفقنده كی كمال جریمۀ الهى همت ماپیدنك شكوه بردیل خیلى عالى عند دوبیجكه خادم مقعد بولنفدوبیز اوسیاسیه دۀ قالبۀ احواله ماروجبنا ولطف فرآوادۀ حضرت همت ماپیدبكدر.

۱۹ حزیران ۱۳۲۷

الداعى
مفتى عجزه قزیسى
على رغب

اعضا
بوراییك بادۀ
سعدى مارسى

اعضا
[imza] محمد

British as he did of his enemies, the gradualists, who were Sendall's closest Cypriot associates, attributed this to the fact that he was 'most popular in Limassol'.⁵³ His name had certainly been elevated there by his prompt and personal attention to the town after the catastrophic flood, and by his efforts for the wine industry, but Limassol was a stronghold of the radical *enotists*, so his popularity there or anywhere else in the island cannot be said to have been politically motivated. Katalanos himself described Limassol schools as following the Greek prototype, whereas, he commented sourly, the Nicosia school was under the regime 'του ραγιαδισμού' (of those who kowtowed).⁵⁴

Before the high commissioner and his lady left for Limassol, Nicosia strove to give them a fitting send-off. This focused appropriately enough on Phaneromeni girls' school. On the day before their departure, the Sendalls were invited there for a special ceremony. The school hall was packed. Pupils and prelates, British officials and legislators jostled for standing room. Familiar faces all around: the Abbot of Kykko, the chief justice, Sir William Smith, who would later join the Sendalls in British Guiana, the reliable Arthur Young, in whose good hands Sir Walter would leave the island, the Heidenstams. Achilleas Liassides read out a resolution in his capacity of mayor of Nicosia, declaring Sir Walter Sendall a great patron of the school. Then Archbishop Sofronios unveiled a column draped in the Hellenic colours. Inscribed on it were the words:

| Ο ΦΙΛΟΜΟΥΣΟΤΑΤΟΣ ΣΕΡ ΟΥΩΛΤΕΡ ΣΕΝΔΑΛ ΜΕΓΑΣ ΑΡΜΟΣΤΗΣ ΤΗΣ ΚΥΠΡΟΥ ΤΟΥΔΕ ΤΟΥ ΤΩΝ ΕΛΛΗΝΙΔΩΝ ΠΑΡΘΕΝΩΝ ΔΙΔΑΣΚΑΛΕΙΟΥ ΕΥΕΡΓΕΤΗΣ ΜΕΓΑΣ | THE FRIEND OF LEARNING SIR WALTER SENDALL A GREAT HIGH COMMISSIONER OF CYPRUS AND A GREAT PATRON OF THE GREEK GIRLS' SCHOOL |

---

53. Katalanos, *Ο Ζήνων*, (Nicosia, 1914), 200.
54. Ibid., 86.

42. A modern Sendall plaque in the entrance hall of Phaneromeni School, replacing the original Sendall column

Loud cheers were followed by 'God Save the Queen' sung in Greek. Sir Walter responded to emotional farewell speeches, emphasising the bright example the school provided. As they left the couple were showered with flowers and farewell gifts.[55] Years later, Sendall's column was placed in an alcove in the grand entrance hall of the new school building completed in 1924. The first Sendall Scholar, Eleni Christou, was still headmistress and remained there until she retired in 1936. Politically incorrect in the atmosphere of the 1950s, the column disappeared. Now a modern plaque has been placed where the column once stood, etched with the same words – an extraordinary tribute to a British governor. There is no record of who attended the gala dinner that evening in the contrastingly English setting of the Nicosia Club, but it is likely that Sir Walter would have made sure that the archbishop, the *mufti* and the Nicosia notables were present, together with the English officials and their wives.[56]

On the eve of their departure from the island, Sir Walter and Lady Sendall climbed for the last time into the ex-Khedival carriage, with its smart white horses, and set out for Limassol. They had been invited to a farewell ceremony at the Victoria Café at 10 o' clock the next morning. The café had been decorated with shields and laurel leaves. It was crowded with Limassolian well-wishers. *Zaptiehs* lined up and raised their swords to create an arch through which the 'popular *archonda*' and his wife were guided, when exactly at ten o'clock they arrived, accompanied by the district commissioner, Roland Michell and Dr. Heidenstam. In a farewell address, the mayor, Ioannis Karageorgiades, tearfully assured the gathering that he was sure the Sendalls would always remember the Cypriots, wherever they went. The Cypriots, and especially the Limassolians, he said, would always remember His Excellency with gratitude. Sendall replied that he and his wife had decided it would not be right to leave Cyprus without visiting Limassol, whose citizens they had, in very unfortunate circumstances, come to know intimately. Schoolgirls presented bouquets on whose ribbons miniature maps of Cyprus and Sendall's name bordered in laurel had been embroidered.[57]

In the afternoon, Sir Walter visited the Limassol girls' school and watched a gymnastics display 'with fatherly appreciation'. The next morning the

---

55. Σάλπιγξ, 26 December, 1897/8 January 1898.
56. Ibid.
57. Ibid.

couple boarded the Austrian Lloyd ship, *Aphrodite,* which flew the Union Jack for the high commissioner. Soldiers (probably all the soldiers) from Polemedia formed a guard of honour, together with the *zaptiehs.* As he disappeared into the crowd on the jetty, hats flew into the air and there were shouts of farewell, 'στο καλό', but as the customs boat pulled out to sea, the crowd fell silent and sad. 'Cyprus wishes them a good journey', this account in Σάλπιγξ, ended, 'and a long and healthy life'.[58]

---

58. Ibid.

43. Labourers working on Acheritou Dam, 1900

EPILOGUE

> *We came to the completed Kouklia dam, a splendid work on the farther side of which the waters are now gathering for the first time. It was curious to see how soon the wild duck have found this new and excellent home, where whole flocks of those beautiful birds now swim.*[1]

So wrote Rider Haggard about his visit to the first new dam to be completed at Kouklia in 1900, just over a year after Sendall's departure.[2] In admiring the excellence of the dam work proceeding and in contemplating the good it would do for the island, he was careful to avoid giving any credit to the successor of his friend, Sir Henry Bulwer. The role of the secretary of state, Joseph Chamberlain, was acknowledged thus

> *To him **and no one else** it is due that the spell of consistent neglect has been broken and that the small sum of £60,000 necessary for the carrying out of these works has been advanced to Cyprus.*[3]

Following suit, Basil Stewart, who toured Cyprus in 1904, dated what little development there had been to the previous six or seven years and attributed them exclusively to the dynamism of the new secretary of state.[4] Most works on the early colonial period in Cyprus pinpoint the arrival of Chamberlain in the Colonial Office as the moment when the island's financial fortunes began to turn in a more positive direction. Hamilton Lang, British consul in Cyprus at the end of Ottoman rule and a fierce critic of the British administration in the 1880s, described Chamberlain as 'the first Colonial Secretary who has had the qualities necessary to treat the question of Cyprus from a business point of view'.[5] Indeed, the Victorian connection with the island seems to have been largely a capitalist venture.[6] The Victorians were such capitalists. What happened in 1895 was a change in tactics. Chamberlain was persuaded that the debt to which

---

1. H. Rider Haggard, *A Winter Pilgrimage*, (London, 1902),148.
2. For an authoritative report on the irrigation works, see J.T. Hutchinson and C.D. Cobham, *Handbook of Cyprus, 1901*, (London 1901), 30-32.
3. Haggard, (1902), 149.
4. Basil Stewart, (1908), 248.
5. 'Cyprus under British Rule', Hamilton Lang KCMG (Ottoman Bank manager in Cyprus, then Constantinople) in *Blackwood's Magazine* No.MXLII, (London and Edinburgh), August 1902.
6. See Diana Markides, 'Bailed in: Strategic financial manoeuvring behind the British acquisition of Cyprus in 1878' (forthcoming).

the British government had committed the island's revenues would best be serviced not only by stringent economy in the way the island was administered, but through modest investment. The island was to be treated as 'an improvable property'. The phrase was used first as regards Cyprus, not by Chamberlain in 1895, but by Sir Walter Sendall in 1893.

Missing from these brief references are the moves made before Chamberlain's arrival on the scene. There is no mention of Sir Robert Wyndham Herbert's special concern at the inadequacies of the administration and the iniquities of 'the Tribute', of his efforts to commute the latter or his move to find and encourage the right man to take over the administration of the island. The material researched for this study indicates that he did find the right man. It was the determination and intelligence brought to bear by the high commissioner in Cyprus to confront the regime proposed by Edward Fairfield and imposed by the Treasury in 1883 that were already producing results between 1893 and 1898. The dextrous manipulation of what few capable staff there were and what little money there was, injected the administration with a confidence in the possibility of growth. The report of the receiver general, Andrew Ashmore, in October 1897, provides a graphic account of the contrasting approaches. In 1895, when he assumed office, regarding collection:

> *No tax collector's district except in Famagusta had been cleared to a later date than March 1885. Every collector carried about with him, packed on a mule, a number of books setting forth all the taxes which ought to have been collected since that date, whether those taxes had been collected or not....The mere mechanical difficulties arising out of these conditions constituted a real hindrance to his work and appreciable sums escaped collection yearly....The first step to be taken was...to write off the books all debts found hopelessly irrecoverable. ....The process of searching old lists, examining the capability to pay of tax-payers imposed much additional work... Of the improvement in collection that has resulted from the process of examination and revision there can be no doubt.*

Regarding the form of taxation:

> *It is in fact less the inability of the tax-payer to meet the amount of the taxes than it is the form in which they have been levied that has*

been the real difficulty......it may surprise the reader to know that there was levied here before the 29 March last an annual tax of 11/3cp a piece on beehives. ..If a man or his wife worked a silk spinning wheel, he had to get a licence to use it and while it was in use, it was sealed up every night before the family went to bed by a petty official and unsealed again to permit work in the morning.[7]

Revenue began to increase after 1895 in spite of the continuing slump in cereal prices worldwide, and rose steadily thereafter. By 1901 revenue had grown so dramatically on 'other heads' that the wine excise was finally abolished. Sendall's discovery of a lucrative market in Hull, the first substantial export of wheat by the government, stood the island in good stead for some years to come. The greatly improved internal communications and the encouragement of shipping boosted the exports to Egypt which, by 1897, was the fastest growing market, taking more or less anything the island would sell.[8]

Dr. George Post, an American professor at the Beirut College, who had known the island in Ottoman times, wrote with enthusiasm after a visit there in 1898, that 'Cyprus is just now an object lesson of the kind of government England can give'.[9] That year, the new high commissioner, Sir William Frederick Haynes Smith, made the only vague official genuflection in Sir Walter's direction. In his inaugural speech to the legislative council, he promised he would try not to do less than his predecessor in the good administration of the island.[10] Within the Colonial Office, there was acknowledgement of the difference Sendall's term had made. Lord Selborne observed in a minute in August 1897, 'Our behaviour in Cyprus up to the advent of the present government was discreditable in the extreme'.[11]

After years of neglect, the speedy improvement in internal communications contributed in all kinds of ways to a better quality of life on the island, but perhaps the most eloquent testimony to that improved quality during Sendall's term, was the greatly reduced crime rate, and more

---

7. A.M. Ashmore, 'Report of the receiver general 'in Draft Annual Report for 1896-1897. An annotation signed by Fairfield asks for the 'paras as to the difficulty in revenue collection to be removed'.
8. Annual Reports for 1897 and 1898 and Jeness, (1962), 171.
9. Jeness, (1971), 90.
10. Σάλπιγξ, 13 April 1898.
11. Minute signed by Lord Selborne, 8 August 1897. He was supporting Sendall's proposals for government investment in a railway. CO67/107, NA.

especially the halving of the number of murders.[12] Not unrelated to these statistics was the growing confidence in the post office. The value of money order transactions carried out had risen abruptly in the last three years.[13] Sendall's penchant for bridge-building created a flurry of construction. The 1897-8 annual report records no less than 30 bridges completed and six underway. Bearing in mind the primitive and diminutive nature of the equipment at the disposal of the Public Works Department at this time, this was an exceptional achievement. A graphic case in point is the absence of road rollers. In 1898, the year of Sir Walter's departure, 23 road rollers were imported into the island.

> Previous to that date the total number of Road Rollers on the island was four, of which two were imported articles and the others of local manufacture from the shafts of antique columns.[14]

It was the high commissioner's continued pressure on Whitehall to increase the public works grant that made this accelerated development possible. Although he did not achieve the fixed annual grant-in-aid he sought, assisted by Chamberlain's own reminders to the Treasury that they actually owed the island the money, he extracted larger grants-in-aid during his term than any other until the sum was finally fixed at £50,000 per annum in 1907. This latter move effectively reduced the Cypriot Tribute by half.

By then, the two further stages of development planned in 1895, the dredging of Famagusta Port and its rail connection to the capital, were in place. World cereal prices soared during World War I and the island flourished as a depot for Britain's armies in the Near East, supplying them, not least, with excellent and indispensable mules. The belated flowering of neoclassical architecture in the island's towns in the aftermath of the war signalled a new modern bourgeois prosperity. But this air of well-being was ephemeral. None of the three major projects born of the Sendall era were successful in the long term. The most soul-destroying feature of the

---

12. Murders: reduction of 50% between 1890 and 1897: 97 murders in 1890 and 49 murders in 1897. See *Annual Report for 1897–1898* presented to both Houses of Parliament in May 1899. [c.- 92887]
13. The value of inland money order transfers rose from £2,555 in 1889 to £8,609 in 1896. By 1898 it had reached £34,290. See 'Statement showing the amount (to the nearest pound) of [post office] money order transactions between 1889 and 1899 in report on the post office, *Annual Report for 1898-1899*, 19.
14. C.V. Bellamy, *A Monograph of the Main Roads of Cyprus*, (Nicosia 1903), 29.

island's financial life, usurious moneylending, remained rampant into the 1930s. The Victorians had worried about, but had not attempted to remedy, the situation. Cash was needed to pay money taxes and moneylenders were a source of cash – expensive cash for the farmers. They vitiated the need to lay aside capital for the agricultural bank sought from time to time by the legislative council.[15] Every available penny was needed for public works.

The Cypriots continued to pay a considerable sum towards the annual interest on the 1855 Crimean War loan to the bondholders for some years after Cyprus ceased being Ottoman territory. The Tribute's belated abolition in 1927 did not prevent the burning down of Government House in the most dramatic protest against British rule four years later. Cypriot resentment then was not essentially about financial management, although it often seemed to be. This first Cypriot revolt brought an end to electoral representation, which had anyway disintegrated into chronic obstructionism. Authoritarian rule, so fashionable throughout Europe in the 1930s, was embellished in 1934 with a purely cosmetic 'Advisory Council',[16] but an elected legislature was never reintroduced. The Cypriot legislative council then would have been in its heyday, in terms of any substantial participation in government in the Sendall years, bearing in mind its activities reported in despatches to London, and described so eloquently by David Hogarth.

It was during Sir Walter's administration that the legislative council came to be perceived as just that, rather than as an 'advisory council', some of its members being appointed, by 1896, to the executive council. After the 1897 elections, a polarisation between gradualist and radical politicians becomes evident. The latter portrayed their opponents as sycophants.

It was a question of politics. Certainly national identity was not an issue. The Greek language and Greek sentiment in Cyprus were taken for granted by the British in the nineteenth century as they were by the 'natives'. Colonial correspondence on the affairs of Cyprus frequently uses the words 'Greek' and 'Turk' to describe the inhabitants of the island; in

---

15. The funds for small works of agricultural development raised from the Field Watchman's tax introduced at the end of the Bulwer era, were referred to then as 'The Agricultural Bank', but a bank was not established. These funds were used in 1897 to subsidise the mail service and subsequently included in the new Public Development Fund.
16. George Georghallides and Diana Markides, 'Constitution-making in post-1931 Cyprus'.

contrast to diplomatic correspondence on the affairs of Crete. On the latter island a substantial threat to the status quo was perceived, therefore great care is taken to use the words 'Christian' and 'Mussulman'. The Turkish flag was flown by Cypriot merchantmen to signify the status of the island. Turkish, British and Greek flags festooned the end of the pier at the ceremony organised to welcome the Sendalls back from leave in January 1896, just as all three flags had flown over Larnaca racecourse in 1879. In the early 1900s, Haggard and Basil Stewart complained bitterly of the ubiquitous presence of the Greek flag all over the island. Sendall made no reference to such things in his correspondence with London. No threat was posed.

Indeed, careful scrutiny of the official correspondence on Cyprus in the 1890s indicates a far greater British concern with the problems created by the awkward cohabitation of a colonial administration with an Ottoman *de jure*, if not *de facto*, jurisdiction. This concern was exacerbated by the Porte's repeated attempts to assert rights within the island. 'I think this is a try on the part of the Turks to establish a right to give instructions to the Government of Cyprus', grumbled Fairfield, on receiving a complaint about the export from the island of antiquities. This complaint, he claimed, was the result of the Sultan keeping 'a sort of unofficial envoy on the island to spy on us'.[17] He was referring to the *cadi*, the manner of whose appointment was so problematical in 1895. The fact that Sendall was careful to underline, in his response to this complaint, that the Cyprus government was guided entirely by the Ottoman law 20 Sefer (24 March 1874) on these matters reflected the importance to the British government as well, of maintaining the legal status quo within the island and indeed within the region. As Sendall left Cyprus, a British-led international force would be supervising the withdrawal of Ottoman forces from Crete while being very careful to emphasise the continuing suzerainty of the Sultan over that island. In both cases the status quo had to be maintained by keeping a careful balance between reassurances to the Christian population that their religious and cultural credentials were not in danger, and reassurances to the Porte that the islands remained Turkish.

Far from rejoicing at the removal of the British forces from the island at the beginning of 1895, the Christian Cypriots were *dismayed*. In fact,

---

17. Minute, Fairfield, 22 September 1892, File 18931 headed 'Exploration of Antiquities', CO67/77, NA.

manifestations of Hellenism increased that year *because* of the withdrawal of the garrison. The purpose was to emphasise the *non*-Ottoman nature of most of the inhabitants in a bid to avoid retrocession to the Porte, which was the greatest fear. Sir Walter's efforts to achieve official British investment in the island were intended precisely to demonstrate that the British were there to stay. These moves towards a more collaborative relationship between governors and governed would begin to be undone by both Cypriots and British after Sendall's departure. The *political* need then of the radicals to demonstrate the nauseatingly collaborative nature of their opponents would lead to less constructive work on legislation and more obstructionism. In the context of *fin de siècle* Greek irredentism, the language of party conflict would increasingly provoke competitive nationalism. Succeeding high commissioners, anyway less inclined to mix with 'the natives', withdrew once more into their ivory towers.

Rider Haggard, writing in 1901, observed that 'in practice, the island is inhabited by two classes only. Between these a great gulf is fixed'. The Cypriots would have agreed with him about the latter. Sendall, a compulsive bridge-builder, was different. Φωνή της Κύπρου (Phoni tis Kyprou) spelt out the difference.

> With him they are able to make themselves understood as, through him, the chasm that existed between rulers and subject and kept those two elements in perpetual misunderstanding has been removed.[18]

The Greek Cypriot historian, Filios Zanettos, writing in the first decade of the twentieth century, considered this his greatest achievement and stressed that Sendall reached out to both communities, a fact borne out by the eloquent petition to the British government signed by the Christian and Moslem leaders of the island for his reappointment.[19]

In governing Hellenic peoples across the Eastern Mediterranean, the British generally have never been so popular as when they are about to depart – *because* they are about to depart. This was not true of the British garrison at Polemedia in 1895 and it was even less true of Sir Walter Sendall.

---

18. Φωνή της Κύπρου, 3 January 1896.
19. Zanettos, 966.

Appendix I

Poem by Vassilis Michaelides
ΤΩ ΑΡΜΟΣΤΗ ΣΕΡ ΟΥΩΛΤΕΡ ΣΕΝΤΑΛ

Ἄν πῆς πὼς δὲν ἔχ'εις καλὴν
καρδκιὰν ἀπὸ τὲς πρῶτες,
λησμονημένον νὰ σὲ δῶ
ἀποὺ τοὺς Κ΄υπριῶτες.

Ἄν ἔν κατάρα ποὺ λαλῶ,
χάρον μου νἄχω τὸν γιαλόν.

Ὅπου κ΄ι' ἄν πᾶς, κ΄αὶ ν' ἀρνηθῆς
τὴν Κ΄ύπρουν, δὲν σ' ἀρνιέται,
γιατ' ἔκαμες κ'' ἕναν καλόν,
ποὺ δὲν ἀλλησμονιέται.

Ἀρνιέσαι το πῶς εἶσ'ἐσοὺ
ὁ γλυτωμὸς τῆς Λεμεσοῦ;

Μακἄρι κ΄ι' ὄπκοιος σὲ μισᾶ
νὰ μὲν καλοκαρτίσῃ·
σὰν σίδερον μέσ' στὸ λαμπρὸν
μέσ' στοὺς καμοὺς νὰ λύσῃ·.

Νἄν' ἡ χαρά του οἱ καμοὶ
κ΄αὶ ἡ ζωή του σταλαμή.

Ὅπου κ΄ι' ἄν πᾶς, οἱ στράτες σου
νἄν δάφνη κ΄αὶ μερσίνι(ν)·
κ'' ὅπου πατᾶς νὰ πλάσκουνται
τριαντάφυλλα κ΄αὶ κρίνοι.

Κ΄αὶ νἄν τὰ χρόνια σου πολλὰ
κ΄αὶ ἡ καρδκιά σου νὰ γελᾶ.

Ἡ Κ΄ύπρου ἐν νὰ σὲ διψᾶ
γιὰ τὴν καλὴν καρδκιάν σου
κ΄αὶ γιὰ δροσ΄ιὰν στὸ στόμαν της
ἐννά 'χ΄η τὄνομάν σου,

νὰ τὸ λαλῆ παντοτινὰ
κ΄αὶ ν' ἀδονοῦσιν τὰ βουνά.

Appendix I

Translation
THE HIGH COMMISSIONER, SIR WALTER SENDALL

*If you say that you don't have
A good heart, among the best,
May you be forgotten
By the Cypriots*

*If it is a curse that I sing
Let me die at sea.*

*Wherever you go,
Even if you deny Cyprus,
Cyprus won't deny you
Because you have done
The best of deeds
That won't be forgotten.*

*Do you deny that you
Are the saviour of Limassol?*

*May whoever hates you
Fare ill,
Like iron in the fire.
May he be lost in misery.*

*Let his joy be sorrow
And his life be brief.*

*Wherever you go, let the way
Be strewn with daphne and laurel,
And where you tread let there be
Roses and lilies*

*And let your years be many
And your heart be glad.*

*Cyprus will thirst
For your good heart
And will be ever refreshed
At the sound of your name.*

*It will be sung forever
And echo in the hills.*

Note: Greek text is taken from Βασίλης Μιχαηλίδης, Ποιήματα, (Limassol Municipal Council: Limassol 1972), 63. The poem was translated by Diana Markides with the help of Sophocles Markides and Eleni Mollinson.

Vassilis Michaelides is often referred to as Cyprus's national bard. He was born in Lefkoniko in about 1860. Settling in Limassol after the British occupation, he worked for the newspapers *Αλήθεια* and *Σάλπιγξ*. He wrote in *katharevousa* and demotic Greek, but also in Cypriot dialect.

Among his poems the best known are *The Ninth of July 1821*, *Chiotissa* and *Anerada* (Fairy). He died a penniless alcoholic in 1917.

Appendix I

Poem by Demetris Libertis

ΤΗ Α.Ε. ΤΩ Μ. ΑΡΜΟΣΤΗ ΣΙΡ ΟΥΩΛΤΕΡ ΣΕΝΔΑΛ

Ἄς προστεθῇ ἕν ὄνομα στήν Ἱστορίαν ἔτι
Ὡς τῶν στηλῶν της κόσμημα, ἀθάνατόν τι ῥῆμα,
Νά μή τό φθείρῃ ὡς ἡμᾶς, ὁ χρόνος καί τά ἔτη·
Νά εἶναι ἐπ' ἀόριστον εὐγνωμοσύνης δεῖγμα
Ὅλων ἡμῶν καί μεθ' ἡμᾶς τῶν μεταγενεστέρων
Τό μεγαλεῖον παριστῶν, τό ὄνομα γεραῖρον.

Οἱ δέ μεταγενέστεροι ὡς θά φυλλολογῶσι
Να ἴδωσι το κόσμημα αὐτό τῆς Ἱστορίας,
Ἀπό τοῦ βάθους τῆς ψυχῆς δάκρυα θ' ἀποσπῶσι
Καί ὑπέρ Σοῦ θά πέμπωσι τῷ Πλάστῃ εὐλογίας,
Ἐπί τῷ ὅτι ἡ Πατρίς ἡ ταλαιπωρουμένη
Οἶδεν ἡμέρας εὐτυχεῖς εἰς Σέ ἐρειδομένη.

Ὦ, ναί. Τό χεῖλος καθενός εὐχάς θά ψιθυρίζῃ,
Πᾶσα καρδία ὑπέρ Σοῦ θά πάλλῃ αἰωνίως,
Τό Ὄνομά Σου συμπαθῶς ἡ μνήμη θά λικνίζῃ.
Ὄντως θά εἶναι ἄληκτος ὁ ἰδικός σου βίος,
Ἀφοῦ ἐργάτης ἀγαθός τῆς Κύπρου ἀνεφάνης
Δέ θ' ἀποθάνῃς, Ἁρμοστά, ποτέ δέν θ' ἀποθάνῃς.

Appendix I

Translation

TO H.E. THE H. COMMISSIONER SIR WALTER SENDALL

Let another name be added to the annals of history
A jewel in its verses, an immortal word,
Not to be consumed like us, by time and years.
To be forever proof of our gratitude
And of those who come after
Seeing the nobility, honouring the name

And our descendants leafing through our history
Will come upon this jewel.
It will draw tears from the depth of their souls
And they will thank God for you.
Our troubled Fatherland
Knew happy days because of you.

Oh, yes. On all our lips, blessings will softly sound
Every heart will always beat for you
Affectionately in our memories you will lie.
Truly you will be immortal
Because you appeared out of the blue to work for Cyprus,
You will be immortal, Commissioner. You will never die.

Note: The Greek text is taken from Σάλπιγξ, December 1897. It was translated into English by Diana Markides with the help of Sophocles Markides and Eleni Mollinson.

Demetris Libertis (1866–1937). If Michaelides was the national bard of Cyprus, Libertis was the poet; he was born in Larnaca, working in later years as a teacher of French and English at the Pancyprian Gymnasium and the English School. He wrote in *katharevousa*, demotic Greek and Cypriot dialect. His four-volume work "Cypriot Songs" has received international acclaim.

Appendix II

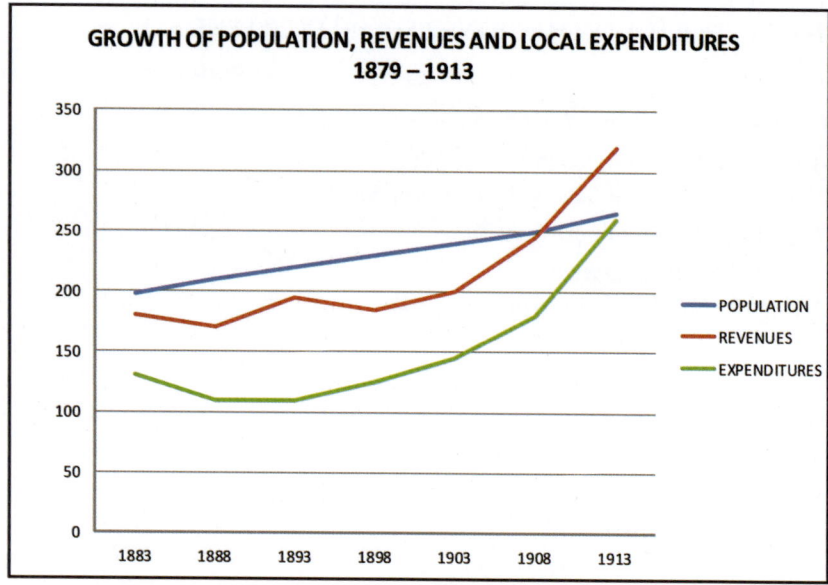

50. Source: Diamond Jeness, *The Economics of Cyprus*, 157

GLOSSARY

archondas	notable, member of leading family
bey	title accorded to a man of rank
cadi/kadi	Muslim judge, interpreter of the law appointed by the Sultan
enotist	person or group who desires and promotes union with Greece
ethnarch	leader of the millet
Evkaf	Islamic pious foundation
Ethniki Etairia	'National Society' formed in Greece in 1878 to promote the incorporation of areas of the Ottoman Empire which held large Greek-speaking populations into the Hellenic kingdom
gymnasium	Greek high school
high commissioner	between 1878 and 1925, when Cyprus was *de jure* part of the Ottoman empire, the governor of the island was termed 'high commissioner'. After it became a crown colony in 1925, he was termed 'governor'
Hadji/Haci	added to the name of someone who has been on the Hadj/Hac (pilgrimage to Mecca). Also added to the name of Christians who had been on a pilgrimage to Jerusalem
i'dade	Muslim high school
ilam	edict
indaba	word from the Natal meaning council
khan	Ottoman inn with stabling for animals
Büyük khan	was 'the great inn' in the centre of Nicosia
klepht	bandit romanticized during the Greek revolution
konak	a large house. It became the term for the residence and office of the Ottoman governor of the area and during British rule, the district office
medjli/mecli idare	Ottoman district council
mesaoria	the central plain of Cyprus. Literally, the plain between two mountain ranges
millet	confessional communities within the Ottoman empire

GLOSSARY

mouhassebedji	accountant general
mukhtar/muhta	headman of the village or quarter of a town. In towns he was also known as *mahalledjis*
mudir	governor of a *nahir*/sub-district in Cyprus and elsewhere in the Ottoman Empire
mufti/muftu	interpreter of the law. The mufti issued *fetvas* or rulings on difficult issues
raya	Ottoman term for non-muslim subjects
rusty'e	Muslim middle school
tekke	Muslim shrine
vakouf/vakf	a trust of property set up by a relative for minors or donated to *Efkav*
verghi kimat	tax on landed property
zaptieh	Ottoman policeman. The term continued into British rule

BIBLIOGRAPHY

ARCHIVAL SOURCES

The National Archives of the United Kingdom at Kew
CO67 Original Correspondence, Cyprus. NA
CO179 Original Correspondence, Natal. NA

State Archives of the Republic of Cyprus
SA1 files CSA
V1 files CSA

University of Birmingham Library
Joseph Chamberlain Collection JC UBL

The British Museum General Archives (BMA)

The National Portrait Gallery Archive (Gallery Records)

Gennadius Library Athens
John Gennadius Archive JGA GL

British Library
Manuscript Collection (Additional Papers)
Dilke Papers, Add.43914 BL
Ripon Papers, Add.43564 BL

House of Representatives of the Republic of Cyprus
Minutes of the Legislative Council 1886–1898 MLC

Courtesy of David Dew
Unpublished diary of Frederick Alexander Breul, a young subaltern with the company of Gloucesters garrisoned at Polemedia, courtesy of his grandson, David Dew. The diary covers the years 1895-1896

NEWSPAPERS

Britain
The Times

Cyprus
Αλήθεια (Alithia)
Ένωσις (Enosis)
Φωνή της Κύπρου (Phoni tis Kyprou)
Σάλπιγξ (Salpinx)
The Cyprus Herald
The Times of Cyprus
The Owl
Kıbrıs (Cyprus)

BIBLIOGRAPHY

PUBLISHED OFFICIAL SOURCES

London
Hansard Debates

House of Commons Parliamentary Papers

[c-3661] *Memorandum on the Finances and Administration of Cyprus, Edward Fairfield, June 1882, Enclosure No.1 in Papers relating to the Administration and Finances of Cyprus presented to Parliament June 1883*

[c-277] *Cyprus (Enforced Sales): A return showing enforced sales of property in the island of Cyprus for the years 1887, 1888, 1889 (a) at the instance of the island government (b) at the instance of Private Creditors*

[c-5251] *Cyprus: Annual Report for the Year 1886–1887*
[c-5749] *Cyprus: Annual Report for the Year 1887–1888*
[c-6189] *Cyprus: Annual Report for the Year 1888–1889*
[c-6764] *Cyprus: Annual Report for the Year 1889–1890*
[c-6764] *Cyprus: Annual Report for the Year 1890–1891*
[c-7053] *Cyprus: Annual Report for the Year 1891–1892*
[c-7411] *Cyprus: Annual Report for the Year 1892–1893*
[c-7876] *Cyprus: Annual Report for the Year 1893–1894*
[c-8076] *Cyprus: Annual Report for the Year 1894–1895*
[c-8580] *Cyprus: Annual Report for the Year 1895–1896*
[c-8805] *Cyprus: Annual Report for the Year 1896–1897*
[c-9288] *Cyprus: Annual Report for the Year 1897–1898*
[cd-227] *Cyprus: Annual Report for the Year 1898–1899*
[cd-510] *Cyprus: Annual Report for the Year 1899–1900*

Cyprus

The Cyprus Gazette 1883-1898
(The Government Printing Office: Nicosia 1899)

Report on the Census of Cyprus taken on 6 April 1891
(The Government Printing Office: Nicosia 1891)

Report on the Census of Cyprus taken on 6 April 1901
(The Government Printing Office: Nicosia 1901)

C.V. Bellamy, *A Monograph of the Main Roads of Cyprus*
(The Government Printing Office: Nicosia 1903)

BIBLIOGRAPHY

Books and Journal Articles

Bağışkan, Tuncer, *Ottoman, Islamic and Islamised Monuments in Cyprus,* (Cyprus Turkish Education Foundation: Nicosia 2009).
Blakely, Brian L., *The Colonial Office 1886–1892,* (Duke University Press: Durham N.C. 1972).
Bryant, Rebecca, *Imagining the Modern, The Cultures of Nationalism in Cyprus,* (I.B. Tauris: London 2004).
Coudounaris, Aristides, *Βιογραφικόν Λεξικόν Κυπρίων,* (Biographical Dictionary of Cypriots) (Nicosia 2010).
Dakin, Douglas, *The Unification of Greece,* (Ernest Benn: London 1972). *The Greek Struggle in Macedonia, 1897-1913,* (Institute of Balkan Studies: Thessaloniki 1993).
Deschamps, Emile, *Στην Κύπρο, τη Χώρα της Αφροδίτης,* (In Cyprus, the Land of Aphrodite) Greek language edition (Laiki Group Cultural Centre: Nicosia 2005).
Duckworth, T.F., *Some Pages of Levantine History,* (Alexander Moring Ltd.: London, 1906).
Enlart, Camille, (translated and edited by David Hunt), *Gothic Art and the Renaissance in Cyprus,* (Trigraph: London 1987) after the original *L' Art Gothique et la Renaissance en Chypre,* (Ernest Leroux: Paris 1899).
Garvin, J.L., *Life of Joseph Chamberlain,* Vol. III., (Macmillan: London 1934).
Georghallides, George and Diana Markides, 'Constitution-making in post-1931 Cyprus', *Journal of Modern Greek Studies,* Vol.13, Number 1, May 1995, 63–83.
Grey, Jeff, *The Destruction of the Zulu Kingdom: The Civil War in Zululand, 1879-1884,* (Longman: London 1979).
Hadjiyiasemi, Androulla, *Lefkara Lace Embroidery,* (Ch.J. Philipides & Son Ltd.: Nicosia 1987).
Haggard Rider, H., *The Days of My Life,* (Longman Green: London 1926), *A Winter Pigrimage: being an account of travels through Palestine, Italy, and the island of Cyprus, accomplished in the year 1900,* (Longman: London 1900)
Harfield, Alan ed., *The Life and Times of A Victorian Officer: Journals of Benjamin Donisthorpe Alsop Donne,* (The Wincanton Press: Wincanton 1986).
Hill, George, *A History of Cyprus,* Vol. IV, (Cambridge University Press: Cambridge 1975).
Hogarth, David, *A Wandering Scholar in the Levant,* (London: John Murphy 1896).
Holland, Robert and Diana Markides, *The British and the Hellenes: Struggles for Mastery in the Eastern Mediterranean 1859-1960,* (Oxford University Press: Oxford 2006).
Hook, Ruth, 'Britons in Cyprus 1878–1914', Ph.D. Dissertation, (University of Texas at Austin, August 2009).
Hutchinson, J.T. and C.D. Cobham, *Handbook of Cyprus, 1901,* (Waterloo and Sons: London 1901).

BIBLIOGRAPHY

Jenness, Diamond, *The Economics of Cyprus: A survey to 1914*, (McGill University Press: Montreal 1962).

Katalanos, Nicolaos, *Ο Ζήνων*, (Zeno), (Nicosia 1914).

Katsiaounis, Rolandos, *Labour, Society and Politics in Cyprus during the Second Half of the Nineteenth Century*, (Cyprus Research Centre: Nicosia 1996).

Kitromilides, Paschalis, 'Greek Irridentism in Asia Minor and Cyprus', *Middle Eastern Studies*, Series 26, Vol. I, 7-8.

Kubicek, Robert, *The Administration of Imperialism: Joseph Chamberlain at the Colonial Office*, (Duke University Press: Durham, N.C.1969).

Lang, Sir H. Hamilton, KCMG, 'Cyprus under British Rule', in *Blackwood's Magazine* No. MXLII, August 1902 (London and Edinburgh: William Blackwood and Sons).

Lewis, Elizabeth Alicia M., *A Lady's Impression of Cyprus*, (Remington: London 1894). 'A Reformation of Domestic Service', *The Nineteenth Century*, Vol. XXXIII, January-June 1893.

Longford, Elizabeth, *Jameson's Raid: The Prelude to the Boer War*, (Weidenfeld and Nicolson: London 1982).

Madella, Albert T., *The Cyprus Sea Post Office* 1906-1932, (Limassol - no date).

MacFarlan, Bill, *The Hunt for the Hasamboulia*, (Gitano: Nicosia 2007).

Markides, Diana, 'Cyprus 1878–1925: Ambiguities and Uncertainties', Faustmann and Peristianis eds., *Britain in Cyprus: Colonialism and Post-Colonialism 1878-2006*, (Bibliopolis: Mannheim Möhnesee 2006). 'Nicosia under British Rule', Demetris Michaelides ed. *Historic Nicosia*, (Rimal Publications: Nicosia 2012).

Medlicott, W.N., 'The Gladstone Government and the Cyprus Convention, 1880-1885', *The Journal of Modern History*, Vol. XII, (June 1940).

Merrillees, Robert S., *The First Cyprus Museum*, (Moufflon Publications: Nicosia 2005).

Michaelides, Agni, *Η Χώρα: Η Παλιά Λευκωσία*, (Old Nicosia) (Nicosia 1985).

Morgan, Tabitha, *Sweet and Bitter Island: A History of the British in Cyprus*, (I.B. Tauris: London 2010).

Packenham, Thomas, *The Boer War*, (Weidenfeld and Nicolson: London 1979).

Papapolyviou, Petros, *Φαεινόν Σημείον Ατυχούς Πολέμου*, (A Bright Interlude in an Unfortunate War), (Cyprus Research Centre: Nicosia 2001).

Pilides, Despina, *George Jeffery : His Diaries and the Ancient Monuments of Cyprus*, (Department of Antiquities, Government of Cyprus: Nicosia 2009, Vol. II).

Sant Cassia, Paul, 'Better Occasional Murders than Frequent Adulteries: Discourses on Banditry, Violence and Sacrifice in the Mediterranean' in Fernando Skurski and Julie Ann Arbor eds., *States of Violence*, (University of Michigan Press: Michigan 2006).

Schaar, Kenneth W., Michael Given and George Theocharous, *Under the Clock*, (Bank of Cyprus: Nicosia 1995).

Severis, Rita, T*he Swedes in Cyprus*, (Cyprus Research Centre: Nicosia 2008).

BIBLIOGRAPHY

Stewart, Basil, *My Experiences of Cyprus*, (Routledge: New York 1908).

Tatton-Brown, Veronica, ed., *Cyprus in the 19th Century AD: Fact, Fancy and Fiction*, (Oxbow Books: Oxford 2001).

Tserkezis, Savvas, *Ημερολόγιον του Βίου μου*, (Diary of My Life), (Marfin Laiki Cultural Centre: Nicosia 2007).

Varnava, Andrekos, *British Imperialism in Cyprus: 1878-1915: The Inconsequential Possession*, (Manchester University Press: Manchester 2009).

Volonaki, Michael, *Η Εκπαίδευσις εν Κύπρω από της Αγγλικής Κατοχής 1878-1912*, (Education in Cyprus since the British Occupation), (Τυπογραφείου Μιχ. Μαντζεβελάκη: Athens 1913).

Yiannoulopoulos, Yiannis, *Η Ευγενής μας τύφλωσις*, (Our Polite Blindness), (Βιβλιογράμμα: Athens 1999).

Wright, Arnold, *Twentieth Century Impressions of Ceylon: Its History, People and Commerce*, (Asian Educational Services: Sri Lanka 1999).

Zanettos, Filios, *Ιστορία της Νήσου Κύπρου*, (History of the Island of Cyprus), Vol. II, (Larnaca 1911).

ILLUSTRATIONS AND CREDITS

Frontispiece: **Sir Walter Sendall,** marble bust in the National Portrait Gallery, sculpted in 1902 by Edward Lanteri (NPG4859). It is exhibited in Room 23

1. **Larnaca, view from the harbour, 1880s** (J.P. Foscolo photograph, Andreas Malecos ed., *Cyprus of J.P. Foscolo*, Cultural Centre Cyprus Popular Bank, Nicosia 1992)

2. **Henry Bulwer's family coat of arms,** (*ex-libris* in a Government House library book, Stavros G. Lazarides, *Souvenir of Famagusta*, The Popular Bank Cultural Centre, Nicosia 1999, 136)

3. **Portrait of Sir Robert Wyndham Herbert,** Permanent Under-Secretary of State for the Colonies: 1871–1892 and for the first few months of Chamberlain's government in 1895. He was the brother of Elizabeth Alicia Lewis (Wikipedia/Wikimedia Commons)

4. **Kyrenia harbour showing the extended mole,** (by Camille Enlart, who visited Cyprus in 1896, photograph courtesy of Haris Yiakoumis, Kallimages, Paris)

5. **The church of Ayios Georgios at Exo Metochi in the Mesaoria plain,** (anonymous, ca. 1905, courtesy of Haris Yiakoumis, Kallimages, Paris)

6. **Gerassimos, Abbot of Kykko 1845-1911,** (Achilleas Lymbourides, *Το Πολύκροτο Αρχιεπισκοπικό Ζήτημα της Κύπρου*, 1900-1910)

7 **Diagram of a wine jar more suitable for tax assessment,** drawn by Sendall (CO67/77, National Archive, Kew)

8. **Potters at Phini,** originally entitled 'Cyprus - Phini women making chatties' (J.P. Foscolo photograph, Andreas Malecos ed., *Cyprus of J.P. Foscolo*, Cultural Centre Cyprus Popular Bank, Nicosia 1992)

9. **The Büyük Khan,** used as a central prison until the new building in Ayios Andreas was completed (Archduke Louis Salvator of Austria, *Levkosia. The Capital of Cyprus*. London 1881, reprinted London 1983; original German edition, Prague 1873, 51)

10. **Sketch of Nicosia Main Drain, 1896,** (SA1:1695/189, courtesy of the State Archive of the Republic of Cyprus)

11. **Sir Walter and Lady Sendall with Phaneromeni School board, girls and staff, 1894,** (J.P. Foscolo photograph, courtesy of The Leventis Municipal Museum of Nicosia)

12. **The road from Kyrenia,** (anonymous, ca.1900, courtesy of Haris Yiakoumis, Kallimages, Paris)

13. **Archbishop Sofronios,** (Achilleas Lymbourides, *Το Πολύκροτο Αρχιεπισκοπικό Ζήτημα της Κύπρου*, 1900-1910)

ILLUSTRATIONS AND CREDITS

14. **Government House, Nicosia, in Sendall's time,** (J.P. Foscolo photograph, Andreas Malecos ed., *Cyprus of J.P. Foscolo*, Cultural Centre Cyprus Popular Bank, Nicosia 1992)

15. **Nicosia within the walls: A khan behind the St. Sophia/Selemiye mosque,** (by Camille Enlart, 1896, photograph courtesy of Haris Yiakoumis, Kallimages, Paris)

16. **Zaptiehs in Famagusta, 1897,** (J.P. Foscolo photograph, courtesy of The Leventis Municipal Museum of Nicosia)

17. **View of Limassol from SS Jumna,** (J.P. Foscolo photograph, Andreas Malecos ed., *Cyprus of J.P. Foscolo*, Cultural Centre Cyprus Popular Bank, Nicosia 1992)

18. **Limassol after the flood,** (from the journal *Black and White*, 19 January 1895)

19. **The Djami Jedit mosque in Limassol before the 1894 flood,** (*The Graphic*, 12 February 1888)

20. **The minaret of the same mosque being demolished by bluejackets from the HMS Arethusa,** (J.P. Foscolo photograph, Andreas Malecos ed., *Cyprus of J.P. Foscolo*, Cultural Centre Cyprus Popular Bank, Nicosia 1992)

21. **The bridge over the river Garrylis built immediately after the 1894 flood** (Altay Sayil's collection). The last three photographs all in Ozay and Selcuk Akif, *Echoes from the Past*. (Terra Cypria, The Cyprus Conservation Foundation, 2008, 39-42)

22. **SS Jumna,** (builder's model, scale 1:48, Merseyside Maritime Museum Collections)

23. **Achilleas Liassides,** (Achilleas Lymbourides, *Το Πολύκροτο Αρχιεπισκοπικό Ζήτημα της Κύπρου*,1900 -1910)

24. **Limassol demonstration in April 1895,** (J.P. Foscolo photograph published in *The Graphic*, June 1895, Tassos A. Andreou collection)

25. **Silted Famagusta port, ca.1897,** (J.P. Foscolo photograph, Andreas Malecos ed., *Cyprus of J.P. Foscolo*, Cultural Centre Cyprus Popular Bank, Nicosia 1992)

26. **Ayios Loukas fair at Famagusta, 18 October1898,** (by an unknown photographer, courtesy of The Leventis Municipal Museum of Nicosia)

27. **Joseph Chamberlain's related political and imperial ambitions,** (cartoon by Harry Firness in J. Enoch Powell, *Joseph Chamberlain*, Thames and Hudson: London 1977, 114-115)

28. **Portrait of Sir Walter Sendall,** (etching in *Westminster Budget*, 23 August 1895)

29. **Doodle composed by Edward Fairfield,** while minuting Sendall's urgent pleas for bridge-building material (CO67/99, NA)

ILLUSTRATIONS AND CREDITS

30. **Peristerona bridge, completed in 1897,** (photograph by F. Fillipos, 2008)

31. **Tennis in the garden at Government Cottage, Troodos,** (J.P. Foscolo photograph, Andreas Malecos ed., *Cyprus of J.P. Foscolo*, Cultural Centre Cyprus Popular Bank, Nicosia 1992)

32. **Entrance to the Konak or Serai in Nicosia,** as drawn by Camille Enlart in 1896, in *Gothic Art and the Renaissance in Cyprus, Camille Enlart*, translated and edited by David Hunt (Trigraph, London, in association with the A.G. Leventis Foundation, 1987) after the original *L' Art Gothique et la Renaissance en Chypre* (Ernest Leroux: Paris, 1899, 395)

33. **Carting antiquities away from Idalion,** (J.P. Foscolo photograph, courtesy of Andreas Coutas)

34. **Dr. Carl von Heidenstam in front of the church built for the leper colony with funds raised by Lady Sendall;** original handwritten caption is "Dr. Heidenstam at the leper farm 1906", Costas and Rita Severis collection, *The Swedes in Cyprus*, (Cyprus Research Centre: Nicosia 2008)

35. **Stamps issued in 1894,** considered especially beautiful because of the new two-tone colour printing. Taken from Hermes St. Frangoudis, *Catalogue of Cyprus Stamps and Postal History 1845-2002,* (Athens 2003)

36. **Athletes who participated in the Pancyprian Games in Limassol in 1897,** (J.P. Foscolo photograph from Tassos A. Andreou, *Λεμεσός Μνήμης*, Nostos: Limassol 2009)

37. **Evelthon Schizas, a Cypriot volunteer in the 1897 Greek-Turkish War,** (Petros Papapolyviou, *Φαεινόν Σημείον Ατυχούς Πολέμου*, Cyprus Research Centre: Nicosia 2001, 433)

38. **Kykko Monastery,** (J.P. Foscolo photograph, Andreas Malecos ed., *Cyprus of J.P. Foscolo*, Cultural Centre Cyprus Popular Bank, Nicosia 1992)

39. **Sketch of the Victoria Scholarship Medal drawn by Sir Walter Sendall,** (CO67/1, NA)

40. **Zaptiehs participating in Jubilee celebrations in London, 1897,** (etching in *The Illustrated London News*, 27 June 1897)

41. **Petition to Queen Victoria in Greek and Ottoman Turkish script by Christian and Muslim leaders,** asking for Sir Walter Sendall to be granted a second term as High Commissioner (CO67/107, NA)

42. **A modern Sendall plaque,** now in the entrance hall of Phaneromeni School, replacing the original Sendall column which disappeared long ago (photograph 2014)

43. **Labourers working on Acheritou dam,** 1900 (H. Rider Haggard, *A Winter Pilgrimage*, 149)

WATERCOLOURS & DRAWINGS - *Thelma Blatchford*

1892: Page 12. *Δουκάνη* (threshing board). This and all agricultural implements shown are from the Fikardou Village Rural Museum, Cyprus

1893: Page 28. *Δουκάνη, λουρικός και ζυγός (threshing board, harness and yoke)*
Page 52. **Anglican Church of St.Paul's**, Nicosia
Page 53. *Φύτη* (Phyti) embroidery. Cotton *σεντόνι* (cover or sheet) woven in typically *Φύδκιωτικο* design, from Cyprus Folk Museum, Nicosia.
Page 58. The Secretariat and Legislative Council Hall

1894: **Page 74. Detail of one of the oldest lefkaritika cutwork (kopta) designs** representing the river *(potamos)* on the edge of the cloth. There are many different designs for the *potamos*, which was always the main feature of the old *lefkaritika*. This one is known as *klonotos monos*. To form the design, threads are cut and removed from the warp and weft of the cloth and then bound in overstitch. Detail taken from *Lefkara Lace Embroidery*

1895: Page 102. *Αλέτρι* (plough) and *στρατούρι* (wooden frame for pack animals)

1896: Page 132. **Early Cypriote (2,600-2,300 BC) cult vessel**. Red polished ware, from Vouni, in City of Birmingham Museum and Art Gallery (as shown in 'Footprints of Cyprus', edited by Sir David Hunt (Trigraph: London 1982)
Page 151. North-east corner of the central prison, Nicosia (drawn March 2012)
Page 156. Government Printing Office completed in 1896 (drawn March 2012)
Page 158. *Rusty'e i'dade* school: Entrance to former Muslim high school, now used as a handicraft centre (drawn March 2012)

1897: Page 170. *Φύτη* (Phyti) embroidery (detail)

End page: *Θερνάκι* (wooden shovel used for winnowing grain) and *Διχάλια* (pitchforks)

INDEX

Abdul Hamid II, Sultan of the Ottoman Empire (1876-1909), 108, n.12 and *vakoufs*, 66 and land claims, 81, poem in praise of, 179 and punitive pogrom against Armenians, 188

Antiquities: 19th century selling of artifacts linked to archaeological digs; Bulwer's collection (Fitzwilliam Museum, Cambridge) and the Bulwer Tablet etched in Cypro-syllabic script, (British Museum); British Museum excavations in 1890s and first cataloguing of Cyprus Museum collection; new legal structure for antiquities proposed, a small subsidy sought from London for Cyprus Museum; fine for illicit digging increased, 159; attempts to restrict antiquities leaving Cyprus were stalled as a result of British Museum influence, 164; new Cypriot awareness, especially in legislature, of need to protect ancient heritage, 165

Ashmore, Andrew, receiver general in Cyprus, 204-5

Attaoullah, Pasha, Mehmet, chief *cadi*, 156-7, 179

Bennett, William, chief clerk, Cyprus, 93

Besant, Walter, novelist and historian, friend of Sendall, 26

Biddulph, Sir Robert, high commissioner and C.-in-C., Cyprus, 1879-1886, 19

Bovill, Sir Elliott, attorney general, in Cyprus, 55

Bowen, Sir George, retired colonial administrator, 27, 46, 49, 75, 191

Breul, Frederick Alexander, subaltern; diary of, 145, 147

British Museum, see under Antiquities

Brown, Samuel, chief engineer, 21, and Kyrenia harbour works, 31; and proposal to dam Garrylis, 97; and 'Alexandria spending ring', 21, n.18, 149

Bulwer, Sir Henry, high commissioner, Cyprus, 1886-92, 16-21; 24 n.26 and 26, 30, 35, 42, 53 and n.40, 55, 57 and n.53 and 54, 80, 93, 126, 138, 149, 184, 203; and 'do nothing policy', 14 n.3; and the Bulwer Tablet, 159 and n.54

Bulwer, Sir Henry Lytton Earle, Ambassador to the Ottoman Empire, Constantinople, 1858-65; 17-18

Calverley, Charles, poet, and brother-in-law of Sendall, 26

Cetshwayo ka Mpande, King of the Zulus 1872-79, who defeated the British in the Anglo-Zulu war of 1879, but was later feted in London as a heroic leader of his people, 57 and n. 54

Chamberlain, Joseph, secretary of state for the colonies, 1895-1903; 13, 122-31, and n. 50, 135, 136, 137, 138-39, 140, 142-5, 149-50, 155, 164, 167, 180-82, 190, 193; pursues commutation of Tribute, 128-9 and n. 50; extracts additional sums from Treasury for public works, 138; rejects amendments to taxation system, 181; refuses to increase education grant, but approves doubling Pancyprian Gymnasium subsidy, 190 and n. 38; changes under, treating the island, 'as an improvable property' (Sendall's words), 203-4

Chamberlayne, Tankerville, 18, 37, 49, 53 n.40, 84; as aide to Bulwer, 18-19; as police commandant, 30; and his book *Lacrimae Nicossiensis*, 30 n.7

Chicago exhibition of embroidery; sales in the US, 74

Christian, Charles, director, Imperial Ottoman Bank in Larnaca, British Museum agent, who lobbied for commutation of Tribute, 127, 159

Christou, Eleni, from Kythrea, a pupil at Phaneromeni girls' school, who was awarded the Sendall Scholarship; later headmistress of Phaneromeni; co-founder of women's association, *Enosis Ellinidhon*; founded and ran boarding school, *Academia Thilion*; 191-2, 200

INDEX

Cobham, Claude Delaval, district commissioner, Larnaca, 16, 31, 61, 84, 133; and on taxes and tithes, 22 n.22; and article criticizing centralizing system of government, 23. n. 23

Connaught Rangers, relief work in Limassol after flood of 1894, 94-5; departure to Malta, ending concept of Cyprus as strategic base, 101, 103-4, 109

Constantinides, Paschalis, MLC; appointed additional member of executive council, 63, 90, 167, 179, 183

Cromer, Lord, British controller-general in Egypt, 1883-1907; 130-31

Cunningham, Frank, 'practical' engineer, promoted in 1888 to replace Samuel Brown; n.11 31, 34,149

Deschamps, Emile, 48-9 and n.35

Dilke, Sir Charles, under-secretary of state for foreign affairs in Gladstone's government, 1880-82, 104, 123, 127

Disraeli, Benjamin, prime minister of Britain, 1868 and 1874-80, 14-15

Duckworth, Rev. H.F., sent as envoy to Cyprus, 1896, by Eastern Church Association, to gain knowledge of Orthodox Church, 76

education: Sendall's particular interest and on local visit to Paphos, he followed new teaching method introduced at boys' school, 38-39; having a background of classical scholarship, he also appreciated Greek education at the Hellenic School in Nicosia, 52; improvement of education one of the two most important issues for the executive council, 61; in annual report of 1892-93 fixed grant for elementary education (unchanged since 1883) highlighted, 70; primary schools increasing, hence need for teacher training; Sendall's special interest in Hellenic School, reformed and extended in 1893, renamed Pancyprian Gymnasium, 70; 1895 Education Act set up two pancyprian boards of education, one Muslim, one Christian, to supervise village schools and ensure teacher qualification, 117; Sendall concerned by deteriorating state of Muslim education; the *Rustye* building having collapsed, the school was rebuilt and reformed, with the support of the chief *cadi* and the *mufti*, 157-8; following provisions of 1895 Education Act, the response in Greek Cypriot schools had been massive, including a 40 per cent rise in the school population between 1896-7, and many new village schools built. Villagers were becoming more willing to send their girls to school and the Phaneromeni girls' school in Nicosia added new classrooms and new subjects offered, 190; Sir Walter's personally-funded Queen Victoria Jubilee Scholarship, enabling a pupil from the Phaneromeni girls' school to pursue further education abroad and return to teach in Cyprus, was awarded to Eleni Christou, 192; this award was balanced by a scholarship for a pupil of the Muslim High School, which had been rebuilt and reformed under his personal supervision, 193.

Enlart, Camille, French medievalist, 153-4, n.42 and illust. 32

executive council: Cypriots demanding participation in this the highest decision-making body, 62-3; Sendall stressing to London the benefits of local informed counsel, 62; officially agreed to in March 1894: problems caused by delays so in 1896 legislative council still protesting annually at absence of Cypriots on executive council, 136; Liassides and Constantinides as prospective permanent 'native' members of, 167; June 1897: first 'additional members' appointed, 179; see also 207.

INDEX

Fairfield, Sir Edward, assistant under-secretary for the colonies, n.19 37, 106, 124, 126, 140, 144,149, 150 and n.35, 204 208; and sent in 1883 on enquiry into financial management of island, 19-21; as Bulwer's defender, 20; and 'imaginary roads', n.11 31; and no investment in irrigation, n.31 46; and prejudice concerning Cypriot appointments on executive council, 63; his modification of statement about possible British withdrawal, 109; and 'do nothing' policy, 116, 142-3

Famagusta: January 1888, protest demands for tax relief, 23; Arthur Young formerly district commissioner for Famagusta, 93; protest meetings later than in other towns, 112-13; a backwater since Ottoman times; medieval city derelict; Venetian harbour silted; malarial flats; but Varosha fertile and trading with Syria, 113-16; local support for Provende's proposed railway project to include Famagusta, 116; tax collection, 204.

Ferzi Effendi, Mustafa, chief *cadi*, 65-67

Francoudes, Socrates, MLC, organised wine-growers' demonstration, 91

Gennadius, Ioannis, wealthy Greek intellectual and diplomat, residing in London, 127,191

Gennadius, Panayiotis, brother of Ioannis, eminent botanist, formerly Greek minister of agriculture, undertook enquiry into agriculture in Cyprus, 127 and n.43, 136, 184-5

George I, King of Greece, 1863-1913; originally a Danish prince, 1st monarch of new Greek dynasty, 174

George, Prince of Greece, son of King George I of Greece, installed by European powers as high commissioner of Crete in 1898, after the Greek-Turkish war of 1897, 179

Giles, Walter, warden, later director, central prison, Nicosia, 150

Gladstone, William Ewart, Liberal prime minister of Britain, 2nd government, 1880-82, 22, 188

Granville, Lord, foreign secretary under Gladstone, 1870-74, 1880-85, 123

Haggard Rider, Sir Henry, widely travelled and prolific author of adventure novels, also involved in agricultural reform and land use, particularly overseas in the British empire; worked for Sir Henry Bulwer when he was governor of the Natal, hence the Cyprus connection, 18 and 19 n.12, n.43 54, and at Kouklia dam, 203, 208-9

Harcourt, Sir William, chancellor of the exchequer in Gladstone's government, 1892-5, 104, n.45 127

Hasanpoulia, bandits, 137-8, 150

Haynes Smith, Sir William Frederick, successor to Sendall as high commissioner, 178, 205

Heidenstam von, Dr Frederik Carl, chief medical officer, Cyprus, 54, n.62 61, 75, 169, 184, 198, 200

Herbert, Sir Robert Wyndham, permanent under-secretary of state for the colonies, 1871-92, 24 n.26; and forced sales 25-7, 57, 124, 129, 204

Hicks Beach, Sir Michael, chancellor of the exchequer, 1895, 128

Hogarth, David, archaeologist and scholar, keeper of the Ashmolean museum, associated with T.E. Lawrence and Arthur Evans, 120

Houloussi, Effendi, the *mouhassebedji*, Turkish delegate to *Evkaf* from before the British administration, 66

Karageorgiades, Ioannis, mayor of Limassol, 200

Katalanos, Nicolaos, Peloponnesian radical, editor of *Evagoras*, newspaper promoting Hellenism and *enosis*, 134, 166-7, 171, 178, 198

INDEX

Kimberly, Lord, secretary of state for foreign affairs, 1882, n.54 57, 62, 190

King, Merton, district commissioner, Nicosia, 121, n.59 161

Kitchener, Lt. Herbert, and water supply, 47 and n.32; and land survey, 140.

Kition, Kyrillos, bishop of, MLC, president of *Ethniki Etairia*, 167, 173, 178, 180, 183

Kykko, abbot of, 38, 53, 76, 145, 183, 198

Kyrenia: harbour works 1886-90 of no help to island's trade, 31; protective mole designed by Samuel Brown but reduced and damaged by storms, 32-33; Chamberlayne's application to be district commissioner of Kyrenia turned down, 84.

Kyriakides, Ioannis, MLC, member of *Ethniki Etairia*, an organiser of winegrowers' demonstration at Parapedi, 91, 173

land registry, forced sales of land, 24 and n.25, 26 and n.31, requirement to survey and register land before buying and selling, 67; Arthur Young, head of in Nicosia, 93; land evaluation bill, 140; pressure for revaluation of property bill, 142

Lang, Hamilton, British consul in Cyprus at end of Ottoman rule, 1863-72, 203

Larnaca: April, 1892: Sendall's arrival in Larnaca, 15-16; Larnaca-Nicosia road 'disgraceful' state, 34; Larnaca people and complaints, 39; route to Troodos via Larnaca, 60; staying in Larnaca 61; salt lake 68-69; foreign consuls, 108; demands for union with Greece, 112; proposal for railway connecting Nicosia to Larnaca, 113; 1896: Sendalls' arrival on steamship from Alexandria, met by town notables 133; tensions resulting from Greek-Turkish war in Thessaly, 177-78

legislative council, 1892: first session with Sendall, 35; 1893: cooperation with Abbot of Kykko, an elected member, 38; refusal to use surplus from locust tax fund for new prison, 42; Bulwer's perception of it as an 'advisory council', 57; Liassides' resolution on surplus, 58; longest session ever ends in May, 60; draft bills submitted to Whitehall, 65; tithes in kind approved, 67-68; 1894: session 'bursting with bills', 84; members combine to reduce wine excise, 87; 1895: Liassides, continuing revolt, urges council to reject budget, 105; 1895: Education Act, first substantial educational reform since British occupation; 117; rapport between Sendall and council, 117; legislative council working constructively, acting as a check on government, 120; 1896: council complains of solicitous words but no practical help from London by investment of any kind to alleviate low prices for crops and high taxes, 136; under Chamberlain's leadership in the colonial office, council finally informed of increased vote for public works and education, 138

Lewis, Elizabeth, sister of Robert Herbert, and author of *A Lady's Impressions of Cyprus*, n.13 19, 27, 31, 49, 53, 57, 61, 66, 76, 94. 191 n.41 and Cypriot needlework and weaving, 73-4

Liassides, Achilleas, MLC, politician who led protests in 1888, 23; betrothed to Theo Paroudi, both pioneering amateur theatre 49, 192; in legislative council, 58; Pancyprian demonstration 112-13; and deputation to high commissioner in Troodos, 90; leading revolt in legislative council, 105; as president of municipal commission, 121; and electoral politics, 167; additional member of executive council, 179; and divide in legislature, 183; as mayor of Nicosia, 198

INDEX

Limassol: flood 1894, 94-101, n. 37-41; Sendall organizing emergency, minaret collapse, fundraising, help from military at Polemidia, 95; proposal to dam river Garrylis 97; antiflood works carried out at Sendall's insistence – no help from London, 136; 1895; military spending important, 90; Sendall impressed by Limassol elected council, 107: civic send-off for Sendalls' departure for home leave, 121; road from Limassol to Paphos completed and bridged by 1897; Sendalls choose to make final journey home from Limassol – visit to girls' school and farewell ceremony, 198-201

Loizou, Eleni, assistant to mistress of Larnaca girls' school, 133

Macheras, abbot of, 76

Maunde Thompson, Edward, secretary and principal librarian of British Museum, 1888-1909, 161, 164

Mavrocordato, Theodore, Levantine police commandant of Limassol district, one of Sendall's prodigies, friend of Rider Haggard, 84 and n.18

Meade, Sir Robert, permanent under-secretary of state for the colonies, 1892-7; 17, 24-5, 86, 129-30, 145, 161, 194

Medlicott, J.H., irrigation engineer, 135-6, 159, 183-4

Metaxas, Dr. Demetris, doctor in Greek army, and secret mission to Cyprus in 1897 to set up branch of *Ethniki Etairia*, 171

Michaelides, Vassilis, poet, who composed poem in honour of Sendall, 121 and Appendix I, 210

Michell, Roland, district commissioner, Limassol, 200

Milner, Alfred, author of best-seller, *England in Egypt*, in 1892, 131

Murray, Alexander, directing British Museum excavations, 159-60

Myres, John, New College, Oxford; involved in cataloguing objects for Cyprus Museum, Nicosia 159-60

Nicosia: Economic crisis in 1888: failure of crops and demand for tax relief – crowd protests at Government House, 23; Büyük Khan used as prison while new prison built 42-3; main drain 46-7, 77; stonemasons in Kaimakli, 48; Deschamps describing avenue beyond wooden bridge over moat as the 'Champs Elysées of Nicosia', 49; rise of suburbs, new Anglican church, 49; Sendalls' life in Nicosia, 49, 52, 53; theatre, 54; key events, 55; April 1895, demonstrations against taxes and Tribute and in favour of union with Greece, 112; 1896: crowd welcoming Sendalls returning from leave, 134; new government offices planned for the site of the old Serai, 151-54; government printing office built, 155-56; museum bill attempted 159-161; Nicosia hospital committee and Cyprus branch BNA, 185; December, 1897 column unveiled at Phaneromeni school on Sendall's departure from Cyprus, 198.

Ohnefalsch-Richter, Max and Magda, archaeologists excavating in Cyprus in 1895, 159

Paphos: protests 1888, 23; lack of police administration, 29-30; crime extensive, 34; Sendall visiting much neglected town, 38; Treasury's refusal of funds for improvements, 44-45; Algernon Ongley appointed police commandant for Paphos, 84; tax arrears greatest in Paphos, 85; Sendall tours Paphos district in September 1894, suggests arrears in kind, 85-6; 91-92; Sendall's tour of inspection - some improvements made, 93-4

INDEX

Paphos, bishop of, 76

Paroudi, Theano, headmistress, Phaneromeni girls' school, 49, 191; and (as Theano Liassides) co-founder of women's association *Enosis Ellinidhon*, 192

Philemon, Georgos, Greek consul in Cyprus, 108 and volunteers for the war in Crete, 174-5; ceremonial welcome on arrival in Limassol, 108

Pierpoint, Robert, British MP, friend of the Sendalls, Liberal politician who had spoken against the Tribute in the House of Commons, 127

Post, Dr George, American professor at Beirut College, who had known Cyprus in Ottoman times and revisited in 1898, 205

prisons: 1893: police administration (including prisons) weakened by ineffective appointments, 29-30; rise in crime rate, 34; need for purpose-built prison a first priority since Bulwer, and land had been purchased and plans drawn up, 35; in Nicosia a new prison under construction by prisoners temporarily housed in Büyük Khan, who had to be transported and guarded to the site distant from the Old City, 42; overcrowded, makeshift prisons mainly housed tax offenders, 69; by 1896 the new central prison was almost complete and a separate short-term block was planned to better supply labour force for public works, 138; new concept of prison administration, appointment of director, three judges in charge of prison policy, 150.

Provende, Charles, entrepreneur, interested in Cyprus railway project, 113, 116-17

Redcliffe, Stratford de: Britain's minister to the Porte, 1842-1858, 17

Ripon, Lord, secretary of state for the colonies, 1892-6, 42, 45, 67, 93, 100; and money owed to the Cypriots by Treasury, 59 and clarifications on executive council, 63

Rossos, Nicolaos, MLC and mayor of Larnaca, 133

Salahi, Effendi, Mehmet, and the awarding of *vakoufs*, 66, appointed trustee of Azizhe Tekke by the sultan, 108 n.12

Salisbury, Lord, foreign secretary in 1878, later prime minister 1886-92 and 1895-1902, 13, 64, 108, 122, 188

Salmon, Rear Admiral Nowell, sent to the Natal in 1884, to the aid of Sir Henry Bulwer at a time of crisis in Zululand, 18

Salt, collected locally from the Larnaca Salt Lake, formerly an important government monopoly under the Ottoman system, 68-69; the Porte claimed an annual Tribute in salt, soon after which, sale of Cypriot salt was prohibited in the Ottoman empire, 69; collecting and guarding mountains of unmoved salt was expensive and problematical, while to acquire salt legally meant long, arduous journeys to depots in Larnaca and Limassol. Hence anyone infringing the salt laws was flung in gaol, causing immense resentment; notably, the *mudir* of Paphos had been murdered while enforcing the salt monopoly, 68; Sendall opened salt depots in all districts, 69

Seager, M.B. Captain, judge with special interest in *Evkaf* affairs, 106 and n.9, 120

Selborne, Lord, under-secretary of state for the colonies under Gladstone, 1895, 124

Sendall, Lady Elizabeth Sophia, wife of Sir Walter, 16, 26, 53, 61, 73, 94, 100, 113,

INDEX

133, 147, 185, 190 and Phaneromeni Girls' School, 49 and the leper colony, 75, 127; and welfare and fundraising, 93 and needlework and hand-weaving 73-74

Sheikh of the whirling dervishes, 53

Shiakalis, Georgos, member of executive council, 63

Smith, George, district commissioner Paphos, 94

Smith, Sir William, chief justice, 1892-6, 138, 198

Sofronios, Phinieus, Archbishop of Cyprus, 23, 52, 63-64, 71, 75, 112, 126, 134, 161, 166, 167, 174, 194, 198; and solidarity with Greek Orthodox bishops, Macedonia, 165

Spencer, Josiah, vicar and government inspector of schools, 75, 190

Stewart, Basil, toured Cyprus in 1904, and his book, *My Experiences of Cyprus*, 'an account of the people, medieval cities and castles, antiquities and history of the island of Cyprus', published in 1908, n.19 179, n.48 193, 203, 208

Swettenham, John, receiver general, 25

Theodotou, Antonios, brother of Theofanis, from the tiny village of Phini, studies in Athens and Paris (medicine); he and his brother pursued radical policies and became promoters and benefactors of education and athletics, 167; nephews of Archbishop Sofronios, likewise from Phini

Theodotou, Theofanis, MLC, see above, (studies in law); 173, 188

Thistleton-Dyer, William Turner, director, Kew Gardens, 127

Troodos: Sendall riding from Troodos to Paphos, visiting Kykko, 38; military road to Troodos and new wine roads, 87; two councillors visit Sendall at Government Cottage to express concerns over troop withdrawals and new tax legislation, 90; 3,000 wine-growers massed at Troodos to present resolution on taxation to Sendall, 92; malarial sourge in Troodos range, 94; Abbot of Kykko invites entire legislative council for special session at the monastery, 145; annual summer migration of government to Troodos and related activities, 145-47; extraordinary meeting of legislature on irrigation held at Kykko Monastery, 183-88;

Tserkezis, Savvas, author of Ημερολόγιον του Βίου μου, (Diary of My Life) 85 n.22, 175 n.12

Tuccarbasi, Hadji Ahmet Derviş Pasha, owner of the *Zaman* newspaper, 157

Warren, Col. Falkland G.E., career soldier and colonial officer who came to Cyprus in 1878 with new British administration, becoming chief secretary. Notoriously involved in excavation and sale of antiquities, leaving the island in 1890, taking many items with him to Canada, where they can still be seen, 21, 93

Wilcocks, William, engineer, author of *Egyptian Irrigation,* 131

Williamson, John, businessman, of the Cyprus Company, Limassol, and agent for British Museum, interested in investing in island's development, 137, 159

Wolseley, Gen. Sir Garnet, first C.-in-C. and high commissioner in Cyprus in 1878. In 1879 rushed from the island to the Natal to take command of the British forces against the Zulus, 17, 93

Yiallouris, notorious bandit, convicted of murdering the *mudir* of Paphos and eventually hanged, 77, 80, 156

Young, Sir Arthur Henderson, chief secretary to high commissioner, subsequently appointed by Sendall to head land registry in Nicosia, 93 and n.34, 133, 137, 140, 182, 195, 198;

INDEX

arguing for railway branch line, 116; and sending memorial from demonstrations to Sendall, 126; negotiating for regular mail service 140

Young, Lady Evelyne Anne, wife of Sir Arthur Young, 93 and n.34, 185

Zanettos, Dr Filios, from Larnaca, radical politician, possibly involved in the *Ethniki Etairia* and active in the organisation of, and author of *Ιστορία της Νήσου Κύπρου*, (*History of the Island of Cyprus*) 1911; n.77 168, 171, 209

Ziyai, Effendi, Hadji Hafiz, Turkish delegate to *Evkaf,* 66; headmaster of the Rusty'e school, member of legislative council, 157